Transition and Transformation
New Research Fostering Transfer Student Success
Volume II

Transition and Transformation
New Research Fostering Transfer Student Success
Volume II

Eileen Strempel & Stephen J. Handel

Blue Ridge | Cumming | Dahlonega | Gainesville | Oconee

Project Editor:
Judith T. Brauer

Published by:
University of North Georgia Press
Dahlonega, Georgia

Printing Support by:
Lightning Source, Inc.
La Vergne, Tennessee

Cover and book design by Corey Parson.

ISBN: 978-1-940771-47-2

Printed in the United States of America, 2018
For more information, please visit ung.edu/university-press
Or email ungpress@ung.edu

CONTENTS

About **NISTS**

The National Institute for the Study of Transfer Students (NISTS) exists to improve the lives of transfer students. Through research, education, and service, we support professionals who directly serve transfer students, as well as those who create transfer policy and conduct transfer-related research. NISTS bridges knowledge, policies, and practice by bringing together a wide range of stakeholders to explore the issues related to the transfer process in order to facilitate student success and degree completion. We partner with two- and four-year institutions, state agencies, higher education associations, foundations, and others committed to transfer student success.

NISTS was founded in 2002 by Dr. Bonita C. Jacobs in response to a lack of professional development opportunities and research literature focused specifically on transfer students. Since that time, NISTS has contributed to the national conversation about transfer students in many ways. NISTS has been awarded multiple grants to conduct transfer-related research and to host symposiums to disseminate the findings. In addition, NISTS advisory board members and staff have produced authoritative transfer-related publications, resources, and presentations. This peer-reviewed monograph is part of an annual series published by the National Institute for the Study of Transfer Students designed to highlight and share promising practices in supporting transfer students.

NISTS held its inaugural conference at the University of North Texas with 300 attendees from over thirty higher education institutions and thirty-two states. More than ten years later, the annual conference brings together nearly 500 attendees from thirty-seven states and two provinces in Canada. The NISTS conference is the only annual gathering of its kind, specifically focused on transfer. It is unique in bringing together a wide range of professionals from across functional areas, institutional types, systems, and sectors to comprehensively focus on transfer research, policy, and practice.

NISTS continues to encourage transfer-related research and best practices in a variety of ways. In 2006, NISTS began offering grants to support transfer-related research, and in 2010 we introduced and awarded the first Barbara K. Townsend Dissertation of the Year Award. In 2013, we introduced an opportunity to recognize outstanding transfer professionals with the inaugural Bonita C. Jacobs Transfer Champions Award. And in 2014, we expanded this award to also recognize Rising Stars, those with a shorter tenure, but whose impact is significant.

The Association for the Study of Transfer Students (ASTS) is the professional organization of the National Institute for the Study of Transfer Students, and the only national association exclusively dedicated to promoting transfer student success, advancing transfer research and facilitating partnerships to enhance transfer. ASTS reaches across departmental and divisional responsibilities and beyond institutional boundaries. Membership is encouraged for higher education professionals charged with providing programs and services to facilitate transfer student success; higher education faculty dedicated to the pursuit of transfer student research and success; higher education administrators committed to ensuring transfer student success; and state and national agency representatives interested in increased transfer student success and degree attainment.

Learn more about NISTS and join ASTS by visiting: nists.org.

INTRODUCTION

Eileen Strempel, Ph.D.

TRANSFER NATION II

The United States of America is blessed with an extraordinarily diverse educational system. Various pathways cross the country in a latticework of two- and four-year institutions, both public and private, for-profit and non-profit. This educational quilt provides an exciting array of possibilities for economic and social transformation. However, successful navigation through this impressive array of educational options remains a bewildering challenge for many students. Within this array of educational routes, the passage between (and among) two- and four-year institutions is perhaps one of the most brilliant structural concepts of our country, but one we have yet to fully actualize as a nation.

Community colleges witnessed their greatest expansion in the 1960s and 70s, an inspired manifestation of the social activism of the time. From 1960 to 1970, community colleges across our country cumulatively grew over 120%, with a new community college being completed at the rate of almost one each week: a simply startling investment in our nation's educational infrastructure (Phillippe and Sullivan, 2005). The noble intent of this astounding venture was to provide affordable educational access combined with geographical convenience for our nation. Decades after this transformative investment, today almost half our nation's students begin their post-secondary education at a community college (American Association of Community Colleges, 2017). Eighty percent of these community college students desire to transfer to four-year institutions in order to obtain a bachelor's or further degree (Horn & Skomsvold, 2011).

Despite these impressive aggregate ambitions, however, only a quarter of these transfer students manage to obtain their goal, even after six years (Jenkins and Fink, 2016).

Juxtapose this slender percentage of student success with the frequently voiced maxim that our nation's only sustained hope for positively affecting economic and social inequality at scale is through education, and the potential of the transfer process is revealed. The challenge of this lofty goal has only increased with time. According to the U.S. Census Bureau, the share of all income going to the 20% of families with the lowest incomes has steadily declined, from 4.8% in 1985 to 3.7% in 2015, while the share of income going to the top 5% of families rose from 16.1% in 1985 to 20% during the same timeframe. The College Board's *2016 Trends in College Pricing Report* notes the upward shift of inequality in family incomes over the three decades from 1985 to 2015, with median incomes for black and Hispanic families at 62% and 64%, respectively, of the median for white families. In 2015, the median family income for families headed by a four-year college graduate was more than twice that of families headed by a high school graduate (College Board, 2016). The specific and important role of transfer in "moving the dial" on income inequality at scale is increasingly evident as vital to the future health of our country and its citizens, as the baccalaureate degree is now the critical credential for sustained economic advancement and full participation in our democracy.

Nevertheless, our educational system is beset by detours and seemingly insurmountable barriers and, as a country, we frequently fail to live up to the aspirational promise of educational public good: access to higher education for all who wish to pursue this opportunity, and not simply for those who can afford it. Despite important investments in two-year institutions, transfer efforts continue to underperform and the difference between the haves and have-nots grows wider.

In this complex educational landscape, one of the most hopeful and promising arenas for whole scale re-imagination and improvement continues to be the point of transfer between two-and four-year institutions. If we effectively improve the transfer process writ large, we will simultaneously transform the lives of our students, families, and communities. The potential societal gains—in a global era of increased economic stratification—are immeasurable, far-reaching, and rooted in one of the most significant moral and ethical imperatives of our time. As a nation we must realize transfer student success as a central component in our quest to foster baccalaureate degree completion.

The articles in this collection are devoted to the re-imagination of the transfer process, with the broader goal of improving educational success for our students. The present volume is a companion to our first work, *Transition and Transformation: Fostering Transfer Student Success*, which focused on highlighting best practices of practitioners serving students in various institutional contexts. Our initial effort was rooted in the lived experience of the practitioner, while this subsequent volume is focused on recent research studies aimed at improving the transfer process. The articles in this collection may be grouped around three expanding circles: 1) why and how to employ research-tested methods for fostering transfer student success at the individual level; 2) how to best foster "transfer student affirming institutional ecosystems" on individual campuses; and 3) how might we improve public policies for transfer students to foster positive change.

RESEARCH-TESTED METHODS FOR EFFECTIVELY FOSTERING INDIVIDUAL TRANSFER STUDENT SUCCESS

Tony A. Lazarowicz's important phenomenological qualitative study, "Transitioning to a Four-Year University: Considerations for Incorporating Schlossberg's Transition Theory into Practice" centers around five central themes that emerged from participants: funding the college experience; transition takes time; support is critical; maturity; and personal responsibility matters. The multi-dimensional transfer student transition experience is then located within the context of Schlossberg's Transition Theory. Lazarowicz posits that the transition for community college transfer students is best facilitated by policies and procedures geared toward increasing the individual student assets enumerated in Schlossberg's 4-S theory (situation, self, strategies, and support), while remaining cognizant of the full transition experience (moving in, moving through, and moving out). Applying this valuable theoretical framework can help institutions intentionally formulate a holistic approach to improving the transition experience of community college transfer students.

Lazorowicz's work is complemented by Mary M. Von Kaenel and Pamela A. Havice's, "A Phenomenological Study of Two-Year College Students' Transition Experiences at a Four-Year Institution." Von Kaenel and Havice's article focuses on four key thematic variables: a student's age (and the resulting impact on the transfer experience); differences in the rigor and pace of the curriculum at two- and four-year institutions; social connections at the new campus; and finally, the presence (or absence) of targeted communication. Participant comments in the study underscore the simultaneous nature of academic and social integration. Students discovered that deeper development of their information networks naturally resulted in forging important social ties, but at the same time these networks provided access to information that helped them to be more successful in their academic study.

Fostering Transfer Student Affirming Institutional Ecosystems

As individual students "transfer up," the pivotal role of the four-year institution moves front and center. Intentional thought is needed to truly foster a transfer student affirming institutional ecosystem that embraces students seeking the next steps towards their baccalaureate degree. Erin E. Shaw's, "Sense Making for Community College Transfers Entering a Public, Liberal Arts University" explores the transition experience of a cohort of transfer students, resulting in a host of wide-ranging recommendations for improvements in both policy and practice on college campuses. This phenomenological study eloquently underscores the need for more high-quality information. The more that is known and understood about the experiences of transfer students, the more effectively institutions may support students as they face academic challenges, find their balance, and ultimately attain their baccalaureate degree.

Jessica Moon Asa, Steve Carignan, Kristi Marchesani, Kristin Moser, and Kristin Woods' article deepens a call to action for four-year institutions with "Transfer Student Choice," a critique of the largely passive transfer student recruitment efforts utilized by many four-year institutions. Instead of relying on information gleaned from websites, student-initiated campus visits, and tables that require a student to be brave enough to approach the college representative, the authors urge institutions to be more proactive and engaging. By utilizing intrusive, longitudinal advising and outreach and providing major-specific, personalized assistance, institutions can help students navigate a complex and overwhelming process. Longitudinal advising ideally addresses the application and financial aid process as key strategies that help students through a bewildering maze. This study strongly emphasizes the important role that family and friends play in providing both emotional and financial support in the college choice process. True recognition of a broad student support network will move institutions towards transfer recruitment efforts that include community and family-focused programming, assuring engagement with both students and their families. While resource intensive, institutional understanding of what drives individual transfer student choice will inform meaningful, active exploration and engagement on the part of transfer students, and ultimately foster levels of transfer student success that all too frequently seem elusive.

Megan M. Chase's "Policy Implementation From a Critical Perspective: Analyzing Transfer Policy Within an Urban Technical College," moves this discussion back to the two-year campus, and utilizes a case study research design that also draws on the tenets of critical race theory. She examines how two-year college practitioners implement a variety of transfer initiatives but finds that these efforts frequently lack grounding in more sustained, cogent, and visible transfer policies and practices. Her study further focuses on the implications of these transfer policies for students from traditionally underrepresented communities.

In her study, "Transitioning: Experiences of Transfer Students," Dalinda Martínez specifically focuses on the post-transfer experience in order to better understand the salient factors that influence bachelor degree completion. By concentrating on both policy and practice, Martínez sheds light on—and offers potential solutions to—the challenges that transfer students face as they enter an environment that does not prioritize them as highly as first-time, first-year students. When universities have a better understanding of the post-transfer experiences of students they will create better policies and programs that address these students' unique needs and challenges.

REFINING PUBLIC POLICIES TO SUPPORT TRANSFER STUDENTS

Kimberly Faris's article "The Completion Agenda and Transfer Students: Divergent Expectations" explores the challenge of aligning public priorities with public policy, and moves our discussion from the institutional level (campus policies, initiatives, and procedures) to the state level. While Faris's study focuses specifically on Texas, her findings are relevant to the policy development process in other states. As this study highlights, the completion agenda focus from our nation's public and policymakers has resulted in large-scale shifts in public policy. Not surprisingly, lawmakers have increasingly rewarded outcome metrics such as graduation, using federal data that only accounts for first-time, full-time students. Unfortunately, the completion metrics frequently selected do not adequately measure transfer student success. Furthermore, as Faris's study poignantly demonstrates, transfer students—rather than the institutions that serve them—are the ones frequently penalized by the very legislation intended to assist them.

Taking a similarly broad perspective, Robin LaSota's mixed methods research project, "Factors, Practices, and Policies Influencing Students' Upward Transfer to Baccalaureate-Degree Programs and Institutions" examines the factors, practices, and policies influencing students' upward transfer to baccalaureate-degree programs and institutions. Focusing on community colleges in Washington, Georgia, and Florida, LaSota compares institutions that have exceeded statewide transfer rates for low-income and underrepresented students with those with average transfer rates. Washington, Georgia and Florida have each experimented with policies to support community college students' postsecondary success over a number of years. LaSota compellingly finds advising the only practice (including common course numbering, curriculum development, and tutoring support, among others) to be successfully and rigorously evaluated for effectiveness. Colleges with higher transfer rates have implemented a range of advising practices, ranging from mandatory advising, early bird advising, and early warning advising systems. In her quantitative strand, transfer intention and full-time attendance were the two student-level characteristics most positively associated with upward transfer probability. This finding implies interventions focused on increasing full-time, continuous enrollment would be extremely beneficial. This focus would necessitate financial aid reforms, especially because community college students tend to be loan averse and also are more likely to work twenty or more hours a week (a factor negatively associated with upward transfer). LaSota's study further enumerates specific strategies for operationalizing an increased shared responsibility for transfer student success between both two- and four-year institutions.

CONCLUSION: FINAL THOUGHTS ON HOW OUR NATION'S TIMELESS ASPIRATIONAL VISIONS MIGHT BE A VISION FOR OUR TIME?

Our country has long correlated educational attainment with transformation, as exemplified by President Lyndon Johnson's famous 1954 University of Michigan commencement speech proclamation, "Poverty must not be a bar to learning, and learning must offer an escape from poverty." This noble sentiment continues to inspire transfer champions, practitioners, policymakers, and researchers as we collectively gather our time, energy, and resources in our quest to build an infrastructure of educational access and success for all. A decade later in 1964, President Lyndon Johnson gave another commencement speech, this time at Howard University. He reiterated his national call to action: "It is not enough just to open the gates of opportunity—all our citizens must have the ability to walk through those gates." Today, the challenge of how best to provide both access and support for higher education in America seems to be not only a timeless aspirational vision eloquently articulated by an inspiring past president, but also a pressing, vital, and potentially healing vision for our time.

REFERENCES

American Association of Community Colleges. (2017). *Community College Fast Facts*. Retrieved from http://www.aacc.nche.edu/AboutCC/Pages/fastfactsfactsheet.aspx

College Board. (2016). *Trends in college pricing 2016.* New York: The College Board. Retrieved from http://trends.collegeboard.org/college-pricing

Horn, L., & Skomsvold, P. (2011). Web tables: Community college student outcomes: 1994–2009 (NCES 2012-253). Washington, DC: U.S. Department of Education, Institute of Education Sciences, National Center for Education Statistics.

Phillippe and Sullivan. (2005). National Profile of Community Colleges: Trends and Statistics. 4th edition. Washington, DC: American Association of Community Colleges.

Jenkins, D., & Fink, J. (2016). Tracking Transfer. New York, NY: Columbia University, Teachers College, Community College Research Center.

Jenkins, D., & Fink, J. (2015). What we know about transfer. New York, NY: Columbia University, Teachers College, Community College Research Center.

SECTION I

RESEARCH-TESTED METHODS FOR EFFECTIVELY
FOSTERING INDIVIDUAL TRANSFER STUDENT SUCCESS

1

Transitioning to a Four-Year University: Considerations for Incorporating Schlossberg's Transition Theory into Practice

Tony A. Lazarowicz, Ph.D.

Abstract

With over 60% of college graduates attending multiple institutions (United States Department of Education, 2006) and many starting at community colleges, the importance of understanding community college transfer students' stories is critical to retention and graduation agendas at colleges and universities nationwide. Specific to community college enrollment, 46% of 2013–2014 academic year college graduates were enrolled in a two-year institution at some point during their undergraduate education (National Student Clearinghouse, 2015). Scholossberg's Transition Theory (1984) has been utilized in higher education literature as a conceptual framework for working with various student populations such as student veterans (Wheeler, 2012; Rumann, 2010); student athletes (Henderson, 2013); and students on academic probation (Tovar & Simon, 2006). Few studies, however, have applied this theory to community college transfer students. This study is intended to help fill that gap by describing the transition of these students using this conceptual framework. At the center of this study was the desire to understand how community college transfer students perceive their transition into a large research, land-grant institutions. This phenomenological qualitative study incorporated journaling and interviews with 12 full-time community college transfer students (21–41 years old) at three points during their first semester (fall 2014) at a large Midwestern research institution. Five themes emerged from this analysis: 1) Funding the college experience; 2) Transition takes time; 3) Support is critical; 4) Maturity; and 5) Personal responsibility matters. The transition experience as indicated by the emergent themes of the participants fit within the context of Schlossberg's Transition Theory. Overall, these transitions were a pathway to move forward, to start a new chapter, and to expand one's opportunities. Consistent with other studies utilizing Schlossberg's Transition Theory, this theoretical framework is valuable when working with community college transfer students. When universities create policies and procedures geared toward increasing student's assets in Schlossberg's 4-S framework (situation, self, strategies, and support) coping resources and are mindful of the full transition (moving in, moving through, and moving out), administrators, staff, and policy makers may facilitate the transition for community college transfer students and provide support to an important and growing percentage of students pursuing higher education.

Community colleges play a significant role within higher education. In the fall of 2014, 45% of undergraduate college students were enrolled in community colleges (American Association of Community Colleges, 2016). While many start at community colleges, a vast majority of community college students (81.4%) desire to obtain a baccalaureate degree or higher (U.S. Department of Education, National Center for Education Statistics, 2011). Despite this goal orientation, most community college students do not earn a four-year degree. What seems clear is that the transfer process poses challenges that many transfer students are unable to overcome.

The research literature that focuses on transfer students is significant, including quantitative studies that examine "transfer shock" and GPA (Cejda & Kaylor, 1997; Cejda, Kaylor, & Rewey, 1998; Ishitani, 2008; Johnson, 2005; Whitfield, 2005), reasons students transfer (Cejda & Kaylor, 2001; Fee, Prolman, & Thomas, 2009), and comparisons of native and transfer students (Conrad Glass, Jr. & Harrington, 2002; Ditchkoff, Laband, & Hanby, 2003; Montondon & Eikner, 1997; Woosley & Johnson, 2006). Studies have also focused on the many challenges these students face as they strive to become successful professionals (McGowan & Gawley, 2006; Townsend & Wilson, 2006; Whitfield, 2005; Woosley & Johnson, 2006). Yet Tatum, Hayward, and Monzon (2006) reveal that many transfer students believe there is minimal assistance and guidance in the transition process from a community college to a four-year university. For example, transfer students feel neglected in campus retention efforts (Townsend & Wilson, 2006). Thus, although there is a robust amount of literature on transfer students, many studies do not reveal what these students require to be successful in their transition and may not deepen our understanding of students' perceptions. "Colleges that successfully cultivate a culture of transfer ensure that their students are well-informed about the transfer process and are supported, both academically and socially" (Miller, 2013, p. 41). Miller's article highlights the important role institutions have in preparing students for success, but questions whether they adequately ensure that community college transfer students earn a baccalaureate degree. Thus, understanding how students' view their transition, what types of experiences are typical for community college transfer students as they transition between institutions, and what types of resources students find helpful would further improve our efforts to serve the educational needs of these students.

THEORETICAL FRAMEWORK

Schlossberg's Transition Theory (1984, 1995, 2006, 2012) provides a theoretical framework to explore key aspects of the experience of transition and the challenges that transfer students face. McEwen (2003) notes, "theory not only helps us to understand what we experience and observe but provides a foundation for practice in student affairs" (McEwen, 2003, p. 154). In comparison to Tinto's (1998) theory of student departure or Astin's (1999) student involvement theory, there is significantly less research on Schlossberg's Transition Theory, and this gap inspired this study, applying Transition Theory to community college transfer students.

Schlossberg's theory has been used to study multiple groups that have transitioned into new settings, including: nontraditional returning students (Schaefer, 2010), students on academic probation (Tovar & Simon, 2006), students withdrawing from athletics (Swain, 1991), students who become professionals (Koerin, Harrigan, & Reeves, 1990), and retiring faculty members (Goodman & Pappas, 2000). Evans, Forney, Guido, Patton, and Renn (2010) pointed out that while this theory was intended for adult development, collegiate staff members should consider this theory and others that may be helpful in working with students.

Transitions are "any event or non-event that results in changed relationships, routines, assumptions, and roles" (Goodman et al., 2006, p. 33), and need to be understood as experiences that can be positively or negatively perceived depending on the individual and the holistic context in that moment in time (McGill & Lazarowicz, 2012).

The three major parts of this theory are: approaching transitions; taking stock of coping resources; and taking charge. (Schlossberg, Waters, Goodman, 1995). The first component, approaching transitions, provides an opportunity to understand the type, perspective and appraisal of the transition, contextual factors, and degree of impact the transition has on the individual's daily life. For the second component, taking stock of coping resources, one can better understand how the person will cope with the transition when they can see both the liabilities (negatives) and assets (positives) within each of the four categories (4S's) of self, support, strategies, and situation. Transition theory posits that it is important to know whether the event is considered planned, unplanned, or a non-event, as this may impact the results within each of the "4S's." If assets outweigh liabilities, then the transition will be less difficult (Schlossberg, Waters, Goodman, 1995). "In the final part, the person experiencing the change begins to use new strategies to manage her or her personal evolution" (McGill & Lazarowicz, 2012, p. 131).

Assessing differences between pre- and post-transition environments may help gauge the impact the transition will have on the student (Goodman et al., 2006). There are two levels of appraisals involved for the individual in transition: the primary is how (s)he feels about the transition in general; and the secondary is how (s)he feels about their resources in dealing with the transition (McGill & Lazarowicz, 2012).

Resources may mean many things within each of the 4S areas. Attending an orientation may be both a strategy and a resource. How an individual feels about the resources can be tied to both the availability and utility of resources that are or are not available. For instance, an advisor is a support. Does an individual feel positive about his or her advisor or not? Similarly, a strategy an individual may have used before transitioning may have included reading between classes, but post-transition, a different class schedule combined with greater distances on the new campus may make the strategy non-viable in a new context.

PURPOSE OF THE STUDY

Schlossberg's Transition Theory has been applied to different higher education student groups, but there are few studies utilizing Transition Theory to explore the experience of community college transfer students.

The purpose of this qualitative study is to apply Schlossberg's Transition Theory to gain a better understanding of how community college transfer students transition to a large land-grant, research university. The focus is to better understand student perceptions of assets and liabilities with respect to community college student support systems, strategies used in the transition to the four-year institution, personal characteristics, and the situation surrounding the transition. Through identification of their perceived assets and liabilities, this study deepens our understanding of the most important challenges and successes that community college transfer students face when transitioning to a large land-grant research university. This study also helps explore what resources community college transfer students identify as the most important to their transition.

LITERATURE REVIEW

The initial purpose of community colleges and junior colleges was to offer students a low-cost opportunity to complete the first two years of undergraduate education with a clear transfer pathway to aligned state universities for the completion of their education (Thelin, 2003). Over time, the mission has grown and varies among institutions to include vocational programs and technical degrees, literacy programs, and adult education, alongside the transfer mission pathway into the larger university system (Cohen & Kisker, 2010). Community colleges serve an important feeder role to four-year institutions because of the inexpensive educational pathway they provide for students wishing to obtain their baccalaureate degree.

Preparing for and Transitioning to a University

While not all students intend to transfer, many students do. Some students arrive intending to transfer, while others may not decide until later. Regardless, staff should consider what types of support they should provide to students to aid in successful transfer. A few types of support mechanisms documented in literature are discussed below.

Packard, Tuladhar, and Lee (2013), discussed strategies faculty members in the Science, Technology, Engineering, and Mathematics (STEM) disciplines at Massachusetts community colleges are using to assist students considering transfer. For one promising practice, students nominated faculty they believe act as transfer champions. They compared faculty who were

7

identified as being highly supportive of their transfer goals with those who were not. Faculty transfer champions—with high frequency—discussed the academic content required to transfer, shared personal experiences, and highlighted the benefits of higher education. Transfer champion professors also gave motivational speeches about transferring and discussed strategies for transferring (Packard, Tuladhar, & Lee, 2013).

To solidify linkages between community colleges and four-year institutions, articulation agreements are extremely important. As Grites (2012) notes, forty states within the United States have some form, policy, or procedure in place that supports articulation among institutions. Although legislated articulation agreements are helpful, Kuh (2008) argues that colleges are not sufficiently held accountable for the development and application of such agreements. For example, if articulation agreements are not properly executed, or admissions and recruitment resources are not distributed adequately to support transfer student needs, transfer students experience negative ramifications. Doyle (2006) finds "acceptance of credit hours in the target institution . . . turns out to be key to students' success— or lack of it," (p. 58) indicative of the importance of articulation agreements among institutions. Similarly, Grites and McDonald (2012) believe "articulation agreements [as well as], programs and services that facilitate students' transition play a critical role in creating a transfer pipeline for students to continue their education beyond a 2-year college" (p. 21).

Although articulation agreements are important, many transfer students often do not understand how they work. Townsend (2008) notes 20% of students are unsure of how many and which courses transferred. This is particularly distressing for students when meeting with advisors to discuss their major courses occur after the student is accepted into their major; sometimes this can be as late as the first semester after transitioning. The problems go beyond articulation agreement concerns. Tatum, Hayward, and Monzon (2006) found many students believe there is minimal assistance and guidance throughout the transfer process. Their findings indicated transfer students desire more assistance throughout the process. Cameron (2005) also found students believe this process could have been much smoother. Some issues relate to financial concerns. Melguizo, Kienzl, and Alfonso (2011) found transfer students experience significant financial strain, as they receive significantly less grant and loan aid to attend college as compared to native students.

Additional studies discuss how to improve the transition experience prior to arrival at the four-year institution. Rhine, Milligan, and Nelson (2000) offer several recommendations that may help alleviate transition difficulties. First, if administrators and staff have a better understanding and appreciation of the difficulties transfer students face, this may allow them to provide improved services. Second, staff should help the students understand the significant differences between the community college and the four-year college. Students should be prepared for the differences in class sizes, grading systems, academic resources, as well as the use of graduate students and teaching assistants in the classroom. Finally, having an understanding of the expectations and experiences of community college transfer students may help administrators and staff address areas of disconnect between the expectations and the realities of transitioning into the new institution.

Transfer and Grade Point Averages

There are many studies that have explored transfer student grade point averages (GPA) in comparison to native student GPAs. Carlan and Byxbe (2000) found that native students experienced fewer troubles and consistently maintained higher GPAs. Carlan and Byxbe (2000) also tracked transfer students after their second semester at the university as well and found that their GPAs tended to level off. Ishitani (2008) found first-year transfer students are more likely to leave as compared with transfer students entering with credit hours levels at the sophomore and junior level. Additionally, transfer students with lower semester GPAs were less likely to persist at their new institution. Cejda, Kaylor, and Rewey (1998) found that students in particular fields may actually experience the phenomenon known as "transfer ecstasy," or an elation of grades after transfer. Cejda (1997) found transfer ecstasy in a number of fields including "education, fine arts and humanities, and social sciences" (p. 285). Meanwhile, Cejda, Kaylor, and Rewey (1998) found students majoring in subject areas within math and science were more likely to experience transfer shock.

Anderson et al. (2012) pointed out that transitions may be stressful. Melguizo, Kienzl, and Alfonso (2011) found grade point averages are not the only thing higher education staff should be concerned about with respect to transfer student success and they should help make the process more seamless by ensuring students do not enroll in unneeded credit hours. In particular, Melguizo et al. (2011) argue "community colleges have the responsibility to provide the academic preparation and transfer curriculum necessary for students to transfer on time, and four-year colleges should work with the students during the transition phase to make the process smoother" (p. 282).

University Challenges

Davies and Casey (1999) found both positive and negative experiences among students who transfer to a university. These researchers conclude that students feel they "need strong support systems, and financial, social and institutional sources all contribute to, or detract from, a good college experience" (p. 70). The transfer students in Cameron's (2005) study felt their social lives were disappointing. Flaga (2006) similarly found students wanted to have a better understanding of the learning resources available to them, and felt the necessity to connect to others academically, socially, and physically before and during the transition period. With time, students adjusted and experienced successful social and physical integration.

Woosley and Johnson (2006) compared the academic and social aspects of transfer students to native students who lived in residence halls. Transfer students did not have significant differences in their academic experiences, but did spend less time in activities, had lower involvement, and lower satisfaction with student activities than their native counterparts. Ishitani and McKitrick (2010) found that native students score significantly higher in "active and collaborative learning, student faculty interaction, and enriching educational experiences" in comparison to transfer students (p. 584).

METHOD

Sampling and Participants

Participants were recruited for the study using purposeful sampling that sought full-time degree-seeking transfer students whose last attended institution was a community college and who had completed a minimum of 12 semester credits at the previous institution. As Creswell (2008) pointed out, purposeful sampling allows for intentional selection of "individuals and sites to learn or understand the central phenomenon" (p. 214). In total, 12 completed the interview process and six of those participants also completed the optional journaling. Information about the participants is provided in Table 1.1. Table 1.2 aggregates additional personal and transfer-related characteristics of the participants, including their current living situation and employment intentions.

Methodology

A phenomenological, qualitative approach was used to understand community college students' perceptions of their transition into a large research, land-grant institution. The general questions above were answered through a series of three individual interviews. Anderson et al. (2012) stressed the importance of studying the transition over several points of time. This study utilizes Seidman's (2013) three-interview series approach:

The first interview established the context of the participants' experience. The second allows participants to reconstruct the details of their experience within the context in which it occurs. And the third encourages the participants to reflect on the meaning their experience holds for them.

A secondary form of data collection, writing a journal, was solicited as a voluntary option for participants. The activity was intentionally loosely structured, as I wanted to give the participants the opportunity to provide unfiltered comments pertaining to their experience. This data collection was complementary to the interviews, and thus both enhanced interview reflections and provided a deeper understanding to the meaning and experience of the transition for these participants. Six people participated in this second data portion of the research.

I used an intentional analysis approach, which Wertz (2011) describes as focusing on the how and what of the experience. Phenomenological studies focus on the most general concept. Through a process of eidetic reduction, these studies determine what the experience includes for everything within that phenomenon, in this case the transition from a community college to a large research institution.

Table 1.1

Participant Information

Name	Academic Major	Age at transfer	Gender	Ethnicity	Children	Relationship Status	Class Standing	Location of Attended Community College
Jefferson	Electrical Engineering	21	Male	Hispanic/Latino; White	0	Single	Junior	In-state
Anastazia	Animal Science	21	Female	Hispanic/Latino	0	Single	Senior	In-state
Elizabeth	History	21	Female	White	0	Single	Junior	In-state
Max	Biological Sciences	22	Male	White	0	Single	Junior	Out-of-state
Mya	Hospitality, Restaurant and Tourism Management	23	Female	Black or African American	0	Single	Junior	In-state
Nadine	Pre-Spanish Education	23	Female	White	1	Single	Junior	In-state
Clark	Psychology	24	Male	Preferred not to answer	0	Married	Sophomore	Out-of-state
Tom	Political Science	25	Male	White	0	Single	Junior	In-state
Nicholas	Business Administration	25	Male	White	0	Unmarried, living with partner	Senior	In-state
Jean	English	25	Female	White	0	Single	Junior	In-state
Suzy	Supply Chain Management	30	Female	White	0	Single	Senior	In-state
Ronnie Lea	Child, Youth and Family Studies	41	Female	White	1	Single	Senior	Out-of-state

Table 1.2

Characteristics of Study Participants

Characteristic	Number (percentage)
Living	
On-campus (Residence Hall)	2 (16.7%)
Off-campus	9 (75.0%)
Off-campus (with parents)	1 (8.3%)
Intending on working	
Yes, On-campus	2 (16.7%)
Yes, Off-campus	8 (66.7%)
No, but may look eventually	2 (16.7%)
No, not intending to work	1 (8.3%)
Transfer cumulative GPA	
4.0	1 (8.3%)
3.5-3.99	7 (58.3%)
3.00-3.49	2 (16.7%)
2.50-2.99	2 (16.7%)
University Transfer Events attended	
Individual Campus visit	4 (33.3%)
None	4 (33.3%)
How to Transfer day	3 (25.0%)
Middle West University Transfer day at previous institution	2 (16.7%)
Red Letter day	0 (0.0%)
Participation in New Student Enrollment	
On-campus	9 (75.0%)
Mail-in	2 (16.7%)
Late Registration	1 (8.3%)
Credits enrolled in during first semester	
12 credits	1 (8.3%)
13 credits	2 (16.7%)
14 credits	6 (50.0%)
15 credits	0 (0.0%)
16 credits	1 (8.3%)
17 credits	2 (16.7%)
Financial Aid	
Grants or scholarships (university/government granted)	7 (58.3%)
Scholarships (private)	1 (8.3%)
Loans (Perkins, Stafford, Direct PLUS, private)	9 (75.0%)
Unsure	1 (8.3%)

Note: all data was self-reported on their initial questionnaire. The only information that could be verified was credits at transfer, which was done by using unofficial transcripts submitted by the participants to the researcher.

[a] The class standing for the university transfer population for the fall 2014 semester was 17.0% first-year; 34.9% sophomore; 36.8% juniors; 11.2% seniors.

Site Description

Middle West University is a large research-extensive institution in the midwestern United States. There are approximately 25,000 students enrolled at this institution with roughly 900 new transfer students each fall. Between 2005–2010, over 50% (2251 out of 4414) of the students who transfer into Middle West University were community college transfer students. Over the past five years, the demographic distribution of the university has been made up of 75% in-state residential students, although the percentage of out-of-state students is increasing slightly each year.

Data Analysis

Phenomenological studies are designed to capture the essence or the meaning of the experience for the participants, and as such some researchers argue for a more flexible, yet scientific approach that allows for an "analytic description of the phenomena not affected by prior assumptions" (Bloomberg and Volpe, 2012, p. 137). Gibson and Brown (2009) clarify there is no perfect definition of how to create themes, only suggestions and guidelines to help researchers make the best decision for their particular study. Strauss and Corbin (1998) articulated that phenomena are the categories that are found within axial coding and they help to explain the experience. Phenomenology is meant to examine lived experiences of a person or group of people and to understand the meaning to the experience (Creswell, 1994), while the explanation of open and axial coding discussed by Strauss and Corbin (1998) provided additional support for open and axial coding.

Validation

Creswell and Miller (2000) provided a list of methods for validation. They admit the list is not exhaustive, but provides a thorough review of many of the most utilized techniques in qualitative research. They included nine methods: triangulation of data sources; member checking; disconfirming evidence; thick, rich description; researcher reflexivity; prolonged engagement in the field; collaboration; peer debriefing; and the audit trail (Creswell & Miller, 2000). Creswell and Miller (2000) pointed out the importance of using multiple validity methods. Six of the nine validity techniques discussed by Creswell and Miller (2000) were accounted for, including: disconfirming evidence, prolonged engagement in the field, thick-rich description, triangulation, member-checking, and peer debriefing.

RESULTS

In conversation, different components that both helped and hindered the transition emerged. A significant percentage of the discussion centered on individual responsibility, the environment, and people that were perceived as important to the transition. Five major themes emerged from the analysis of the data: funding the college experience; transition takes time; support is critical; maturity and personal responsibility matter.

Theme 1: Funding the College Experience

One of the key reasons the participants chose to start at the community college was due to finances. Out of the 12 participants in the study, 10 cited finances as one of the top reasons they began at a community college. Anastazia noted her financially-based decision was tied to family circumstances while Jean appreciated the added value of a scholarship she received at the community college.

While the cost was discussed by many, there were other funding aspects that surfaced as well. Most students were very conscious of the increased cost in attending the university and this awareness was an important part of their transition, particularly as most students were struggling to find ways to be successful students while avoiding significant amounts of debt. Jean received a specific university grant and pointed out that she likely would not have come to Middle West University without the grant. Anastazia considered other schools, but they did not provide as much financial aid, while Mya focused her search only on Middle West University because she received a tuition discount because her mother worked there.

Most of the students interviewed needed to subsidize the cost of attending college by working. During their first semester at the university, 9 of the 12 participants were employed. Most were working to avoid taking out loans and to pay bills. While some had loans, most were debt adverse and thus tried to pay as much as possible by working. Nicholas emphasized this point, "I don't want to be in so much debt that I take out big loans so I would compensate by just working full-time."

When choosing where to live, 10 out of the 12 chose to live off-campus. Three specifically noted that living off-campus was due to cost. Suzy pointed out that "living at home is the most economical choice at this point." Some discussed the importance of using alternative travel (biking, public transportation, off-campus parking lots) to campus to avoid paying for parking permits. Every person mentioned the importance of finances in their decision to transfer to a university, and recognized the costs involved in pursing their bachelor's degree.

Theme 2: Transition Takes Time

The second theme that surfaced was the notion that the transition takes time. Many felt overwhelmed at the beginning of the transition process. This feeling surfaced in multiple ways. Many felt overwhelmed from the initial point of researching possible transfer institutions, to transitioning, to well into their first semester at the institution. Jean pointed out that "I think that might have been the overload of information too. I just didn't even know what to look at." Many who did participate in campus tours were overwhelmed with the sheer size of Middle West University.

Two of the participants were from out-of-state community colleges. Max indicated that he did not initially have a feeling of being overwhelmed before arriving at Middle West University because he had utilized online resources to learn about the university. Once he arrived at the institution, however, he felt overwhelmed. The notion of when the transition ended varied for each participant. Many believed it would be at the end of the first semester before they felt like they could say the transition was over. Anastazia was unsure of when the transition would really end, stating "I don't know. I don't know if the transition is over for me yet." At the same time, Mya felt "like it's not going to be over until I walk that stage." Some argued that transitions never end.

Some participants discussed not knowing what to initially expect with regard to their academics. In terms of classes or the campus environment, many felt nervous and believed it would take time to adjust. About three months into the semester, Jefferson felt like he was "gaining some momentum and direction" with regard to his classes. Nadine found herself becoming more comfortable about half-way through the semester. For most participants, the notion that the transition takes time was related to three key insights: acclimating and learning the new environment, understanding the resources and support systems that existed on campus, and developing an increased sense of confidence in one's own abilities.

Participants did not view negatively the time it took to transition to the university. In fact, nearly all of the participants ultimately found the transition to be a positive experience and felt their experience was fairly smooth and seamless, despite some of the challenges that they experienced. Elizabeth stated, "overall this semester has been fun but a serious challenge."

Theme 3: Support is Critical

All of the participants highlighted a wide variety of supports that they relied on to transition successfully. Supports ranged from personal to work-related to institutional. Support was discussed both at the community college and university levels and was found in both active and implied support mechanisms. In fact, the word "support" was mentioned over 250 times within the interviews while "resource" was used over 170 times. One aspect of support that was talked about a lot was academic advising. The word "advise/adviser/advising" appeared over 280 times in the transcripts. The participants highlighted the need for support throughout the process.

Community college advising. Many participants had mixed advising experiences at their community college. All of the participants felt that advising was critical for an effective transition. Some of the participants—including Anastazia and Nicholas—discussed the difficulties they experienced with their community college advisors, noting their advisers seemed to use an instruction manual for advising as opposed to individualizing the experience. Nicholas attended two different community colleges and discussed the lack of consistency among messages he received from his advisors, particularly on transferability of courses. However, not everyone's experience with advising at the community college was poor. Clark noted that his advising was effective and he enrolled in the right classes. While the advising experiences of the participants were mixed, nearly all indicated they enjoyed their overall experience at the community college.

University advising. Another important support that was discussed frequently was advising at the four-year university. All of the participants of this study were pleased at this point with their advising experiences at

Middle West University. No one highlighted any poor experiences thus far, although not everyone viewed the role of the adviser the same.

The advisers at the university were considered knowledgeable and were able to articulate how credits transferred, although a number of participants wished the credit evaluation process would take less time. A few participants did not know how some of the credits had transferred, even after the semester had started. At the end of the semester, several students were still trying to determine how some of their credits would count toward their degree requirements.

Elizabeth did not use an adviser regularly when at the community college, but she heeded the advice of others as she transitioned to her new institution. She had been told to meet with advisers to "build a relationship, and always make sure you're on the right track. It's an adjustment to always meet with an advisor, but it's nice that I can have a support group that will keep me on track."

Other institutional supports. While the advisers at the four-year institution were generally helpful, other supports and resources were also discussed. Nearly all participants noted that it is hard to identify what resources exist and where those support units may be located. Tom could have used "a little more hands on information as to the resources that are available . . . I know the resources are there, but to find out about them or to discover how I can utilize them, that's a little more."

Additional resources that were considered important by the participants included the library, the accessibility of wireless internet, and online resources. Participants also specifically highlighted the helpfulness of the financial aid office. Having a good understanding of their financial situation and understanding the process for receiving financial aid were important. Mya felt that the staff in the financial aid office were open, accessible, and straightforward. Jefferson said he visited the financial aid office frequently and emphasized that the staff there were "super nice."

The institutional support that every participant highlighted was the weekly Transfer Connections email. "The Transfer Connection includes timely reminders, events on and around campus, and helpful suggestions." (University of Nebraska-Lincoln, 2015). Each student made different use of this email, but everyone appreciated this regular communication.

Family support. Family played a critical role, but that role varied for individual participants. For instance, two participants had the responsibility of children, compared with others who still lived with their parents. One was fully enrolled in online courses in order to be with his spouse who was studying abroad. All of the participants felt a need for their family to be supportive of their decision to pursue the bachelor's degree. Nearly all of them said that had their family not been supportive, they would have strongly reconsidered attending the university.

One of the ways families provided support was financial. This financial support included small things, such as purchasing school supplies, to larger-scale support, such as rent-free housing and providing a dependent child scholarship. Sometimes the support the family provided was not financial; in fact, most of the time it was in other forms. For some, it was providing free child care, while for another it was acting as a rolemodel to her child, and for others it was academic support and motivation. Seven of the participants had family members who had received bachelor's degrees, and those family members provided emotional as well as crucial academic support. For instance, Jean's mother had helped her review her degree audit to ensure she understood what courses she still needed.

Family may also be a distraction. For instance, Ronnie Lea discussed the support she received from her son, however, he also proved a distraction when he was sick or when she needed to attend his school activities. Similarly, Nadine was living at home, and occasionally ran into family distractions that were unintentional and problematic. Overall, the general message was clear. Family was vital to the transition process by providing a wide variety of supports. Whether financial, emotional, or physical support, the added value of having close family support helped community college transfer students in this study to feel successful as they started at Middle West University.

Support from friends. The support from friends was noted consistently as important, although different, from the support role of family. The participants shared a variety of benefits from their network of friends. Anastazia's roommate was already a student at Middle West University, with knowledge of the campus, such as navigating the busses and using the library. Jean and Tom discussed the internal emotional role that the support of friends had on their transitions. Some friends provided needed academic support. Nadine met friends from class to review problems for math and Spanish, while Jefferson worked with friends for his chemistry review. Tom noted that he did not study with anyone at the community college and this was something he hoped to do at the university. He joined various study groups, which he found to be quite helpful. Clark, a military veteran who suffers from a traumatic brain injury as a result of combat, was in a unique situation. Clark was completing his coursework via distance education because he was currently out of the country. Clark highlighted the important role his wife played, supporting him and keeping him focused, noting this was especially important with online classes.

Socializing was also a consistent form of support for many of the participants. Some, like Elizabeth, talked about having social nights with their roommates while others talked about experiencing aspects of the city with new friends. Nadine found support from friends at work in similar life situations with balancing children, and they often share family events. Jean talked about the important support her church network provided in her transition to Middle West University. Nicholas and Mya talked about the importance of spending time with their significant others.

Support from work. Out of 12 participants, nine were working. Nearly all participants valued the flexibility and support that employers and coworkers provided. This support manifested in a variety of ways. For some, the employer was flexible with scheduling hours to ensure the student was able to go to class or study as needed. Mya's boss had a graduate degree and helped her by critiquing her resume. Tom juggled multiple jobs throughout his time at the community college as well as during his time at the university. His employers have been extremely flexible, and he articulated the importance of communicating with his supervisors in advance in order to ensure that he could balance his studies with his jobs.

Theme 4: Maturity

The next theme related to the participants' views of themselves. This theme relates to the focus of Transition Theory on coping resources and the accurate appraisal of the assets and limitations of each individual. All participants viewed themselves as being more mature at the point of transfer to Middle West University. The time at the community college had allowed them to create a more refined vision of who they wanted to become and what they wanted to do. Some of the participants believed they would not have been mature enough to start at a four-year institution and felt that being a community college transfer student provided them with an excellent opportunity to be more focused on their academics when they transferred.

Many of the participants compared themselves to the other students in their classes that had started at Middle West University. They believed they valued their educational experience more than many of their classmates. Some attributed their maturity to age, but also thought they had a broader range of life experiences because they had been at multiple institutions.

Those who were more traditional age, such as Anastazia, had a slightly different viewpoint concerning their maturity. She felt she was mature, but she sought out experiences in part because she wanted to continue to grow and mature. She felt she was too mature to live in the dorms, and she wanted to grow from adult responsibilities such as paying bills on her own "rather than just paying the school and getting it over with."

Some participants highlighted frustrations with Middle West University that they believed originated from being viewed as older. For instance, a few believed some professors geared assignments toward traditional-aged students and did not account for those in a different life circumstance. In other portions of campus life, some felt student organizations were mostly geared toward the traditional-aged student starting at Middle West University, and felt less inclined to participate in those organizations.

For many, the sense of being more mature was a different experience for them at the four-year institution versus at the community college. At the community college, participants experienced a broader range of students, so they felt they blended in more easily. As Ronnie Lea stated, "for me to walk up and say, 'I'm a non-traditional student' was pointless because almost everyone in my class was non-traditional."

Theme 5: Personal Responsibility

The final theme that emerged in the study was the role of personal responsibility. This theme surfaced as participants discussed what the transition meant to them. They appreciated the support from a broad spectrum of people and campus departments, but in the end they knew that they needed to personally own the responsibility of pursuing a bachelor's degree. Nadine pointed out that she had to prove she could do it for herself.

The participants used different strategies to navigate their transition. These strategies varied, but each deployed strategies they hoped would help them have a better transition experience. In fact, when asked how they felt about the strategies they had used to navigate the transition, all of the participants felt confident that their strategies were effective. No one highlighted any ineffective strategies.

Many participants discussed the decision to take a lighter course load during their first semester in the university. While they may have been able to take on more credits, there was a sense of wanting to ease into the transition and understand the resources and system before taking more classes. There were two students who wished they would have taken a lighter load, as one ended up dropping a course and felt that the 17 credits he was enrolled in were too many for his first semester.

Other strategies included effective communication. Many mentioned the need to communicate frequently with their advisers, professors, and employers about what they needed to be successful or to receive guidance. Some communicated their needs to family members to ensure they could continue to pursue their goals. Many participants underscored the importance of being willing to ask questions or asking others around their classrooms if they would be willing to study together. Many pointed out they had to be willing to seek guidance from various offices on campus such as advisers, the education abroad office, and financial aid.

Some found that they needed to find places on campus to study to aid in their transition. Most had never utilized their community college as a place to study and instead went home. Now, even those students that commuted were looking for places to study. Locations such as the library, college-specific facilities, and the veteran's center were widely mentioned as ideal locations for studying. Because the students were spending more time on campus, they began to embrace the role of a student more than they had at the community college. At the four-year institution they were finding themselves taking on more responsibility and studying more to ensure they were successful in their transition to the university.

The transition to the university meant a lot to the participants, because obtaining a bachelor's degree was viewed as a major milestone. As Max remarked, the transition is a "big step" in moving forward towards degree attainment goals while Nadine believes "Every step counts because it gets you closer." A number of participants talked about the newfound focus and pleasure of taking classes directly related to their career path and what they want to do the rest of the lives. Mya began contemplating important questions, from "What am I supposed to get from this class?" to "How am I supposed to add this to my career?" Many connected the meaning of their transition to their career potential, but this was particularly important for the non-traditional students who had worked for years in unsatisfying jobs. As both Ronnie Lea and Suzy commented, this transition to the four-year institution would allow them to pursue careers that they felt passionate about pursuing and that provided more financial stability.

DISCUSSION

This study sought to better understand the transition experience of community college transfer students by applying Schlossberg's Transition Theory. At this particular institution, there was minimal data on any transfer students, and certainly not specifically about community college transfer students. There was a strong interest in understanding their experience and how it may have connected to the theoretical underpinnings of Transition Theory.

Schlossberg's 4S Coping Resources

Schaefer (2010) found students needed a better understanding of the educational process, were motivated by their career aspirations, and required complex support. The need for better understanding of the educational process is connected to the support and information gathered prior to transitioning. Similar to Schaefer's study, transfer participants discussed their bewilderment and confusion about how to access resources. Likewise, these participants were career-driven, which relates to the strategies they used to navigate their transition.

Rumann's (2010) dissertation highlighted the experience of student veterans returning to a community college. One of the themes that emerged in his study centered around the interactions and connections with others, including key relationships with family, military peers, civilians, the veteran affairs certifying official, faculty, and college peers. Rumann found "family relationships and interactions as being integral to managing their transitions back to the civilian world and college." This study also found similar results with regard to the positive impact of family.

DiRamio, Ackerman, and Mitchell (2008) studied military veterans, and similar to this study, found that student veterans had a higher level of maturity in comparison to other students. While their study attributed their higher maturity level to world travel and cultural experiences, this current study ascribed this higher maturity to the multiple institutions navigated and the broader life experiences of community college transfer students. Community college transfer students felt they had a clearer vision of their educational goals compared to their native peers.

DeVilbiss (2014) studied the transition that conditionally-admitted students experience through the lens of Schlossberg's Transition Theory and found a need for support, particularly from people and services on campus. These supports included teachers, new friends, a college transition class, welcome week events, and other university services. This study also found this to be true for community college transfer students. Community college transfer students talked about the importance on their successful transition of advisers, the value of friendships and of students in their classes, and the significance of support service offices across campus.

Archambault's (2010) dissertation found students felt less confident with their ability to cope with change and had lower views of self. Transfer students in this study felt overwhelmed and were unaware of some of the resources that were available. These feelings of being overwhelmed did impact their experience, but most felt that they were able to cope with the transition fairly well.

Three-phase Transition Process

Archambault (2010) asserted that early in the transition students focus on the process of moving *into* the transition, rather than moving *through* the transition. She perceived students were being pushed into a phase they were not ready to transition into yet. Transfer students in this study were likely to be in the "moving in" phase, since they were still adjusting to the new environment, learning the system, and determining how the university worked. The "moving through" period "begins once learners know the ropes" (Anderson et al., 2012, p. 57). Few participants felt like they "knew the ropes" and this finding suggests the moving in phase may take more time for transfer students than universities realize. Universities often push students to become involved and to take advantage of opportunities early in the semester before they have "learned the ropes" of the institution and while they are still transitioning into their new educational environment.

In discussing the "moving in" stage of a transition with respect to a new job, Anderson et al. (2012) discuss the role that an official orientation can serve to assist with the transition, and highlight the finding that individuals must learn expectations and norms. With respect to applying Transition Theory to higher education, Patton and Davis (2014) demonstrate the importance of the receiving university providing a supportive environment and a structured and detailed orientation. Flaga (2006) highlights the need for enhanced orientation programs that provide information related to their major, adviser, and campus. While some of the participants who participated in orientation had recommendations for improvement, their input aligns with this recommendation.

The presented literature and the results of this study underscore the importance of the three-phase transition process articulated by Transition Theory. The moving in phase of the transition for a community college transfer student begins the moment the student makes the decision to transfer to a university, through the early part of their time at the new university, and includes their learning "the ropes" of the institution. The moving through phase may not happen as early as anticipated. Students frequently discussed being overwhelmed and many did not know about the resources even at the end of their first semester. Additionally, many felt extremely overwhelmed with the demands of navigating new locations and buildings while also learning new policies and procedures. Several felt the transition would be over near the end of the first semester, believing they understood their new institutional context and how to best navigate through the transition.

The moving out phase may begin at different times for different individuals. Participants mentioned the concept of a constant transition, something that Anderson et al. (2012) addressed in their study. They theorized that moving out may not be complete for a student until they graduate; if that happens to be the case, then the process of moving through the transition may last longer than some of the students anticipated.

Anderson et al. (2012) noted the model itself helps partially answer "why different individuals react differently to the same type of transition and why the same person reacts differently at different times" (p. 63). The transition is experienced differently by each individual, thus creating inherent challenges when using a standard "one-size-fits-all" approach for community college transfer students.

Limitations

Given the qualitative framework of this study, it is important to address potential limitations in generalizing conclusions beyond this research. This study examined the experiences of 12 participants who transferred to the same university, six from the same primary community college feeder institution to this university. However, over 980 students transferred into Middle West University during the period of this study, so there are many voices not captured in this analysis. However, the sample generally reflects the two-year institutional breakdown of community colleges transfer students into Middle West University.

Nearly all of the students who transferred entered with junior or senior standing. Only two of the participants entered with sophomore standing, so I potentially missed the viewpoints of community college transfer students with lower numbers of credit hours in this study. This may have been due to the fact that participation in this study was limited to those who were 19 years of age or older. Many of the students viewed themselves as non-traditional, as working students and perhaps less involved. It is possible that a more traditional-aged transfer student would have a different type of transition in comparison to those who participated in this study.

An unanticipated limitation for this study was the fact that a number of the students did not feel their transition was complete. This raises the question of the best time to capture the transition experience, whether this is during the transition or after the transition is complete. Data was captured at three separate times throughout the first semester of the community college transfer students, with simultaneous journaling from half of the participants. Interviewing participants upon completion of their first semester, rather than during the first semester, may have highlighted different perspectives from a reflective standpoint.

Recommendations

The recommendations made in qualitative studies are limited in scope, however, there were instances in which the findings from this study contributed to the research literature in this area. This section focuses on recommendations as derived from the use of Schlossberg's Transition Theory as a framework to describe the transition experiences of community college transfer students.

Recommendations for community colleges. The most important student service discussed at the community college level was that of academic advising, although participants had mixed reactions towards their advising experiences. Given the priority participants placed on strong academic advising, community colleges should ensure community college advisors are properly trained and provided adequate resources. There are strong indications that the experiences of students with advising would have been more consistent and positive if additional staff development was put into place. Cuseo (2012) highlighted national data that indicates students place the academic advising ahead of any other support centers in community colleges.

Archambault (2010) noted faculty members are in a position to play an important role in helping students transition, and Cuseo (2012) recommended connecting students with faculty mentors. While some participants did mention meaningful relationships with faculty, many did not. For the few community college transfer students who did discuss transfer with a faculty member, most found it helpful.

Cuseo (2012) provided additional recommendations ranging from the importance of delivering timely transfer workshops to developing a physical space for a transfer center. A few participants in this study agreed with the idea that a transfer center would have been helpful. Engaging students while at the community college may help them embrace the role of being a student more fully. Most of the Middle West University participants discussed that as they transitioned to the university they felt more like college students.

Recommendations for universities. One of the observations made was that it did not appear that sending and receiving institutions worked together, as Middle West University participants believed there was a lack of collaboration between the community college and the university. Based on this, a more substantive collaboration could be crucial for helping to foster a positive transition. Flaga (2006) noted there is an incentive for four-year universities to have an active role with community college transfer students through all phases of their college experience, both at the community college and the four-year university. Students in this study frequently discussed their perception that they lacked accurate information from their community college advisers, and a more collaborative approach might ameliorate this limitation.

DiCesare and Younger (2015) shared an ongoing training model being utilized within the Minnesota State Colleges and Universities System. This model annually brings together advisers and transfer specialists for a conference, includes an annual orientation training for new specialists, and hosts regional transfer meetings to discuss updates that pertain to particular regions within the state. Since the implementation of these programs overall satisfaction has risen, and perceptions of the overall ease of transfer have improved.

While at the community college, a few Middle West University participants took advantage of campus visit days that included visiting with university staff. Flaga (2006) recommended regular visits from universities to their feeder community colleges. Four-year institutions need to cultivate relationships with students considering transferring, and need to make regular and intentional visits to the community college. Advisers from four-year institutions should visit community colleges and meet with students to discuss their questions, provide resources, and recommend transferable coursework at the community college.

Most community college transfer students have financial concerns. The students in this study discussed—at length—the impact finances have had on their academic journey. Participants were predominantly concerned about the lack of scholarships and financial aid, the higher cost of tuition at the four-year institution, and a perceived need to work to pay their bills. If institutions restructured their financial aid packages, they may attract and retain more community college students. As Archambault, Forbes, and Schlosberg (2012) note, financial challenges may be real or perceived, but this perception creates a cascading impact on a student's choice to work or reduce credit hour loads.

At a recent National Institute for the Study of Transfer Students conference, transfer professionals observed many orientation programs were not mandatory for transfer students (Marling, 2015). Flaga (2006) highlighted the need for enhanced orientation programs that provide opportunities for intentionally connecting transfer students to their major, adviser, and to the campus. Marling and Jacobs (2011) stressed transfer orientations play an important role in retaining and graduating students. Middle West University orientation participants had recommendations to improve the orientation program, and their remarks corroborate this suggestion. Orientation programs are a source of accurate information and provide introductions to support systems for students before classes begin.

Recommendations for Schlossberg's Transition Theory. This study relied on several key aspects of Schlossberg's Transition Theory. In Schlossberg's five themes, the notion of the transition taking time corresponds to the 3-phase model of moving in, moving through, and moving out. "Support is critical" connects to one of the four coping resources. "Maturity" intersects with the self-coping resource while "personal responsibility" maps onto the strategies coping resource. "Funding the college experience" is related to the situation coping resource. The following section briefly highlights implications for the use of Transition Theory.

The transition process. The transition process as described in Schlossberg's Transition Theory is a 3-phase process: moving in, moving through, and moving out. The cycle of transition is continual, and as one moves out of a transition, they are simultaneously moving into a new transition.

Examining the initial phase of moving in, it is important to understand the amount of new information being processed at a given time. In this study, students described this initial phase of transition with words such as confused, overwhelmed, overloaded, and intimidated. This model may help institutions conceptualize where students are in the transition process and how to adapt the type of support provided to better correspond with their phase of transitioning. If an advisor or other institutional figure perceives a student is lacking motivation, yet has seemingly adapted to their new role and program, that student may need to be treated differently than the student who has yet to grasp the difference in being a student at the community college and being a student at the university. Anderson et al. (2012) furthermore assert that a student's perception of the scope of the transition may impact the magnitude of the effects. If roles, relationships, or routines are dramatically altered during the transition, this could negatively or positively impact the individual more or less depending on the size and duration of the change.

The 4S coping resources. McGill and Lazarowicz (2012) extensively discussed the application of the 4S coping resources within advising. This study examined all four of the coping resource categories (situation, self, support, and strategies), which emerged within the coding phase of the data analysis.

Within the situation coping resource, there are a number of salient characteristics. Timing is a key element that references a student's perception of whether the timing was right. Whether the student was admitted during their first application or deferred may impact a perception of timing. Transferring timed to accommodate a move for a partner or the completion of an associate degree may also impact both a student's overall transition and the perception of their transition. The 4S model "partially answers the question of why different individuals react differently to the same type of transition and why the same person reacts differently at different times" (Anderson et al., 2012, p. 63). Students experience transition in a variety of ways, thus a review of assets and liabilities within the 4S model enhances understanding of individual responses. Students will be better served and their transition experience improved when informed with this understanding.

Recommendations for future research. Given the increasing number of individuals who attend community colleges, along with an intensified federal spotlight on community college education as an affordable pathway to a four-year degree, research that examines the transition experiences between community college and a four-year institution thus becomes increasingly crucial.

Further disaggregating the community college transfer student population will provide potentially meaningful future research. This study included both in-state and out-of-state transfer students, traditionally and post-traditionally aged students, and those living both on- and off-campus. By refining demographic pools of participants, results may show trends and information that would inform subsequent tailoring of services and support.

This research attempted to capture the transition of students as it occurred and examined this transition at multiple points in time as recommended by Anderson et al., (2012). However, a retroactive analysis of a student's transition after graduation may provide a significant amount of useful data. Capturing the student's voice after they graduate or drop out may inform understanding of what salient aspects of Schlossberg's 4S model were prevalent in their experiences, while examining how the subsequent transition experience from college to the workplace may offer additional valuable insights.

CONCLUSION

The findings of this study suggest possibilities for improving the transition experience for community college transfer students. Consistent with the findings of other studies that have used Schlossberg's Transition Theory, this is a valuable theoretical framework for working with community college transfer students. Transfer student policies and procedures should intentionally foster the increase of student assets in Schlossberg's 4S coping resources and should remain mindful of the full scope of transition (moving in, moving through, and moving out). Informing administrators, staff, and policy makers with research grounded in Transition Theory will improve the transition of community college transfer students and provide support to significant and growing numbers of students in higher education.

REFERENCES

American Association of Community Colleges (2016). *2016 community college first facts.* Retrieved from http://www.aacc.nche.edu/AboutCC/Pages/fastfactsfactsheet.aspx

Anderson, M. L., Goodman, J., & Schlossberg, N. K. (2012). *Counseling adults in transition: Linking Schlossberg's theory with practice in a diverse world* (4th ed.). New York, NY: Springer Publishing Company.

Astin, A. W. (1999). Student involvement: A developmental theory for higher education. *Journal of College Student Development, 40*(5), 518–529.

Archambault, K. L. (2010). *Improving transfer student preparation: Transition theory and organizational change in one community college.* (Doctoral dissertation). Retrieved from ProQuest Dissertations and Theses database. (UMI No. 3490359)

Archambault, K., Forbes, M., and Schlosberg, L. (2012). Challenges in the transfer transition. *Advising transfer students: Issues and strategies* (2nd ed.). 105–118. [Monograph].

Bloomberg, L. D., & Volpe, M. (2012). *Completing your qualitative dissertation: A road map from beginning to end.* (2nd ed.). Thousand Oaks, CA: SAGE Publications, Inc.

Cameron, C. (2005). Experiences of transfer students in a collaborative baccalaureate nursing program. *Community College Review, 33*(2), 22–44. doi:10.1177/009155210503300202

Carlan, P. E., & Byxbe, F. R. (2000). Community colleges under the microscope: An analysis of performance predictors for native and transfer students. *Community College Review, 28*(2), 27–42.

Cejda, B. D. (1997). An examination of transfer shock in academic disciplines. *Community College Journal of Research and Practice, 21*(3), 279–288. doi: 10.1080/1066892970210301

Cejda, B. D., & Kaylor, A. J. (1997). Academic performance of community college transfer students at private liberal arts colleges. *Community College Journal of Research and Practice, 21*(7), 651–659.

Cejda, B. D., & Kaylor, A. J. (2001). Early transfer: A case study of traditional-aged community college students. *Community College Journal of Research and Practice, 25*(8), 621–638. doi: 10.1080/106689201316880795

Cejda, B. D., Kaylor, A. J., & Rewey, K. L. (1998). Transfer shock in an academic discipline: The relationship between students' majors and their academic performance. *Community College Review, 26*(3), 1–13.

Cohen, A. M., & Kisker, C. B. (2010). *The shaping of American higher education: Emergence and growth of the contemporary system.* San Francisco, CA: Jossey-Bass.

Conrad Glass Jr., J., & Harrington, A. R. (2002). Academic performance of community college transfer students and "native" students at a large state university. *Community College Journal of Research and Practice, 26*(5), 415–430. doi:10.1080/02776770290041774

Creswell, J. W. (2008). *Educational research: Planning, conducting, and evaluating quantitative and qualitative research.* (3rd ed.). Upper Saddle River, NJ: Pearson Education.

Creswell, J. W., & Miller, D. L. (2000). Determining validity in qualitative inquiry. *Theory Into Practice, 39*(3), 124–130.

Cuseo, J. (2012). Facilitating the transfer transition: Specific and systemic strategies for 2- & 4-year institutions. *Advising transfer students: Issues and strategies* (2nd ed.). 135–152. [Monograph].

Davies, T. G., & Casey, K. L. (1999). Transfer student experiences: Comparing their academic and social lives at the community college and university. *College Student Journal, 33*(1), 60–71.

DeVilbiss, S. E. (2014). *The transition experience: Understanding the transition from high school to college for conditionally-admitted students using the lens of Schlossberg's transition theory.* (Doctoral dissertation). Available from ProQuest Dissertations and Theses database. (UMI No. 3618529)

DiCesare, L. & Younger, T. (2015, February). *Student transfer survey results and transfer initiatives.* Session presented at the annual conference of the National Institute for the Study of Transfer Students, Atlanta, GA.

DiRamio, D., Ackerman, R., & Mitchell, R. L. (2008). From combat to campus: Voices of student-veterans. *NASPA Journal, 45*(1), 73–102.

Ditchkoff, S. S., Laband, D. N., & Hanby, K. (2003). Academic performance of transfer versus "native" students in a wildlife bachelor of science program. *Wildlife Society Bulletin, 31*(4), 1021–1026.

Doyle, W. R. (2006). Community college transfers and college graduation: Whose choices mater most? *Change: The Magazine of Higher Learning, 38*(3), 56–58.

Evans, N. J., Forney, D. S., Guido, F. M., Patton, L. D., & Renn, K. A. (2010). *Student development in college: Theory, research, and practice.* (2nd ed.). San Francisco, CA: Jossey-Bass.

Fee, J., Prolman, S., & Thomas, J. (2009). Making the most of a small midwestern university: The case of transfer students. *College Student Journal, 43*(4), 1204–1216.

Flaga, C. T. (2006). The process of transition for community college transfer students. *Community College Journal of Research and Practice, 30*(1), 3–19. doi: 10.1080/10668920500248845

Gibson, W. J., & Brown, A. (2009). *Working with qualitative data.* Thousand Oaks, CA: SAGE Publications, Inc.

Goodman, J., & Pappas, J. G. (2000). Applying the Schlossberg 4S transition model to retired university faculty: Does it fit? *Adultspan Journal, 2*(1), 15–28.

Goodman, J., Schlossberg, N. K., & Anderson, M. L. (2006). *Counseling adults in transition: Linking practice with theory* (3rd ed.). New York, NY: Springer Publishing Company.

Grites, T. J. (2012). Introduction. In T. J. Grites & C. Duncan (Eds.), *Advising student transfers: Strategies for today's reality and tomorrow's challenges* (11–13). [Monograph Series 24].

Grites, T. J., & McDonald, N. L. (2012). General influence on the transfer landscape. In T. J. Grites & C. Duncan (Eds.), *Advising student transfers: Strategies for today's reality and tomorrow's challenges* (21–28). [Monograph Series 24].

Henderson, M. M. (2013). *Coming to terms: Career development experiences of NCAA division I female student-athletes in transition.* (Order No. 3557564, The George Washington University). ProQuest Dissertations and Theses, 154. Retrieved from http://search.proquest.com/docview/1346181178?accountid=8116. (1346181178).

Ishitani, T. T. (2008). How do transfer survive after "transfer shock"? A longitudinal study of transfer student departure at a four-year institution. *Research in Higher Education, 49*(5), 403–419. doi: 10.1007/s11162-008-9091-x

Ishitani, T. T., & McKitrick, S. A. (2010). After transfer: The engagement of community College students at a four-year collegiate institution. *Community College Journal of Research and Practice, 34*(7), 576–594. doi:10.1080/10668920701831522

Johnson, M. D. (2005) Academic performance of transfer versus "native" students in natural resources & sciences. *College Student Journal, 39*(3), 570–579.

Koerin, B. B., Harrigan, M. P., & Reeves, J. W. (1990). Facilitating the transition from student to social worker: Challenges of the younger student. *Journal of Social Work Education, 26*(2), 199–208. Retrieved from http://www.cswe.org/Publications/JSWE.aspx

Kuh, G. D. (2008, December 12). Diagnosing why some students don't succeed. *The Chronicle of Higher Education, 55*(16), A72.

Laanan, F. S (1996). Making the transition: Understanding the adjustment process of community college transfer students. *Community College Review, 23*(4), 69–84.

Marling, J. (2015, February). *Closing session: Advancing the transfer agenda.* Session presented at the annual conference of the National Institute for the Study of Transfer Students, Atlanta, GA.

Marling, J. L. & Jacobs, B. C. (2011). Establishing pathways for transfer student success through orientation. In M.A. Poisel & S. Joseph (Eds.), *Transfer students in higher education: Building foundations for policies, programs, and services that foster student success.* 71–87. [Monograph No. 54]. Columbia, SC: University of South Carolina, National Resource Center for the First-Year Experience and Students in Transition.

McAtee, A. B., & Benshoff, J. M. (2006). Rural dislocated women in career transition: The importance of supports and strategies. *Community College Journal of Research and Practice, 30*(9), 697–714. doi:10.1080/10668920500207858

McEwen, M. K. (2003). The nature and uses of theory. In S.R. Komives, D.B. Woodard, Jr., & Associates, *Student services: A handbook for the profession* (4th ed.). 153–178. San Francisco, CA: Jossey-Bass.

McGill, C. M., & Lazarowicz, T. (2012). Advising transfer students: Implications of Schlossberg's transition theory. In T. J. Grites & C. Duncan (Eds.), *Advising student transfers: Strategies for today's realities and tomorrow's challenges, 24.* 131–133. [Monograph].

McGowan, R. A., & Gawley, T. (2006). The university side of the college transfer experience: Insights from university staff. *College Quarterly, 9*(3). Retrieved from http://www.senecac.on.ca/quarterly/2006-vol09-num03-summer/gawley_mcgowan.html

Melguizo, T., Kienzl, G. S., & Alfonso, M. (2011). Comparing the educational attainment of community college transfer students and four-year college rising juniors using propensity score matching methods. *Journal Of Higher Education, 82*(3), 265–291.

Miller, A. (2013). Institutional practices that facilitate bachelor's degree completion for transfer students. *New Directions for Higher Education, 2013*(162), 39–50.

Montondon, L., & Eikner, A. (1997). Comparison of community college transfer students and native students in an upper level accounting course. *Community College Review, 25*(3), 21–38.

National Student Clearinghouse (2015). *Snapshot report—contribution of two-year institutions to four-year completions.* Retrieved from http://nscresearchcenter.org/snapshotreport-twoyearcontributionfouryearco mpletions17/

Packard, B., Tuladhar, C., & Lee, J. (2013). Advising in the classroom: How community college STEM faculty support transfer-bound students. *Journal of College Science Teaching, 42*(4), 14–20.

Patton, L. D., & Davis, S. (2014). Expanding transition theory: African American students' multiple transitions following hurricane Katrina. *Journal of College Admission*, (222), 6–15.

Rhine, T. J., Milligan, D. M., & Nelson, L. R. (2000). Alleviating transfer shock: Creating an environment for more successful transfer students. *Community College Journal of Research and Practice, 24*(6), 443–453. doi:10.1080/10668920050137228

Rumann, C. B. (2010). *Student veterans returning to a community college: Understanding their transitions.* (Doctoral dissertation). Retrieved from http://lib.dr.iastate.edu/etd/11583/

Schaefer, J. L. (2010). Voices of older baby boomer students: Supporting their transitions back into college. *Educational Gerontology, 36*(1),67–90. doi:10.1080/17419160903057967

Schlossberg, N. K. (1984). *Counseling adults in transition: Linking practice with theory.* New York, NY: Springer Publishing Company.

Schlossberg, N. K., Waters, E. B., & Goodman, J. (1995). *Counseling adults in transition* (2nd ed.). New York, NY: Springer Publishing Company.

Seidman, I. (2013) *Interviewing as qualitative research: A guide for researchers in education and the social sciences* (4th ed.). New York, NY: Teachers College Press.

Strauss, A., & Corbin, J. (1998). *Basics of qualitative research: Techniques and procedures for developing grounded theory.* (2nd ed.). Thousand Oaks, CA: SAGE Publications, Inc.

Swain, D. A. (1991). Withdrawal from sport and Schlossberg's model of transitions. *Sociology of Sport Journal, 8*(2), 152–160. Retrieved from http://journals.humankinetics.com/ssj

Tatum, B. C., Hayward, P., & Monzon, R. (2006). Faculty background, involvement, and knowledge of student transfer at an urban community college. *Community College Journal of Research and Practice, 30*(3),195–212. doi: 10.1080/10668920500322400

Thelin, J. R. (2003). Historical overview of American higher education. In S.R. Komives, D.B. Woodard, Jr., & Associates (Eds.), *Student services: A handbook for the profession* (3–22). San Francisco, CA: Jossey-Bass.

Tinto, V. (1998). Colleges as communities: Taking research on student persistence seriously. *The Review of Higher Education, 21*(2), 167–177.

Tovar, E., & Simon, M. A. (2006). Academic probation as a dangerous opportunity: Factors influencing diverse college students' success. *Community College Journal of Research and Practice, 30*(7), 547-564. doi: 10.1080/10668920500208237

Townsend, B. K. (2008). "Feeling like a freshman again": The transfer student transition. *New Directions for Higher Education, 2008*(144), 69–77.

Townsend, B. K., & Wilson, K. B. (2006). "A hand hold for a little bit": Factors facilitating the success of community college transfer students to a large research university. *Journal of College Student Development, 47*(4), 439–456. doi: 10.1353/csd.2006.0052

University of Nebraska-Lincoln. (2015). Transfer student resources. *First-Year Experience & Transition Programs.* Retrieved from http://success.unl.edu/transfer

U.S. Department of Education (2006). *The toolbox revisited: Paths to degree completion from high school through college.* Retrieved from http://www2.ed.gov/rschstat/research/pubs/toolboxrevisit/toolbox.pdf

U.S. Department of Education, National Center for Education Statistics (2011) 2004/09 Beginning Postsecondary Students Longitudinal Study (BPS: 04/09) retrieved from http://nces.ed.gov/programs/digest/d11/tables/dt11_347.asp

Wertz, F. J. (2011). A phenomenological psychological approach to trauma and resilience. In F. J. Wertz, K. Charmaz, L. M. McMullen, R. Josselson, R. Anderson, & E. McSpadden (Eds.), *Five ways of doing qualitative analysis* (124-164). New York, NY: Guilford Press.

Wheeler, G. D., Malone, L. A., VanVlack, S., Nelson, E. R., & Steadward, R. D. (1996). Retirement from disability sport: A pilot study. *Adapted Physical Activity Quarterly, 13*(4), 382–399.

Wheeler, H. A. (2012). Veterans' transitions to community college: A case study. *Community College Journal of Research and Practice, 36*(10), 775–792. doi:10.1080/10668926.2012.679457

Whitfield, M. (2005). Transfer-student performance in upper-division chemistry courses: Implications for curricular reform and alignment. *Community College Journal of Research and Practice, 29*(7), 531–545. doi: 10.1080/10668920590953999

Woosley, S. A., & Johnson, N. J. (2006). A comparison of the academic and cocurricular outcomes of residence hall transfer students and nontransfer students. *Journal of College and University Student Housing, 34*(1), 25–30.

Tony A. Lazarowicz, Ph.D. *is the Assistant Director of the College of Arts and Sciences Academic and Career Advising Center at the University of Nebraska-Lincoln.*

2

A Phenomenological Study of Two-Year College Students' Transition Experiences at a Four-Year Institution

Mary M. Von Kaenel, Ph.D. & Pamela A. Havice, Ph.D.

Abstract

Two-year college students experience challenges as they transfer to a four-year institution. To investigate these documented challenges, the present study used Weidman's Model of Undergraduate Socialization (1989), Tinto's Model of Student Integration (1993) and Deil-Amen's (2011) notion of socio-academic integrative moments to examine these transitions. A qualitative phenomenological study was conducted to explore the experiences of twelve two-year college students during their transition to a four-year university in the fall of 2013. The results included three themes, which were developed through an iterative data analysis process. These emergent themes focused on the importance of a transfer student's age in their ability to make a successful transition; dealing with the academic rigor of the new institution; and finding ways of making new social connections at the receiving institution.

Introduction

Two-year college students experience unique challenges as they transfer to a four-year institution. Given the growing popularity of community colleges and the fact that these institutions are more likely to enroll students from underserved groups—among the fastest growing populations in the U.S.—understanding the barriers they face is essential to increasing educational success rates in two- and four-year institutions. Unlike students who begin college at a four-year institution, community college students who wish to earn a baccalaureate degree must transfer in the middle of their undergraduate careers to achieve this goal. These students must acclimate to a new institution at the very time they are tackling the most demanding collegiate coursework. Describing the experiences of students who must go through this transition would seem to be a rich research domain, but there is little available evidence that delineates the academic and social challenges that transfer students face when they arrive at the four-year institution. This study begins to address this gap in the literature, using several well-established conceptual models, including Weidman's Model of Undergraduate Socialization (1989) and Deil-Amen's (2011) notion of socio-academic integrative moments to examine the factors that help or hinder students' transfer transitions.

The Importance of the Community College

Students enroll in two-year colleges for a variety of reasons: lower costs, geographic convenience (often closer to home for many students), and flexibility regarding course offerings (Karp, Hughes, O'Gara, 2010). For these reasons, enrollment in the two-year college sector is expected to grow significantly. According to a report by the National Center for Education Statistics (2012), between 2000 and 2010, enrollment at two-year institutions grew from 5.9 to 7.7 million students and is expected to reach 8.8 million students by 2021.

Two-year colleges are also an important point of access for students who might not otherwise have access to higher education. For example, students who enroll at two-year colleges are more likely to come from lower socio-economic backgrounds and to be the first in their family to attend college (Laanan, 2007). The American Association of Community Colleges (Mullin, 2012) documented that for the academic year 2007–2008, two-year or community colleges enrolled 1.7 million students who were living at a socio-economic level considered at poverty level and that the enrollment figure accounted for 41% of the total number of enrolled low-income postsecondary students. The AACC also identified other characteristics that put two-year college students at risk for completing their educational goals. These characteristics include delaying college attendance after high school graduation, part-time enrollment in college, financial independence, significant family responsibilities (such as caring for dependents), and the lack of a high school diploma (Mullin, 2012).

Given the prevalence of these risk factors among students who attend community colleges, students who start postsecondary education at a two-year college may be underprepared for the academic rigor of the four-year institution following transfer. Karp et al. (2010) noted "community colleges tend to enroll students who are more academically, economically, and socially disadvantaged than do other postsecondary institutions" (p. 70).

Researchers have also discovered that the challenges students face in making the transition from a two-year to a four-year postsecondary education institution have both academic and social dimensions. For example, students may find it difficult to become socialized to the new school, to learn new systems and processes at the receiving institution or to address increased academic rigor at the receiving four-year institution (Berger & Malaney, 2003, Karp et al., 2010). Moreover, unlike students who begin college at a four-year institution directly from high school, two-year students who wish to earn a baccalaureate degree must survive, in the words of Townsend and Wilson (2009), a second "first-year experience" at the receiving institution (p. 410).

Despite the importance of the transfer process for many students— and the unique socialization and transitional circumstances they face—the research literature does not sufficiently describe the unique challenges of these students. For example, empirical studies on student socialization have focused on the traditional four-year college undergraduate experience. These studies confirm the importance of socialization within a new academic environment as a pivotal factor influencing student academic success (Karp, 2011). However, the transition from the two-year to the four-year institution—and the kinds of socialization challenges that transfer students face—has not been the subject of much research. While some studies include various conceptual frameworks to explain certain student outcomes, no study has specially investigated the impact of the transfer transition on student socialization.

Relevant Conceptual Frameworks

Tinto's Model of Student Integration (1993) was one of the first to examine student persistence and retention at postsecondary institutions, and his "interactionalist framework" (Deil-Amen, 2011, p. 56) has been a consistent theoretical perspective for numerous researchers. Tinto's model is based on the belief that a subjective sense of belonging and membership is an important part of college students' decisions, and thus part of the students' outcomes. Congruence with the institution's academic and social systems acts to reinforce students' commitment to their institution and educational goals.

According to Tinto's model, integration is divided along two dimensions. One dimension is academic integration, which represents the connection students make to the academic and intellectual environment of the institution. The second dimension, social integration, operates when a student makes connections to the social environment via interactions with other groups (Tinto, 1993; Karp et al, 2010; Townsend & Wilson, 2009). Tinto's (1993) original conception of student persistence and success defined academic and social integration as operating largely separately. Moreover, his model was rarely applied to students attending two-year colleges because of a common belief that such students would not have either the time or opportunity to become involved on campus with clubs or other groups. Attendance patterns for two-year college students assumed they were away from campus except for periods of time for classes.

Nevertheless, other researchers have seen the value of Tinto's constructs for students attending two-year institutions, especially if these constructs are viewed as occurring simultaneously within a given student's experiences. Townsend and Wilson (2009) used a longitudinal approach to investigate the two-year college transfer student experience after an extended period of time enrolled at the four-year institution. Townsend and Wilson's (2009) study recognized that the typical two-year college student had different experiences once they enrolled at the larger four-year institution and that standard measures of social integration, such as joining a club or group on campus, may be more relevant while they were at the two-year school. These researchers also noted that older, nontraditional transfer students did not experience as many social connections as the younger two-year college transfer students.

Karp, Hughes, and O'Gara (2010) assessed the connection between social and academic integration and found that such integration did occur for students attending two-year institutions. Using Tinto's integration framework, they focused on how beginning college students at two-year schools experience social and academic integration. Karp et al. (2010) used in-depth interviews with students at two urban community colleges to examine how students actually became engaged at the institution and how that sense of attachment to the institution was related to persistence. One key finding was that community college students could, and did, develop attachments to their postsecondary institution. These researchers outlined how students reported their sense of belonging and how that also influenced their academic integration.

Karp et al. (2010) also found that students' information networks helped them make connections throughout the two-year college campus, noting that such networks "appear to have helped students feel at home on campus while giving them the tools necessary for successful degree completion" (p. 76). Moreover, they found that students' social relationships increased the likelihood that they take advantage of a campus service or program, especially if they had a connection to faculty or staff associated with that program.

The findings of Karp et al. (2010) are noteworthy because the research documents a link among information networks, socio-academic integrative experiences, and socialization experiences. What is not clear from their study is how the concept of using information networks as a mechanism for socialization and for experiencing socio-academic integrative moments could be applied to the four-year college setting. If two-year college students develop information networks that can influence their socio-academic integrative experiences, and impact their socialization to the campus, do they have these same experiences after they transfer to the four-year institution?

A conceptual model that may bridge differences in how two- and four-year institution students experience college was developed by Weidman (1989). His theory emphasizes socialization as a process through which an individual learns to adopt the values, skills, norms, attitudes, and knowledge needed for membership in a given society, group or organization (Weidman, 1989, 2001, 2006). Weidman's model delineates a process that helps frame students' experiences as they become immersed in the social and academic culture of their transfer institution. He further defines the socialization process as incorporating such processes as "interaction," "integration," and "learning." Also residing conceptually under the umbrella of the socialization experiences, the model includes the core elements of "knowledge acquisition," "investment," and "involvement."

According to Weidman (1989), the core socialization experience is related to the normative contexts of the academic program. Related to this study, the normative contexts of the academic program were understood to be the standard schedule of classes a full-time student would experience as an undergraduate. Moreover, the academic program would correspond to the student's program of study for their intended major at the four-year university.

Deil-Amen (2011) extended both Tinto's (1993) and Weidman's framework to a study of two-year college students, examining the relationship between integration and persistence. Deil-Amen (2011) developed a conceptual framework that incorporated social and academic elements as pivotal for the success of students attending two-year institutions. She concluded that "the concept of a 'socio-academic integrative moment' can be used to describe opportunities for specific instances of interaction in which components of social and academic integration are simultaneously combined" (p. 72). Her study considered how the concepts of academic and social integration should be modified or altered in order to apply more appropriately to two-year students, while also considering the relevance of class, race, and ethnicity in the integrative process. Deil-Amen (2011) suggested that socio-academic integrative moments had social benefits such as a stronger sense of fit or belonging to the institution, or a more concrete or self-confident image of themselves as a two-year college student. Deil-Amen also noted that socio-academic integrative moments had informational benefits. This is an important concept for the present study because socio-academic integrative moments include critical points of "information exchange where students' strategies for attaining goals are improved" (p. 73). Access to crucial information enhanced feelings of congruence and focus on shared goals amongst students. Socio-academic integrative moments, then, are connected to information networks in that students used their academic setting (i.e., in the classroom) to extend their social connections as they sought critical information.

An important dimension of Deli-Amen's conception of socio-integrative moments come from Karp and Hughes' (2008) qualitative study of two-year college students. The students reported greater feelings of integration or sense of belonging to the institution if they were involved in information networks. They defined information networks as "a group of social ties that helped them understand college life" (p. 73). Karp and

Hughes (2008) posited that information networks facilitated the transfer of institutional knowledge and procedures and that student participation in such networks encouraged integration. Thus, information networks and socio-academic integrative moments can be construed as mechanisms fostering a greater connection to the institution. If two-year college students connect to information networks after transfer to a four-year school, they could experience an increased sense of fit to the receiving institution.

METHODOLOGY

Conceptual Framework

The research design for this study was derived from an interpretivist paradigm, grounded in constructivism. In *Assumptions about the Nature of Social Science*, Burrell and Morgan (1979) reviewed broad assumptions that underpin the foundations of social science research, especially subjective versus objective dimensions. According to these researchers, the subjectivist dimension stresses the importance of the "subjective experience of individuals in the creation of the social world" (Burrell & Morgan, 1979, p. 3). Moving deeper into the analysis leads to the interpretive paradigm, a paradigm most concerned with understanding the individual's subjective experiences in the social world (Burrell & Morgan, 1979; see also Crotty, 1998).

For the questions posed in the current study, the underlying assumption is that knowledge is constructed by individuals. This suggests a methodology grounded in phenomenology, which aligns well with interpretivist and constructivist assumptions. Describing the "lived experiences" of a person or groups of individuals regarding a similar phenomenon is the heart of this interpretation. In describing the experiences of individuals across a similar phenomenon, we have the potential to "universalize" that phenomena; understanding the elements common across a range of individual understandings (Van Manen, 1990).

The phenomenon under study in this research project was the experience of students as they transitioned from a two-year college to a four-year institution. As noted by Crotty (1998), individuals who experience the same phenomenon may construct knowledge about that phenomenon differently than other individuals with the same experience. Thus, in-depth semi-structured interviews provided the detailed qualitative responses regarding the phenomenon as described in detail by each participant.

Research Design and Data Collection

The research was conducted on the main campus of a large, public four-year institution in the southeastern United States. South University (a pseudonym) had a total enrollment of 18,963 for fall 2013 semester. Of that number, the total enrollment of new undergraduate transfer students for the fall 2013 semester was 1,106.

A total of 12 transfer students were interviewed for this study. These individuals transferred to the four-year institution in fall 2013, had previously attended a two-year college in the same state, and, at the time of the interview, were enrolled full-time in a degree program at the four-year institution. Table 2.1 provides additional information about each participant's gender, age, number of credits earned at the two-year institution, and GPA earned in the first semester at the four-year institution.

Data for this study was collected in four ways: (a) semi-structured interviews, (b) analysis of relevant documents, (c) direct observations of transfer students, and (d) the development of the primary researcher's professional journal. The twelve interviews lasted between 12 minutes to 41 minutes and were recorded and transcribed. The interview focused on the student's socialization experiences regarding the academic and social environment of the four-year institution; how they gathered information and learned to navigate the institution's technical and institutional systems; and the kinds of emotions students felt in establishing social connections to other students at the institution. The interviews were held on campus during the spring 2014 semester. At the end of each interview, each participant received the approved incentive, a $25 VISA gift card.

Table 2.1: Characteristics of Study Participants

Name	Age	Credit hours earned at two-year colleges (s)	Academic program at South University	GPA fall 2013 semester South University
Holly	20	55	Food Science	2.30
Thomas	21	92	Biological Sciences	3.68
Fiona	21	49	Animal and Veterinary Sciences	2.37
Joe	22	60	Psychology	2.0
John	22	43	Pre-Business	2.0
Jake	22	60	Computer Science	1.45
Alex	22	52	Civil Engineering	3.30
Elliott	22	45	Parks, Recreation and Tourism Management	2.33
Debbie	26	86	Animal and Veterinary Science	2.69
Chuck	31	88	Biosystems Engineering	3.66
Jim	39	71	Biological Science	2.60
Gus	43	58	Forest Resource Management	3.33

The second type of data collection was document analysis. During interview sessions, each participant was asked how they obtained information about institutional deadlines, rules, policies, and procedures. The purpose was to gain a better understanding of how each participant approached the task of becoming familiar with the four-year campus and how they developed their own sources of information and their overall socialization to the environment. Documents, such as email messages and web pages, were analyzed for content and construct value, which refers to the generally understood purpose for the information (content) and the value of the document(s) to student's academic and/or social integration. During interview sessions, participants were able to identify specific ways they obtained key information, such as academic deadlines. Although their answers revealed a variety of sources, the majority of participants indicated that email communication provided by the institution was the most important source of information. Participant's responses regarding documents and email indicated they understood the supportive intent of the institution's efforts to provide key information in a timely manner.

Data collection included two additional elements: direct observations of new transfer students on campus and a research journal of professional experiences by the lead researcher. The purpose of direct observations was to examine the ways new students interact with other students on campus in various locations (Creswell, 2009; Patton, 2002). The principal investigators use of a research journal was key to help recognize personal biases and provided a vehicle for "bracketing out" or setting aside biases and any pre-determined thoughts about the participants, such as prejudging any student's academic outcomes based on the two-year college they attended prior to enrollment at the research site (Moustakas, 1994).

RESULTS

Developing Textual, Structural, and Composite Descriptions

Interview transcripts, relevant documents, observation notes, and entries from the professional journal were analyzed using a five-step protocol. The first step focused on the professional research journal. Writing in the research journal served as a strategy to present or expose researcher bias towards transfer students or the institutions under question. The second step focused on an analysis of the interview transcripts and other documents to create an outline of significant statements, which, taken together, would constitute a description of how participants experienced the phenomenon of transfer. The third step combined the significant statements into larger units of information, forming "themes." The fourth step involved the development of a "textural description," which, as conceptualized by Creswell (2007), provides an account of the participants as they transition from a two-year college to a four-year university. From the information gained during the interviews with participants, the following textural description was developed:

Two-year college transfer students experienced academic challenges during their first semester at the four-year institution. Students needed to have self-reliance to stay up with the academic demands. Adjusting socially and making connections to new groups took initiative on the part of each student, challenging them to look outside their normal social groups and make new connections.

The fifth step was to create a "structural description," which Creswell (2007) describes as the "how" of the experience, as well as the relevant context for the phenomenon being analyzed. This study's structural description was developed as follows:

> Two-year college transfer students experienced a physical setting that was large and unfamiliar, and felt out of place because their cohort peers were already a year or more ahead of them in enrollment at the university. Living off-campus, they learned to navigate various systems and where to go to get assistance for logistical issues.

The final step in the process was to develop the overarching meaning or essence of the transfer student's experience after transitioning to the four-year institution. According to Creswell (2007), the researcher should "write a composite description of the phenomenon incorporating both the textural and structural descriptions" (p. 159). Integrating both the textural and structural descriptions, the following composite description was developed:

> The academic adjustment from the two-year college environment to the four-year university was more difficult than expected and making social connections to the new campus was crucially important for students to feel they were making a successful transition.

Transfer Themes

Applying a phenomenological research perspective, "themes" can be understood as the "structures of the experience." Van Manen (1990) pointed out that "when we analyze a phenomenon, we are trying to determine what the themes are, the experiential structures that make up the experience" (p. 79). The development of themes was accomplished by analyzing the transcript data and highlighting significant statements from each participant's responses during the interviews. Gathering the significant statements into clusters of meaning allowed the lead researcher to identify critical or overarching categories that described the participants' transition experiences. These categories then became the themes for this study.

The first theme concerned the importance of participants' age on the extent to which they were able to make new social connections. Three of the twelve participants were between 11 to 20 years older than their peers as entering transfer students. The older the student, the wider the gap they experienced when they attempted to make social connections. Jim, age 39, commented on his attempts to get involved socially with campus groups:

> I tried joining an organization last semester and I didn't feel very comfortable because it was thirty 20-year-olds and I, so it was harder to stay involved in the group because there seemed to be a lot more communication between the other students than they shared with me. It's been a challenge to try to stay involved.

All of the participants lived off-campus. The three oldest participants also had family dynamics to contend with while they transitioned to South University. Living off-campus, because he was an older student who was married and had a family, created restrictions for Gus, age 43, when he considered making social connections at South via clubs. He depended on riding the campus bus to get to classes, and had limited transportation after hours to use to return to campus for a club or group meeting.

Although the majority of the participants were much younger, age remained a factor in how they described their effectiveness in establishing social connections at South University. Several participants noted that since their peers had started at South as first-year students, they already had established groups of social connections. Joe, age 22, felt he had a harder time meeting new people at South because he was already a junior in credit hours and in years of school, and noted that his peers who started at South as first-year students had established social groups he did not think he could break into without a lot of extra effort. He said:

> So, I know it has been a little bit harder for me to meet and socialize because I came in as a junior instead of a freshman going as a regular student, like 18 or 19 years old, I came in later as a junior, older, so it was a little harder for me to connect because most of the people in my age group or whatever had already been here for two years or more. They had established a network of friends and so [I] found that to be difficult to break into.

Age also impacted academic connections. One older student indicated he had experienced differences in how he was treated in the classroom setting. Jim, age 39, said:

I've had to adjust my thinking, because I'm an older student and most of the other students are half my age. I've noticed that I'm not usually perceived as a traditional student so when conversations in class occur, I'm usually the kid picked last or excluded, or what I say isn't respected as much as other things people in the same age group [say].

The second theme concerned academic rigor. All of the participants noted the academic challenges of transferring to the senior institution and commented on the difficulties they encountered with making the adjustment academically. After their first semester of enrollment, only four of the twelve study participants had a cumulative 3.0 GPA or higher. The remaining participants were closer to the 2.0 or 2.5 GPA (see Table 2.1).

During the interview, participants were asked to describe their academic experiences during their first semester at the four-year institution. Although most participants indicted their academic experiences were positive, they also learned, through experience, that academic expectations were higher at South University than they had anticipated. Several participants commented on the faster pace and the higher level of critical thinking that was required if a student was to be successful in class.

The third theme highlighted the importance of establishing new social connections for participants to make a positive transition to the four-year institution. Most participants said that they met other students during study sessions, tutoring sessions, or group meetings associated with a particular class. Students even used academic assignments to reach out to other students via social media, ultimately connecting with even more students who were enrolled in the same or similar courses. Numerous examples were noted during a review of the interview transcripts, where participants described campus academic settings as common locations for meeting other students and making new social contacts. Thomas, age 22, commented on how he met other students and described what can be considered an example of socio-academic integrative moments:

Well, primarily through my classes, with some of the students I would regularly sit next to in class, we would sometimes form study groups. When you start doing upper-level classes, you're with students who are in the same major as you so you'll be taking multiple classes with them.

While students also talked about specific social events and described their level of involvement with such activities, all mentioned academic settings as the most prominent or popular place to meet other students.

DISCUSSION

The current study takes a blended perspective to form a conceptual framework based on the construct of socio-academic integrative moments, information networks and socialization to describe the transition experiences of two-year college students. A blended conceptual framework allows for a more nuanced approach to investigating the research questions, while allowing the strengths of various theoretical approaches, such as those of Tinto (1993), Weidman (1989), and Deil-Amen (2011), to inform and advance our understanding of the challenges that two-year students face following their transfer to a four-year institution.

The participants in this study responded candidly to questions about their transition from a two-year college to a four-year university. Their responses supported the development of significant statements, providing a deeper understanding of the transfer experience. All of the participants, to a varying degree, were challenged by the academic rigor and pace at the four-year university. As a result, many expressed the opinion that they had to change their approach and develop better skills in order to be successful. Participants also expressed a desire to take more initiative with academic assignments and learn to be more self-reliant.

Socially, participants had different experiences depending on their age. The older the student, the more challenging it was for them to feel that they fit in with the other students in class. For some, the age difference impacted their campus interactions and how much effort they put into establishing new connections. Participant comments supported the notion that students experience academic and social integration experiences simultaneously. Numerous examples were provided by the study participants, indicating they made new connections in class and learned about a campus social event by hearing about it from other students while sitting in class. Participant comments also supported the perspective that information networks were comprised of social ties and were used to gain information that helped them be more successful on campus.

It should come as no surprise that information networks and social relationships play a critical role in the adaptation of students in postsecondary educational institutions. Sociologists have noted for decades the importance of social capital as expressed in elaborated connections throughout communities as an important variable in advancing the benefits of a privileged, well-resourced community. What is compelling in this research is that the power of "networking" can have clear benefits for individuals in less well-resourced communities. Support for this point, as related to this study, comes from research on Latino/a college choice. Chain migration, or chain enrollment theory, is a perspective based on research on the immigrant experience (Pérez & McDonough, 2008). MacDonald and MacDonald (1974) explained that chain migration refers to methods used by migrant workers to obtain work information via their social ties to groups of other migrant workers. More recent research on college choice examined the ways Latino/a students made decisions about college enrollment. Person and Rosenbaum (2006) noted that Latino/a students in their study frequently cited the influences of family and friends in their college choice decision process. From the earlier research on immigrant patterns, Person and Rosenbaum (2006) applied the concept of chain migration to the college choice process, noting that "we expect students to choose colleges where a primary social contact is or has enrolled, enroll with members of their network, and look to contacts for assistance once enrolled" (p. 52). Chain migration theory, then, relates to the current study in that new transfer students coming from a two-year college may tap into their own social networks for information about student life and academics at the larger four-year institution. Moreover, given the attractiveness of community colleges for students from underrepresented groups, noted earlier, the importance of social networks may be key for their ability to transfer in a timely fashion and to meet their educational goals at the four-year institution.

The results of this study add to the body of literature seeking to gain a better understanding of how transfer students experience the challenges faced when they continue their journey towards earning a baccalaureate degree. Further studies are needed to continue identifying key elements that support transfer students along this postsecondary pathway.

REFERENCES

Aud, S., Hussar, W., Johnson, F., Kena, G., Roth, E., Manning, E., Wang, X., & Zhang, J. (2012). *The condition of education 2012* (NCES 2012-045). Washington, D.C.: U.S. Department of Education, National Center for Education Statistics. Retrieved from http://nces.ed.gov/pubsearch.

Barnett, E. A. (2011). Validation experiences and persistence among community college students. *The Review of Higher Education, 34*(2), 19–230.

Berger, J. B., & Malaney, G. D. (2003). Assessing the transition of transfer students from community colleges to a university. *NASPA Journal, 40*(4), 1–23.

Brim, O. G., Jr. (1966). Socialization through the life cycle. In O.G. Brim Jr. & S. Wheeler (Eds.), *Socialization after childhood: Two essays*. New York, NY: John Wiley.

Burrell, G. & Morgan, G. (1979). *Sociological paradigms and organisational analysis: Elements of the sociology of corporate life*. London: Heinemann.

Carnevale, A. P., & Rose, S. J. (2011). *The undereducated American*. Washington, Dc.: Georgetown University Center on Education and the Workforce. Retrieved from http://cew.georgetown.edu/undereducated/

Carnevale, A. P., Smith, N., & Strohl, J. (2013). *Recovery: Job growth and education requirements through 2020*. Washington, D.C.: Georgetown University Center on Education and the Workforce. Retrieved from http://cew.georgetown.edu/publications/reports/

Creswell, J. W. (2007). *Qualitative inquiry and research design: Choosing among five approaches* (2nd ed.). Thousand Oaks, CA: SAGE Publications, Inc.

Creswell, J. W. (2009). *Research design: Qualitative, quantitative, and mixed methods approaches* (3rd ed.). Thousand Oaks, CA: SAGE Publications, Inc.

Crotty, M. (1998). *The foundations of social research: Meaning and perspective in the research process*. London: SAGE Publications, Inc.

Deil-Amen, R. (2011). Socio-academic integrative moments: Rethinking academic and social integration among two-year college students in career-related programs. *The Journal of Higher Education, 82*(1), 54–91.

Dowd, A. C., Pak, J. H., & Bensimon, E. M. (2013). The role of institutional agents in promoting transfer access. *Education Policy Analysis Archives, 21*(15), 1–44.

Holley, K. A., & Taylor, B. J. (2009). Undergraduate student socialization and learning in an online professional curriculum. *Innovative Higher Education, 33*(4), 257–269.

Karp, M. M. (2011). Toward a new understanding of non-academic student support: Four mechanisms encouraging positive student outcomes in the community college. *Community College Research Center.* [Working Paper No. 28.] Retrieved from http://ccrc.tc.columbia.edu

Karp, M. M., & Hughes, K. L. (2008). Information networks and integration: Institutional influences on experiences and persistence of beginning students. *New Directions for Community Colleges, 2008*(144), 73–82.

Karp, M. M., Hughes, K. L., & O'Gara, L. (2010). An exploration of Tinto's integration framework for community college students. *Journal of College Student Retention, 12*(1), 69–86.

Laanan, F. S. (2007) Studying transfer students: Part II: Dimensions of transfer students' adjustment. *Community College Journal of Research and Practice, 31*(1), 37–59.

Martinez, M., & Fernandez, E. (2004). Latinos at Community Colleges. *New Directions for Student Services, 2004*(105), 51–67.

MacDonald, J. S., & MacDonald, L. D. (1974). Chain migration, ethnic neighborhood formation, and social networks. In C. Tilley (Ed.), *An urban world.* New York, NY: Little, Brown and Co.

Moustakas, C. E. (1994). *Phenomenological research methods.* Thousand Oaks, CA: SAGE Publications, Inc.

Mullin, C. M. (2012, February). *Why access matters: The community college student body.* AACC Policy Brief 2012-01PBL. Washington, D.C.: American Association of Community Colleges.

Museus, S. D., & Neville, K. M. (2012). Delineating the ways that key institutional agents provide racial minority students with access to social capital in college. *Journal of College Student Development, 53*(3), 436–452.

National Student Clearinghouse Research Center (2012). *Transfer and mobility: a national view of pre-degree student movement in postsecondary institutions.* [Signature Report.] Retrieved from http://www.studentclearinghouse.info/signature/2/NSC_Signature_Report_2.pdf

Nuñez, A. (2009). Latino students' transitions to college: A social and intercultural capital perspective. *Harvard Educational Review, 79*(1), 22–48.

Padgett, R. D., Goodman, K. M., Johnson, M. P., Saichaie, K., Umbach, P. D. (2010). The impact of college student socialization, social class, and race on need for cognition. *New Directions for Institutional Research, 2010*(145), 99–111.

Patton, M. Q. (2002). *Qualitative research & evaluation methods* (3rd ed.). Thousand Oaks, CA: SAGE Publications, Inc.

Pérez, P. A., & McDonough, P. M. (2008). Understanding Latina and Latino college choice: A social capital and chain migration analysis. *Journal of Hispanic Higher Education, 7*(3), 249–65.

Person, A.E., & Rosenbaum, J.E. (2006) Chain enrollment and college enclaves: Benefits and drawbacks of Latino college students' enrollment decisions. *New Directions for Community Colleges, 2006*(133), 51–60.

Person, A. E., Rosenbaum, J. E., & Deil-Amen, R. (2006). Student planning and information problems in different college structures. *Teachers College Record, 108*(3), 374–396.

Rosenbaum, J. E., Deil-Amen, R., & Person, A. E. (2006). *After admission: From college access to college success.* New York, NY: Russell Sage Foundation.

Shields, N. (2002). Anticipatory socialization, adjustment to university life, and perceived stress: Generational and sibling effects. *Social Psychology of Education, 5*(4), 365–392.

Smith, J. A., Flower, P., & Larkin, M. (2009). *Interpretative phenomenological analysis: Theory, method and research.* London: SAGE Publications, Inc.

Tinto, V. (1993). *Leaving college: Rethinking the causes and cures of student attrition* (2nd ed.). Chicago, IL: University of Chicago Press.

Tinto, V. (1997). Classrooms as communities: Exploring the educational character of student persistence. *Journal of Higher Education, 68*(6), 599–623.

Townsend, B. K., & Wilson, K. B. (2009). The academic and social integration of persisting community college transfer students. *Journal of College Student Retention, 10*(4), 405–423.

Van Manen, M. (1990). *Researching the lived experience: Human science for an action sensitive pedagogy.* Ontario: The State University of New York.

Weidman, J. C. (1979). Nonintellective undergraduate socialization in academic departments. *The Journal of Higher Education, 50*(1), 48–62.

Weidman, J. C. (1989). Undergraduate socialization: A conceptual approach. In J. Smart (Ed.), *Higher Education: Handbook of Theory and Research (Vol V)*, 289–322. New York, NY: Agathon.

Weidman, J. C., Twale, D. J., & Stein, E. L. (2001). Socialization of graduate and professional students in higher education: A perilous passage? *ASHE-ERIC Higher Education Report, 28*(3), 1–139.

Weidman, J. C., (2006). Student socialization in higher education: Organizational perspectives. In C. Clifton & R. Serlin (Eds.), *The SAGE Handbook for Research in Education: Engaging ideas and enriching inquiry*, 253–262. Thousand Oaks, CA: SAGE Publications, Inc.

Weidman, J. C. & Stein, E. L. (2003). Socialization of doctoral students to academic norms. *Research in Higher Education, 44*(6), 641–656.

Yarbrough, B., & Brown, M. H. (2003). Understanding organizational socialization: Insight for academic advisors. *NACADA Journal, 23*(1 & 2), 66–73.

Mary M. Von Kaenel *is the Director of Bridge to Clemson and Transfer Academic Programs at Clemson University.*

Pamela A. Havice *is a professor of Educational and Organizational Leadership Development in the College of Education at Clemson University.*

SECTION II

FOSTERING TRANSFER STUDENT AFFIRMING
INSTITUTIONAL ECOSYSTEMS

3

Sense Making for Community College Transfers: Entering a Public, Liberal Arts University

Erin E. Shaw, Ph.D.

Abstract

This transcendental phenomenological study describes the experiences of mid-year community college transfer students as they entered a public, liberal arts university (hereafter referred to as PLAU), using Louis's (1980) model of Sense Making in Organizational Entry as a framework for the analysis. Eight mid-year community college transfer students transferred to a university for the first time in January 2013, and each participated in three in-depth interviews. I explored how they came to be community college transfer students, their transition experience, and their reflections on what being a transfer student meant to them. The findings offer participant profiles crafted from their life histories and a phenomenological analysis of their transition experiences and their reflections on that transition. The experience of being a mid-year community college transfer student encompassed five themes: (1) facing academic challenges, (2) finding balance, (3) becoming independent, (4) feeling lost, and (5) feeling pressed for time. Community colleges and universities can benefit from the analysis of the stories and experiences of these participants, as they shed light on the lived experience of being a mid-year, first-semester transfer student on a four-year campus.

Purpose of the Study

This study explores the experiences of community college students who have transferred mid-year to a PLAU. Transferring from a community college to a four-year university may be a difficult process, as the student must adapt to different institutional, academic, and social experiences at the new school in order to succeed and graduate. Laanan (2004) found "for transfer students, coming to a four-year college or university requires numerous adjustments to the new environment and institutional culture, including larger classes and campus size, increased academic rigor, new friends, and a new location" (p. 332). As newcomers to the university, transfer students must make sense of their experiences in the new organizational environment (Louis, 1980). According to Louis's model, to accomplish this "sense making," newcomers draw on past experiences, personal predispositions, as well as the interpretations of others to understand the new organization.

Studies on transfer student experiences at four-year universities provide advice on ways to foster transfer. Advice typically centers on improving advising, articulation agreements, and transfer guides to avoid loss of transfer credits or increased time to graduation. Additional attention is focused on orientations and other programming to aid academic and social integration (Peska, 2009; Townsend & Wilson, 2006; Whorton, 2009). However, universities must understand their own students' experiences to appropriately apply this advice to assure that the recommendations are relevant and meaningful to that school (Davies & Casey, 1998). By understanding what transfer students experience at that university, the institution could make changes specific to their school. Universities have the opportunity to influence the entry and transition experiences of new transfers by coaching them how the university implements processes such as academic advising, credit evaluation, parking, class registration, and scholarship application and renewal. The purpose of this transcendental phenomenology was to understand transfer students' entry and sense-making experiences over the course of their first semester at PLAU.

LITERATURE REVIEW

The existing literature on community college transfer student experiences at the university is generally categorized in three main areas: (1) processes and places, (2) academic experiences, and (3) social experiences. Participants in several studies noted the difficulty of navigating the transfer process (Andres, 2001; Britt & Hirt, 1999; Cameron, 2005; Davies & Casey, 1999; Laanan, 2007). Transfers lacked information about different aspects of the transfer process and coped with inconsistent distribution of information upon acceptance (Britt & Hirt, 1999; Davies & Casey, 1999; Kelly, 2009; Owens, 2010). Transfer students also reported being surprised by the lack of communication between the university and the community college (Andres, 2001; Flaga, 2006; Owens, 2010). They wished the advisors at the community college and the university would communicate with each other in order to share consistent information such as transfer course equivalencies, articulation agreements, and degree requirements (Andres, 2001; Flaga, 2006; Owens, 2010).

At the university, community college transfers may also encounter increased levels of academic rigor, larger class sizes, more competitive classroom environments, faculty who may be more focused on research rather than teaching, and classes taught by teaching assistants (Davies & Casey, 1999; Laanan, 2007; Townsend, 1995; Townsend & Wilson, 2006). However, some transfers students found in retrospect that the community college was too similar to high school (Davies & Casey, 1999; Kerr, 2006). Townsend (1995) identified community college students who fell behind academically at the university because their community college courses were less rigorous.

Many transfers felt they received high-quality instruction at the community college by instructors who enjoyed teaching (Townsend, 1995) and offered individualized attention (Davies & Casey, 1999). Students also appreciated small classes, caring faculty, and personalized relationships with instructors (Balzer, 2006; Townsend & Wilson, 2006). Some reported the rigor of the community college course matched or surpassed the university course (Pak, Bensimon, Malcom, Marquez, & Park, 2006), though many transfers found the university to be more difficult in comparison to the community college (Cameron, 2005; Kerr, 2006; Pak et al., 2006; Townsend, 1995). Adjusting from smaller to larger class sizes was also a common theme (Balzer, 2006; Davies & Casey, 1999; Flaga, 2006; Kelly, 2009; Nowak, 2004; Townsend & Wilson, 2006). In large classes, students tended to feel less connected to classmates and to the professor (Davies & Casey, 1999) and sometimes felt like just a number (Townsend & Wilson, 2006).

At the university, transfers reported feeling alone and alienated (Harrison, 1999; Peska, 2009; Townsend & Wilson, 2008), and had trouble making friends or forming study groups (Britt & Hirt, 1999; Townsend & Wilson, 2006). Some transfers found it difficult to make friends at the university because non-transfer students had already established friendships in their first year through formal first-year and residential living programs, and were perceived as less willing to make new friends (Townsend & Wilson, 2006; Zubernis, McCoy, & Snyder, 2011). Especially disadvantaged were commuters, parents, and post-traditional aged students who departed campus for work or family after class (Austin, 2006; Davies & Casey, 1999; Kodama, 2002; Rice; 2008; Townsend & Wilson, 2006). Transfers sometimes felt out of place or alone and worried about fitting in (Owens, 2010; Rice, 2008; Townsend & Wilson, 2006). Several researchers determined transfers best connected by finding their niche, either by joining student organizations, becoming involved, or developing a social support system (Harrison, 1999; Owens, 2007; Zubernis, McCoy & Snyder, 2011).

Little is known about how mid-year transfers experience the transition to the university. According to Peska (2009), getting involved is more complicated for mid-year transfers because there are fewer opportunities for them to become involved academically and socially. Peska found not all student organizations accepted new members mid-year, and there was less of a campus-wide focus on helping students form friendships in the spring semester. When comparing fall and mid-year transfers, he found a difference between their feelings of isolation, where mid-year transfers living on campus mentioned how alone they felt on their floor because everyone already knew one another (Peska, 2009). Britt and Hirt (1999) also found mid-year transfers experienced increased difficulty making friends because they felt the other students had already formed friendships in the fall semester.

RESEARCH QUESTIONS

The central research question of this study was: How do community college transfer students experience their entry and transition into PLAU? With three interviews per participant, I sought to understand: (1) What details and experiences in the life history of each transfer student contributed to their being a community college student transferring to PLAU? (2) How do transfer students describe their entry and sense-making experiences transitioning to PLAU? and (3) What does being a transfer student mean to them after they have transitioned to PLAU?

METHODS AND PROCEDURES

I used the qualitative research methodology of transcendental phenomenology to explore the entry and sense-making experiences of community college transfer students as they transitioned to a four-year university. As a theoretical framework, Louis's (1980) model of Sense Making in Organizational Entry influenced the research questions, interview guides, and my pursuit of the study. Husserl's (1965) transcendental phenomenology provided the methodological framework for this study. Seidman's (2006) three-interview series provided analytical direction for the data collection procedures and the creation of participant profiles that were created from participants' first interviews. Finally, the study used Moustakas's (1994) modification of the Stevick-Colaizzi-Keen method of phenomenological data analysis to analyze participants' second and third interviews.

Sampling. For this study, I used criterion sampling and recruitment by referral sampling techniques. Interested students who attended transfer student orientation had the opportunity to sign-up in person to participate in the study. Simultaneously, I asked staff members who work with transfer students to refer anyone they thought might be interested. To be included in the sample, participants had to be mid-year transfer students who had only attended community colleges prior to entering PLAU for the first time in January 2013. Criterion sampling in a phenomenological context is important because the researcher must ensure all participants have experience with the phenomenon being studied (Creswell, 2007; Moustakas, 1994). The sample was planned to include the first 15 community college transfer students who indicated their interest in the study, scheduled, and then completed the first interview. Of the 61 transfer students who entered the PLAU in Spring 2013, twelve had only attended community colleges prior to transferring. Of these twelve transfer students, eight agreed to participate in the study.

Interviews. In this study, data were primarily collected through one-on-one interviews. I used in-depth interviews and multiple interviews with each participant, common in phenomenological research (Creswell, 2007; Moustakas, 1994). I followed Seidman's (2006) Three-Interview Series model of three one-on-one interviews per participant, each up to 90 minutes in length, to structure my interview timeline and questions.

I interviewed students over the first ten weeks of the semester to allow the participants to fully experience the transition to the university before the final interview. Holding the third interview earlier in the semester might have limited the students' experiences. I believe the extended timeline added to the richness of the stories the transfers shared about the experience of entering and making sense of a new organizational culture.

Organizing the Data

I recorded each interview using a digital recording device and personally transcribed each audio recording verbatim to maximize my familiarity with the data and to capture exactly what each participant said. I read each transcript while listening to the interview, to ensure the text was accurate before starting my analysis. As a researcher in the phenomenological research tradition, I used the epoche process to reflect on my own views, biases, and knowledge about transfer students before starting the analysis. I then bracketed the knowledge contained in the current literature of transfer student studies, by attempting to not read or think about any of the current literature during the entire data analysis process. For those several months, I also tried to push from my mind my prior knowledge of the literature as I read the participants' words. The only knowledge I relied upon was from the eight participants' experiences and their meaning-making. I remained open to the experiences they described by using epoche to clear my own thoughts and to view their words with an open mind. I let these data speak for themselves. Once these data were analyzed and the textural and structural descriptions of the group's experiences were written, I returned to the literature for comparison. Only at that point did I explore connections between the findings of this study and what has been discussed in prior research studies.

Analyzing the Data

Seidman's profiles. To craft the participants' profiles, I read and re-read the interview transcript for each participant's initial interview. Then I examined the individual stories of how each student came to enroll at a community college. Keeping the participants' stories in the original order, I reduced the text according to Marshall (1981) and Seidman (1985). Marshall mentioned researchers tend to focus on the minutiae when they are marking words, sentences, or paragraphs rather than letting the data dictate the length of the significant statement. She argued "you get chunks of meaning which come out of the data itself," which may or may not follow a rule of only being one word, sentence, or paragraph long (p. 397). In my first review of the profiles, I marked sections of the text I considered significant to each story. In his research, Seidman (1985) reduced the text by omitting: "1) repetitious material; 2) ad hominem material; 3) unconnected material; 4) material that would make the participant vulnerable; [and] 5) material that, if taken out of the total context of the interview, was not fair to the participants" (Seidman, 2006, pp. 23–24).

In my study, I followed the following principles. First, I printed a hard copy of the transcript from each participant's first interview. For each transcript I marked chunks of text that pertained to the interview questions. For this first iteration, the majority of the participant's words were highlighted. The paper process then moved to the computer. From the original transcript file, I created a new file in Microsoft Word and removed the interviewer's words from the transcript. Next, I highlighted the text in Word that I had marked on the paper copy and removed the remainder. According to Seidman (2006), the length of the final version should be one-third to one-half the length of the original transcript.

For the second iteration, I used track changes in Microsoft Word to note any deletions I made as I further reduced the text. I removed unnecessary transition words, false starts and stutters, and verbal idiosyncrasies that a person may have said but would not typically use in writing (e.g., uh, like, really, just, you know, so). Also, at this point I started excluding passages that contained material that had already been shared earlier in the transcript. I carefully shortened the number of words used to tell each story while maintaining each story's point and main details. I attempted to keep the participant's voice intact, so their stories still sounded like they were telling them. This required including improper grammar, pauses or sighs, sound effects, talking in third person, and other characteristics of an individual's speech beyond the verbal idiosyncrasies noted above.

Seidman (2006) advocated that the profiles should be told in first person to keep the reader close to the participant's perspective. He also suggested the researcher keep the stories' original order, since reordering the text would move segments out of context. Although sections of text were removed as part of the data reduction process, I kept each interview transcript in the original order as it was told. I bracketed any of my words that were used to replace text for clarification. If I added words for explanation or context, these were placed in parentheses. Ellipses for omitted material or quotation marks for the entire interview were not used so the text would be easier to read. Quotation marks in the profile reflect statements made by the participant to reflect when the participant was quoting someone else or speaking in third person. Each profile was reviewed one final time to remove any remaining redundancy or unconnected material. I also made sure that the crafted profile was fair, dignified, and accurately represented the entire original interview, mindful of the additional criteria emphasized by Seidman (2006).

Moustakas' transcendental phenomenological analysis. The approach of transcendental phenomenology includes epoche, phenomenological reduction, imaginative variation, and synthesis of the composite structural and textural descriptions into the essences of the phenomenon (Moustakas, 1994). Epoche means, "to stay away from or abstain," (Moustakas, 1994, p. 85) and it entails setting aside or "bracketing" all of my preconceptions and biases so I could focus on the research question and the data before me without the influence of my own assumptions. Phenomenological reduction requires marking each statement that relates to the topic at hand in a verbatim transcript. Only repetitive or irrelevant statements are removed. The remaining statements are the invariant meaning units or horizons of the experience, which are clustered into themes and reduced to textural descriptions of the experience. Each individual's textural description is formed using this process. Next, imaginative variation is used to determine the structural descriptions of the experience. This step involves looking at an experience from a variety of perspectives and creatively examining which underlying structures might explain how the participants experienced what they did. Moustakas' (1994) instruction to consider "the universal structures that precipitate feelings and thoughts with reference to the phenomenon, such as the structure of time, space, bodily concerns, materiality, causality, relation to self, or relation to others" (p. 99) informed this study. A structural description for each individual is formed through imaginative variation. The textural descriptions are brought together to form a composite textural description of the group. Next, a composite structural description for the group is formed from the individual structural descriptions. Finally, the composite textural descriptions and the composite structural descriptions were synthesized into the overall essences and meanings of the experienced phenomenon.

I used in-depth phenomenological interviewing combined with a narrative style analysis to create a profile as the final product of Interview One. I did so to introduce the reader to each participant and their individual experiences. I hoped this approach would connect readers to the participants, fostering a sense of engagement with individual and collective experiences at the university and the meanings ascribed to being a transfer student.

For the transcripts from Interview Two and Interview Three, I followed Moustakas' (1994) modified Stevick-Colaizzi-Keen method of phenomenological analysis, which includes epoche, transcendental phenomenological reduction, and imaginative variation.

Epoche. To understand my preconceptions and biases, I needed to examine my personal background. Through my job, I developed a sense of rapport with the transfer students prior to their arrival on campus. I hoped being communicable, helpful, and reliable with students would encourage them to participate in my study. I also hoped they would be more likely to share open and honest feelings, reflections, and experiences about the positive and negative aspects of their transition. I actively listened to my participants' words rather than anticipate what they might say based on preconceived ideas. Additionally, I recognized that my presence and position in interviews might influence my participants' answers.

Each time I prepared to analyze the data I collected, I reminded myself to push my experiences and perspectives from my thoughts, and tried to view the participant's words with an open mind. If I caught myself returning to my own experiences while reading one of the interviews I would look up or take a break to clear my head and then return to my analysis.

Horizonalization. The next step in phenomenological reduction is horizonalization, which is the process of giving equal value to every statement made by a participant. After considering each statement, the text can be reduced by removing repetitive or irrelevant statements. Before horizonalizing the data, I read each verbatim transcript while listening to the recording of the interview to confirm the transcripts were accurate. I went through each transcript individually, repeating these steps. I read each sentence and asked myself, "Is this significant in describing the experience of transferring to PLAU?" I marked all sentences that pertained to the phenomenon being studied. Next, I cut these statements verbatim and pasted them into a Microsoft Excel spreadsheet. For each statement, I removed any verbal idiosyncrasies and in some cases I removed parts of the quote as indicated by the use of ellipses. I compared the statements in Excel and further removed any sections that were repetitive or irrelevant.

The non-repetitive, non-overlapping statements that remain are called "invariant meaning units" (Moustakas, 1994, p. 122). Moustakas defined horizons or meaning units as "the textural meanings and invariant constituents of the phenomenon" (p. 97). When horizonalizing, it was essential that I treated every statement equally and did not give more weight to some statements over others. The final product was a spreadsheet of non-repeating significant statements. I printed the spreadsheet, cut each statement out, re-read each statement, and clustered the statements into themes. Then I wrote a textural description for each individual, detailing what they experienced while transferring to PLAU.

Imaginative variation. The next step of phenomenological analysis constructs each structural description. This step involves looking at a participant's invariant meaning units from different angles and creatively examining which underlying structures, themes and qualities may have connected how they experienced their actions.

Composite textural and structural descriptions. Once the individual textural and structural descriptions were completed, I created another spreadsheet of all of the individual textural descriptions separated by the individual themes. I printed the paragraphs, cut them out, and clustered them into new, composite themes. Then I reviewed the individual textural descriptions and crafted a composite textural description detailing what the shared group experience of transferring to PLAU entailed. After the textural description, I wrote a composite structural description of the underlying dynamics of the group's experience. For this description, I employed the universal structures that contribute to the way a person experiences a phenomenon (Moustakas, 1994).

Synthesizing and arriving at the essence. Once the composite textural and structural descriptions were written, I reviewed them both and described the phenomenological synthesis of the meanings and the essences of the experience. After completing all of these steps for Interview Two, I completed the same steps for Interview Three.

FINDINGS

The experience of being a mid-year community college transfer student encompassed the following themes: (1) facing academic challenges; (2) finding balance; (3) becoming independent; (4) feeling lost; and (5) feeling pressed for time. For the community college transfer students in this study, the experience of entering and making sense of a public, liberal arts university was a steep learning curve that included adapting academically, adjusting to this planned but palpable life change, filling in missing information, and trying to connect with other students, faculty, and staff.

When students began at PLAU in January, they discovered that the classes were more difficult than they anticipated. Though the class content was understandable, the volume of assigned reading and high academic expectations far exceeded their community college courses. They had to learn new ways to study, while coping with less time spent on review and less reinforcement of missed homework deadlines. They had to complete outside readings, engage in self-directed study to understand the material, and make the connections between their work outside of class with what the professor said in lecture. They felt surrounded by peers who seemed to always be studying.

Each participant struggled to find the balance among studying, finding time to plan for the future, eating, sleeping, exercising, spending time with friends, or getting involved. Living a healthy lifestyle was a challenge, but one that the participants fought for as a goal. This took on a variety of forms, including taking back some time for personal reading and writing, catching up on sleep, cleaning and cooking for themselves, working on their mental health issues, working out, joining a student organization or two, and making friends.

Despite being a little older and having already figured out the campus and processes at a community college, the participants shared similar experiences with first-year students. The participants were also going off to college, having to make friends, learning to navigate a new campus, and figuring out how to live with other people who are not family. The participants felt the community college allowed them to segue from high school to PLAU, but as one participant said, "it was a big jump," to the university.

Another essence was feeling lost. Sometimes the participants were physically lost navigating their way around campus. In the classroom, they felt lost regarding faculty expectations. In order to adapt more quickly in their classes, they relied on feedback from their professors in the form of edits and grades. Another change was that some professors only provided syllabi electronically, and never discussed it in class. This made it a challenge for students to clearly understand what was expected of them.

Despite having entered the university with all different levels of credits, all participants felt the lack of time. Some felt left behind by students their own age, as they had already made friends, joined organizations, and survived a semester or more of classes. Others felt thrown into their major courses, and felt the pressure of having fewer total semesters to figure out PLAU, confirm their major, complete their graduation requirements, and line up their career path.

IMPLICATIONS FOR THEORY

This study added the application of Louis's (1980) model of Sense Making in Organizational Entry to the community college transfer student experience at the four-year university. The model guided the research questions of the study, though the data was analyzed on its own in a phenomenological context. I set aside my knowledge of the model, personal experiences and biases, and the prior research. This allowed me to view the words of the participants with an open mind and capture their experience of the phenomenon.

I found the model proved very applicable to how and what transfers experienced entering PLAU. Newcomers undergo change, contrast, and surprise as they enter a new organization. For example, the participants experienced a similar change of physical surroundings; a contrast between the academic rigor at the community college and the university; and some surprises between what they anticipated at PLAU and what they actually experienced.

Under Louis's (1980) model, newcomers make sense of their new organization through the lens of their past experiences and personal dispositions, as well as the interpretations of others and the organization's way of doing things. The participants in this study had very different personal histories, yet each one was influenced by their backgrounds and their personal tendencies as they tried to make sense of the people, places, and processes of PLAU. They wished for more instruction as well as feedback from faculty, in order to make better sense of their classes. Those with friends already at PLAU felt they benefitted from knowing someone already familiar with the university. After sense making, newcomers next attribute meaning to what they experienced entering the new organization, and from that experience, they choose a behavioral response and set expectations for their next transition as they reassess their view of the setting. For the participants, transferring meant arriving at the institution that would award their baccalaureate degree. It also meant having to explain to everyone around them that they were a transfer student and what that meant. One participant remarked that transferring taught him the valuable skill of adapting to challenges as you enter a new place. He thought these skills would benefit him in the future when moving to a new job or town. In their view of the setting, many of the participants felt as pleased with PLAU as they had anticipated. Sometimes participants' transitions were rockier than expected and for others it went more smoothly, but many of their expectations were met.

Many of Louis's (1980) ideas about the experience of transitioning to a new organization were also relevant to this study. When entering a new organization, Louis posits that newcomers were likely to experience "disorientation, foreignness, and a kind of sensory overload." This dislocation was experienced by all of the participants in this study. Participants were navigating a new campus, feeling like a brand new student when everyone else was established on campus, and feeling overloaded with information from the orientation process. Additionally, PLAU relies more heavily on email communication, at a volume higher than most of the participants were used to receiving. Different departments, individual faculty and staff all sent emails and announcements to keep students informed. Unfortunately, many of these announcements are composed with current students in mind, students already well acquainted with campus. A few participants in this study mentioned feeling completely lost when university emails and announcements were sent out because they did not have a frame of reference to know what the message was discussing. For example, event announcements might be laden with acronyms or include abbreviations for buildings or locations.

Louis (1980) believed the structures of time and space created problems for newcomers because they had no frame of reference to use to construct their new reality. In this study, the way time was spent at the community college was very different from how participants spent time at PLAU.

Transfer students carried campus maps with them or wandered around until they found places, because they had to construct in their minds where things were located and the connections those locations had to classes, friends, and campus resources.

The content of socialization as described by Louis (1980) includes role-related content and a general understanding of the organizational culture. Community college transfers need to understand the ways in which a university might be different than their previous school, and they need to know what is expected of them in their new role as a transfer student. It is the university's responsibility to share expectations and to help the newcomer understand the culture of the institution. Louis (1980) advocated for employers to provide "timely formal and informal feedback" (p. 247) so newcomers know how they are doing in their new role. For example, professors should give timely feedback in the form of graded assignments, so new transfers can learn from their mistakes, identify areas they need to study more carefully, and gauge whether they adequately prepared for the assessment. Without timely feedback—either in grades or conversations with the professor—a transfer will not be able to alter their behavior in time for the next assignment. The transfers in this study experienced this in their classes, and they struggled to know what the professor was looking for in the assignment or exam.

IMPLICATIONS FOR POLICY AND PRACTICE

There are potential implications for policy and practice that emerged from this study. Based on the academic experiences of the participants, it might help if transfers are forewarned about what to expect at the university. Community college faculty and advisors could inform potential transfers about the level of rigor at university. Faculty members at a community college have attended at least one university to earn their degrees and they can use their alma mater as a frame of reference when talking to students interested in pursuing a baccalaureate degree. Even if the community college's courses closely match the university's classes, students may be transferring in with only upper-level and major courses to complete, which generally are more rigorous than the general education courses at either institutional type.

Community colleges serve students with different levels of ability in the same classroom, and thus face a challenge preparing future transfer students for the rigor at a university. If possible, community college classes could include more reading, critical thinking, and class discussion in the general education courses. Having students practice leading a class discussion (individually or in small groups) would also teach students valuable skills that could translate to the workforce or the university classroom.

More could be done to bridge faculty between institutions, such as inviting a community college class to "sit in" on a lecture at the university. Faculty from the university could partner with local community college faculty to co-teach a lecture or workshop. If either institution has a guest speaker, they could invite the corresponding department to attend the lecture and experience the other campus environment.

Most universities do not have the staffing resources to house an academic advisor on main feeder community college campuses. However, advisors from feeder schools could meet annually or quarterly with the university transfer advisors to assure accurate information is being distributed and students are being effectively advised.

The transfer admissions staff could invite prospective transfer students to campus events prior to their start at the university. For example, spring transfers who will enter PLAU in January might be admitted months in advance. The university could invite these admitted transfers to get acquainted with campus by attending sporting events, concerts, or other student activities. Ideally, the university would pair transfer students with a current student who previously transferred, so they can begin to make friends.

At the university, transfers have to make sense of their classes quickly in order to succeed. To aid in this transition, professors could take time with new transfers to discuss class expectations in more detail than is typically covered in a syllabus. In some university classes, when homework is assigned, it may not be graded. This contributes to a transfer's confusion and anxiety when they try to discover how they are doing in their courses but have not received graded feedback to guide them. Transfers use professor feedback to gauge whether they are learning the appropriate material for exams and papers and to adapt their behavior. Observing what other students are doing and listening to the professor's comments in class may be helpful cues, but may also be misinterpreted. At the community college, homework was emphasized and transfers were reminded frequently about deadlines.

If newcomers rely on this prior experience to make sense of a new place, then at the university transfers might not understand the importance of homework if it is not emphasized in the same way.

Andy found that homework was not really mentioned at PLAU. He knew everyone was studying, but his "homework" included the reading for his English classes. Completing the reading before class was essential for discussion and was also important for his critical analysis in papers due later in the semester. In Andy's other classes, his homework might be 10% of his grade. No longer having homework emphasized in the same way and not having deadlines reinforced was an adjustment, especially for transfers like Gary who did not recognize reading assignments as homework. Gary commented that in high school having homework worth 5% of his grade was not worth his time. At PLAU, even if Gary completed his assigned work, additional reading and ungraded—yet still important—assignments may have gone untouched.

The importance of homework and self-study at PLAU needs to be discussed and reiterated during orientation and before a transfer student begins classes. An advisor should specifically follow up on this area when checking in with transfers after a few weeks into the semester.

At PLAU, academic departments track paper usage with printing and copier codes. Departments are allotted a limited amount of paper, and there has been a campus-wide focus on sustainability. Posting a syllabus, class assignments, and announcements via email saves a substantial amount of paper across all courses on campus. Students, however, were unhappy with having only electronic distribution of important course materials, believing that paper documents were the best way to effectively communicate information about course expectations and assignments. Universities following similar sustainability practices should include an explanation and a reminder during transfer orientation that syllabi and class materials will only be distributed electronically.

Another implication for practice centers on assuring a new transfer connects to the faculty and to students in their major as early as possible. If department chairs were notified as a transfer student in their major was admitted, they could reach out and welcome the student, helping the transfer feel noticed and appreciated. If the student had major-specific questions, they would now have another point of contact in addition to their academic advisor. The department chair would also be alerted to how many transfers had been admitted into their major, and this could prove informative as the chair makes course capacity/availability decisions.

On the student side, early contact with the department chair may help them develop a clearer understanding of how long it will take to graduate. If transfer students clearly understand why it may take them longer to graduate, then they are more likely to be accepting of this extended timeframe. By having early contact with the department chair, they could make an informed decision about whether to transfer, even while knowing the path to graduation was going to take longer than expected.

A professional advisor writes graduation plans that adhere to pre-requisites and the anticipated course rotation schedule. However, department chairs are the ones who could accelerate the transfer's path to graduation by allowing them to take a pre-requisite and the next course simultaneously. Faculty members have intimate knowledge of what is taught in each class and can specifically explain the sequencing of courses or what knowledge a student must master to understand concepts in the next class. The professional advisor creates the graduation plan while the faculty member provides the academic context, and informed by this context, perhaps the student will feel less pressured to squeeze an unreasonable course load into a shortened amount of time.

Appraising faculty about their students is helpful, especially if the academic cohort of each student is included on the class roster. This information would tell a professor who was in their class and when they started at the university. For example, at PLAU the cohort codes show whether the student entered as an undergraduate first-year student or undergraduate transfer as well as which year and semester they entered. Faculty see how many transfers are in the class and if any students— whether they were first-year students or transfers—were new to the university that semester.

If the initial points of contact at a university are the admissions person and the transfer academic advisor, it benefits students if these people understand the basic steps of financial aid. Financial aid rules change frequently, so it's important for a transfer student to stay in touch with the financial aid office. However, if a staff member understands which documents must typically be submitted and the approximate processing time, he/she could help ease the new transfer's anxiety about what needed to happen and when.

Andy shared two suggestions to better serve transfer students. First, he said he would have benefitted from a major-specific packet of information. In practice, each transfer who had declared a major would be handed a packet upon arrival that included details about major course content, student organizations related to that major, faculty research areas, any journals or publications produced by that department, undergraduate research opportunities, and the contact information for the department office including the department chair and department administrative assistant. Another idea is to create a corps of former transfer students who would be willing to volunteer and serve as a major-specific resource for new transfers. If a transfer student volunteer could be recruited for each major, then new transfer students would have an ambassador to welcome her/him into the major. Ideally, this volunteer would help the new transfer connect to major-related student organizations, activities, and share advice on successfully navigating major courses at the university.

Revisiting the town/gown relationship results in several recommendations. First, once at the university, orientation staff should teach new transfers about where the university is situated in relation to the town. In Fall 2013, a bus tour around town was added to the orientation schedule. However, due to time constraints, weather, and darkness, a bus tour in the spring did not occur. Rethinking the spring orientation schedule to include a bus tour during the day might help new spring transfers learn the main areas of town outside of the campus. Second, providing a map of the streets that feed into campus would give transfers a resource to reference when their friends invite them to off-campus locations. In addition to information about on-campus living options, transfers should be provided resources on rental agencies, utility companies, popular eateries, and recreational opportunities. Similar to a Chamber of Commerce relocation guide for a new employee, the university could do more to help transfer students adjust to their entire surroundings beyond the classrooms and campus buildings.

University employees should take a step back and imagine navigating the campus and the university website and other processes from a transfer student perspective. By viewing the university environment from this vantage point, staff could clarify points of confusion. This is an implication for practice that would benefit all new students. However, mid-year transfers have a tight window of time to figure out the university, and stand to benefit the most from having clearer environments to navigate.

Along the same lines, buildings at PLAU are not always labeled. A few have newer signs on one side of the building and others have some portion of the name in stone somewhere on the outside structure. Building markers should be posted outside of buildings during the first week of school in each semester and the university should prioritize funds for permanent signage. Clearly identifying the buildings on campus will benefit transfer students as well as newcomers and guests attempting to navigate the campus.

Spring Orientation covers a substantial amount of information in a short amount of time, and this can be overwhelming to new transfers. There is a finite amount of orientation time, yet transfers are missing pertinent information. Therefore, current orientation offerings should be re-evaluated and possibly shortened or eliminated to create space for the following topics to be covered: how to print documents on campus, how to access shared network drives, how to locate computer labs while fostering an awareness of their procedures, and how to navigate online course management software. Whenever possible this information should be presented during an extended orientation during the semester, reviewed one-on-one by an academic advisor, and also described through emails. While these implications might be very specific to PLAU, any university should consider what information is absent from its transfer student orientation.

Another implication based on my findings was focusing more attention on student health. PLAU students (except for transfers with an AA degree) are required to complete a Personal Well-Being requirement, which includes a health class and a physical activity class. PLAU's Wellness Committee has created a zone in the library to help relieve stress, and perhaps a next focus should be on surviving rigorous academics while still sleeping and eating.

An additional recommendation is to consider effective strategies that connect interested students to faith-based organizations. PLAU does not distribute information to incoming students about faith services. They direct interested students to the religious organizations section of the student organization website. A student may email the contacts listed for the organization to discover when services are offered. However, as Andy pointed out, getting connected to a faith-based organization was essential for him, yet he would not have thought to seek out this information if it were not for his friends. At the same time, James wanted to go to church upon arrival to campus but he did not know where to find services and without a contact person, he was afraid to go alone. As a public university, PLAU should find a way to link interested parties to all the resources that will help students feel engaged. Several of the participants in this study considered their faith-based organization to be essential to their adjustment, so more exploration of policies in this area is needed.

IMPLICATIONS FOR RESEARCH

As my study has reinforced, transferring mid-year can be challenging and deeper exploration into the influence of term of entry is still needed (Peska, 2009). Additional research should be conducted at small and medium-sized universities. In addition, new research should involve the insights of transfer students from a wider set of backgrounds and experiences. The participants in this study had different socioeconomic backgrounds and were from urban, rural, and international locations, but did not vary significantly in age, ethnicity, or racial diversity. More studies should be conducted on the experiences of different underrepresented transfer student populations at all types of institutions and certainly at public, liberal arts universities.

Beyond time of entry and institution type, future studies should conduct additional document and discourse analyses, focusing on the ways in which the university communicates with transfer students. For example, comparing staff and faculty intentions behind printed or online material versus transfer students' interpretations of this content could help clarify any miscommunication or unintended interpretations.

Another opportunity for research relates to the concept of academic difficulty. Many participants expected PLAU to be academically rigorous but they shared that the class content was similar to the community college, while the amount of reading or writing at PLAU was overwhelming. More needs to be uncovered about how transfers define academic rigor to help better prepare students and manage expectations. Furthermore, it would be interesting to examine what a student considers "doable" or "not too difficult" in comparison to the expected and earned grades at the end of the first semester. Several participants in this study mentioned low GPAs in high school and at the community college. At PLAU, I wondered if they were aiming for a 2.0 GPA (in order to avoid probation) or closer to a 4.0 GPA. Qualitatively, hearing more about a transfer's reflections on past academic performance and current academic behaviors would provide an interesting view into the transfer student experience.

More research is needed on transfer students' social experiences, particularly for individuals who did not know anyone at the university. Much of the literature mentions the challenges of loneliness or difficulty making friends at the university (Britt & Hirt, 1999; Harrison, 1999; Peska, 2009; Townsend & Wilson, 2008); however, more could be learned about students who never made a friend. Other participants noted how miserable they would have been without pre-existing friendships with PLAU students.

CONCLUSION

Community colleges and universities can benefit from the experiences of these participants, as they shed light on the everyday lived experience of being a spring transfer student in their first semester on the four-year campus. Transfers have already been in college somewhere, having attended different higher education institutions for various lengths of time. Transfers reach the university at different ages with varied life experiences, with a wide range of readiness and preparation to take the next step in their educational journey. The more that is known and understood about the experiences of transfer students, the more universities can do to help them succeed and attain their goal of earning a baccalaureate degree.

REFERENCES

Andres, L. (2001). Transfer from community college to university: Perspectives and experiences of British Columbia students. *The Canadian Journal of Higher Education, 31*(1), 35–74.

Austin, S. A. (2006). A successful university-foundation partnership to assist non-traditional transfer women. *Journal of College Student Retention: Research, Theory, & Practice, 8*(3), 275–295. doi:10.2190/9203-NU72-21R7-R363

Balzer, J. (2006). *Community college and university degree partnership programs: A qualitative study of the student experience.* (Doctoral dissertation). Retrieved from http://scholarsarchive.library.oregonstate. edu/xmlui/bitstream/handle/1957/3147/Doctoral%20Dissertation%20 -%20J.%20Balzer.pdf?sequence=1

Britt, L. W., & Hirt, J. B. (1999). Student experiences and institutional practices affecting spring semester transfer students. *NASPA Journal, 36*(3), 198–209. doi:10.2202/1949-6605.1086

Cameron, C. (2005). Experiences of transfer students in a collaborative baccalaureate nursing program. *Community College Review, 33*(2), 22–44. doi:10.1177/009155210503300202

Creswell, J. W. (2007). *Qualitative inquiry & research design: Choosing among five approaches.* Thousand Oaks, CA: SAGE Publications, Inc.

Davies, T. G., & Casey, K. L. (1998). Student perceptions of the transfer process: Strengths, weaknesses, and recommendations for improvement. *Journal of Applied Research in the Community College, 5*(2), 101–110.

Davies, T. G., & Casey, K. L. (1999). Transfer student experiences: Comparing their academic and social lives at the community college and university. *College Student Journal, 33*(1), 60–71.

Flaga, C. T. (2006). The process of transition for community college transfer students. *Community College Journal of Research and Practice, 30*(1), 3–19. doi:10.1080/10668920500248845

Harrison, P. L. (1999). *Transition experiences of community college transfer students: A qualitative study.* (Doctoral dissertation). Retrieved from ERIC (ED461395).

Husserl, E. (1965). *Phenomenology and the crisis of philosophy* (Q. Lauer, Trans.). New York, NY: Harper & Row.

Kelly, K. (2009). *Student perceptions of the higher education transfer process from two-year to four-year institutions: A qualitative study viewed through the lenses of student departure, social network, and complexity theories* (Doctoral dissertation). Available from ProQuest Dissertations and Theses database (UMI No. 3370305).

Kerr, K. H. (2006). *The experience of being a transfer student at a four-year university.* Paper presented at the Association for the Study of Higher Education 2006 Annual Conference.

Kodama, C. M. (2002). Marginality of transfer commuter students. *NASPA Journal, 39*(3), 233–250. doi:10.2202/1949-6605.1172

Laanan, F. S. (2004). Studying transfer students: Part I: Instrument design and implications. *Community College Journal of Research and Practice, 28*(4), 331–351. doi:10.1080/10668920490424050

Laanan, F. S. (2007). Studying transfer students: Part II: Dimensions of transfer students' adjustment. *Community College Journal of Research and Practice, 31*(1), 37–59. doi:10.1080/10668920600859947

Louis, M. R. (1980). Surprise and sense making: What newcomers experience in entering unfamiliar organizational settings. *Administrative Science Quarterly, 25*(2), 226–251. doi:10.2307/2392453

Marshall, J. (1981). Making sense a personal process. In P. Reason & J. Rowan (Eds.), *Human Inquiry* (395–399). New York, NY: Wiley.

Moustakas, C. E. (1994). *Phenomenological research methods.* Thousand Oaks, CA: SAGE Publications, Inc.

Nowak, M. (2004). *Understanding the community college transfer student experience from the student voice.* (Unpublished doctoral dissertation). Boston College, Massachusetts.

Owens, K. (2007). *Community college transfer students' experiences of the adjustment process to a four year institution: A qualitative analysis.* (Doctoral dissertation). Retrieved from ProQuest Dissertations and Theses database. (Publication No. AAT 3292569).

Owens, K. (2010). Community college transfer students' adjustment to a four-year institution: A qualitative analysis. *Journal of The First-Year Experience & Students in Transition, 22*(1), 87–128. Retrieved from http://fyesit.metapress.com/content/u01037m522012u71/

Pak, J., Bensimon, E. M., Malcom, L., Márquez, A., & Park, D. K. (2006). The life histories of ten individuals who crossed the border between community colleges and selective four-year colleges. Los Angeles, CA: University of Southern California. Retrieved from http://cuedev.usc. edu/tools/The%20life%20histories%20of%2010%20individuals%20 who%20crossed%20the%20border%20from%20community%20 colleges%20to%204%20year.pdf.

Peska, S. F. (2009). *Timing is everything: A comparative study of the adjustment process of fall and mid-year community college transfer students at a public four-year university.* (Doctoral dissertation). Retrieved from https://www.ideals.illinois.edu/handle/2142/14557

Rice, T. (2008). *Riding out the waves: Community college transfers graduating with bachelor's degrees.* (Doctoral dissertation). Retrieved from http://etd.ohiolink.edu/view.cgi/Rice%20Tamara.pdf?bgsu1206385493

Seidman, E. (1985). *In the words of the faculty: Perspectives on improving teaching and educational quality in community colleges.* San Francisco, CA: Jossey-Bass.

Seidman, I. (2006). *Interviewing as qualitative research: A guide for researchers in education and the social sciences* (3rd ed.). New York, NY: Teachers College Press.

Townsend, B. K. (1995). Community college transfer students: a case study of survival. *The Review of Higher Education, 18*(2), 175–193.

Townsend, B. K., & Wilson, K. B. (2006). "A hand hold for a little bit": Factors facilitating the success of community college transfer students to a large research university. *Journal of College Student Development, 47*(4), 439–456. doi:10.1353/csd.2006.0052

Townsend, B. K., & Wilson, K. B. (2008). The academic and social integration of persisting community college transfer students. *Journal of College Student Retention, 10*(4), 405–423. doi:10.2190/CS.10.4.a

Whorton, S. S. (2009). *Academic self-efficacy, academic integration, social integration, and persistence among first-semester community college transfer students at a four-year institution.* (Doctoral dissertation). Available from ProQuest Dissertations and Theses database (UMI No. 3355166).

Zubernis, L., McCoy, V. A., & Snyder, M. (2011). *Starting over again: Counseling considerations for transfer students in higher education.* Retrieved from http://counselingoutfitters.com/vistas/vistas11/Article_11.pdf

4

The Impact of Active Exploration on Transfer Student Choice

Jessica Moon Asa, Ph.D.; Steve Carignan, Ph.D.; Kristi Marchesani;
Kristin Moser, Ph.D.; & Kristin Woods, Ph.D.

Abstract

An increasing body of research on community college transfer has emerged in higher education literature, primarily focused on the process of adjustment after transfer to four-year institutions. Less understood is the decision-making process that community college students undertake while deciding on a transfer institution. The present study examines transfer decision-making, drawing on a mixture of quantitative and qualitative analysis to better understand how students think about and prepare for transfer to a four-year institution.

Community colleges are key providers of undergraduate education, although the traditional path of transfer from two-year degree granting institutions remains anemic. Community colleges enroll some 45% of undergraduate students in the United States (American Association of Community College Students, 2013). Of these students, the National Center for Education Statistics reported 81.4% of first year community college students in the 2004–2009 cohort indicated a desire to obtain a bachelor's degree or above; however, only 21.1% actually achieve transfer within five years (NCES, 2011). This gap between educational aspirations and outcomes offers both a challenge and an opportunity for higher education.

The economic impetus for increasing the successful completion rate at both the associate's and the bachelor's level is compelling. Recent reports by the Organization for Economic Co-operation and Development (OECD) ranked the United States sixth in the world for the percentage of citizens ssociate's degree or higher (OECD, 2008). United States workforce pment projections indicate the need to develop a more highly-icated workforce to remain globally competitive. The projected need for ducated workers requires the United States to increase the production of workers with associate's degrees by 25.1% annually and those with bachelor's degrees by 19.6% (Reindl, 2007).

A clearer understanding of the transfer process is urgent, not just from the traditional standpoint of access (Baum, Ma, & Payea, 2013) but also in light of recent federal initiatives related to degree production (White House, 2009). On an institutional level, competition for students has never been greater among private, public, and for-profit institutions (Altbach, 2010; Selingo, 2012; Kirp, 2009). Greater understanding of the transfer process will enable institutions to increase market share by expanding the proportion of students who achieve their transfer goals. The present study examines transfer decision-making, drawing on a mixture of quantitative and qualitative analysis to better understand how students think about and prepare for transfer to a four-year institution.

LITERATURE REVIEW

An increasing body of research on community college transfer has emerged in higher education literature, primarily focused on the process of adjustment after transfer to four-year institutions. Less understood is the decision-making process that community college students undertake while deciding on a transfer institution.

Community College History

Junior colleges have been present in the American educational system since the early 1900s, with the primary purpose of preparing students for transfer to four-year institutions (Johnson, 1973). Local control, local funding, and strong connections to secondary schools characterized junior colleges in the early years; however, a shift in emphasis to relationships with area housing, employment, human service, and related organizations led to a new focus on adult and continuing education and vocational-technical offerings beginning in the late 1930s (Witt, Wattenbarger, Gollattscheck, & Suppiger, 1994). Comprehensive community colleges, supported by national legislation and funding in the late 1950s and early 1960s encouraged states to build vocational programs, broadened the mission of existing junior colleges and boosted their enrollments (Iowa Department of Education, 1992).

In the fall of 2012, approximately 40% of undergraduate students in the United States (7.2 million) were enrolled in two-year institutions (Aud et al., 2012). After decades of rapid increases in two-year college enrollments, the last years of the 2000s saw slight decreases; however, enrollments are expected to top 8 million by 2021 (Juszkiewicz, 2014; Aud et al., 2012).

The growth in community college enrollments throughout the twentieth century corresponded with a diversification of students entering higher education, and opened doors to students from low-income and working-class families, women, minorities, and those with marginal secondary school academic performance (Cohen & Brawer, 2008). While postsecondary access has improved through the community college pathway, educational outcomes such as graduation rates have not kept pace (Bailey, Calcagno, Jenkins, Leinbach, & Kienzl, 2006).

College Choice

Hossler and Gallagher (1987) developed a widely used three-step model of college choice, beginning with the predisposition phase during which young students develop attitudes and aspirations about college from family, friends, and community members. The second stage, search, takes place in mid to late high school when students gather information about potential institutions in relation to their abilities and occupational interests, resulting in a more focused list of options (Terenzini, Cabrera, & Bernal, 2001). Finally, students enter the choice stage and make an enrollment decision, taking into consideration institutional, financial, and personal factors.

Parents and families influence students in a variety of ways during the first and second stages of this model, as they shape attitudes about postsecondary education and provide access to financial and social resources, thus shaping the group of institutions from which students ultimately choose (Hossler & Stage, 1992; Hossler, Schmit, & Vesper, 1999; Terenzini, Cabrera, & Bernal, 2001). While the families of first-generation and low-income students may provide support and encouragement related to college aspirations in the predisposition stage, they are often unable to provide guidance grounded in experience with higher education as their children search and choose institutions. In a study of first-generation and low-income Chicana students, Ceja (2006) found that students relied heavily on their families for support and encouragement while navigating the college search, but they were often challenged during the choice process, as they were largely on their own, while also managing the expectations of their parents.

Recent research supports the idea that college choice works differently for students traditionally underrepresented in higher education (Bergerson, 2009), and recognizes differences in access to information, financial resources, and social capital (Cabrera & La Nasa, 2001). This highlights the significant role of socioeconomic status in students' college choice pathway, with low SES students much less likely to complete high school graduation, meet minimum college entrance requirements, and navigate college application processes. However, family involvement and school-based interventions show results in reducing gaps between low and high SES students on these three measures (Cabrera & La Nasa, 2001). Institutional agents such as faculty members and college administrators also positively impact the college aspirations and postsecondary access of low-income and minority community college transfer students by providing college information and psychological support (Dowd, Pak, & Bensimon, 2013). Therefore, personal and institutional agents have the ability to impact college choice and access for students with limited social and financial resources.

Students who transfer from community colleges to four-year universities are faced with multiple decision points on their path through higher education. Community college students have cited a number of reasons for choosing a two-year institution out of high school, including lower cost, proximity to home, and the ability to work while enrolled in college (Nora & Rendón, 1990). Students with a lack of parental support, lower socioeconomic status, limited access to resources (Cabrera & La Nasa, 2000), lower levels of prior academic achievement, and degree objectives below a bachelor's degree (Kurlaender, 2006) are also more likely to choose a community college rather than a four-year institution after high school.

Proximity to home and family seems to have a particularly influential role in community college choice, both in terms of determining which institution students attend and whether they progress to postsecondary education (Lopez Turley, 2009). In a study of Ohio college-bound students, those intending to pursue a bachelor's degree were more likely to begin at a two-year college the closer in proximity they lived to a two-year institution and the further away they lived from a four-year institution (Long & Kurlsender, 2009).

Latino students are much more likely than their White and African American peers to choose a community college (Adelman, 2005), controlling for prior academic achievement, socioeconomic status, and educational objectives (Kurlaender, 2006). For many first-generation Latino students, family members, peers, and high school contacts were influential in the college choice process (Perez & McDonough, 2008; Ceja, 2006), highlighting the importance of relationships and related social capital.

Students who decide to begin the postsecondary journey at a two-year institution are at higher risk of leaving higher education before reaching the bachelor's degree, even when controlling for selection variables such as academic performance and demographic characteristics (Long & Kurlsender, 2009). A critical decision point arises soon after the initial transition to college concerning transfer. When considering all community college entrants, transfer rates to four-year institutions have ranged from 21 to 23% for students in the 1990 through 2008 cohorts (NCES, 2011). That rate increases to 36% when only including community college students who expect to complete a bachelor's degree or higher, with non-traditional aged and lower SES students transferring at even lower rates (Bradburn, Hurst, & Peng, 2001). Given these low rates of transfer, clear and timely information about transfer options and processes are especially important for students enrolled in community colleges.

Across institutional type, the college choice process creates common stressors for students, including concerns about application essays, standardized tests, uncertainty while waiting for responses from universities, and pressure from parents and family members (Vultaggio & Friedfeld, 2013). Some of these concerns are delayed for students who begin at an open access community college, but may arise prior to transfer. For first-generation students, stress arises from the need to navigate the college choice process on their own due to their parents' lack of postsecondary experience and information. This can be partially alleviated through the assistance of siblings and other family contacts with college experience (Ceja, 2006). Identifying stressors experienced by students at various points in the decision-making process and tapping into key sources of support will assist four-year institutions in more effectively reaching community college transfer students.

METHOD

The purpose of this study was to understand the transfer decision-making process of community college students in order to inform enrollment management strategies in higher education. The study had two primary research questions: 1) Which factors most influence community college students to choose a particular university as their transfer destination? and 2) How do students perceive four-year institutions when making the decision to transfer? The study was conducted at four public, Midwestern community colleges in the fall of 2013 and the spring of 2014. Two of the colleges were located in urban regions, two were located in a small city or rural area. All four of the selected schools had arts and sciences programs and all four offered residential living options. Data were collected in two ways: a qualitative study consisting of twenty-one student interviews and a quantitative study consisting of a thirty-item survey distributed electronically to arts and sciences students at the four study sites.

Participants for the qualitative portion of the study were identified by academic advisors at their community college. All students interviewed were enrolled in an arts and sciences major, which was viewed as an indication of potential intent to transfer to a four-year institution. Interviews consisted of a series of structured questions and lasted 15 to 45 minutes. The resulting dialogue was audio recorded, transcribed, and analyzed for common themes. Names were changed to protect the identity of participants. Transcripts and themes were triangulated through member checks within the research team.

Participants for the quantitative survey were also enrolled in arts and sciences programs at the four sites. An analysis was conducted on 1,029 completed surveys. Response rates by institution ranged from 6.1% to 16.5%, for a total response rate of 9.7%. The bulk of the respondents (65.3%) were 18 to 24 years old, with an additional 14.2% indicating they were between the ages of 30 and 39. The community college students surveyed were predominantly female (67.7%), with 4.9% stating they had served in the Armed Forces. Three-fourths of the respondents (75.3%) were full-time students, and almost half (47.6%) indicated that they worked 20 or more hours per week while going to school. Over half of the respondents (60.1%) lived within 20 miles of the institution they attended, with another 20.1% living between 20 and 50 miles from their community college. When asked about degree aspirations, 44.0% stated that they aspired to complete a bachelor's degree, and an additional 27.9% desired to complete a master's degree.

RESULTS

Quantitative Analyses

The quantitative results of this study address the first research question ("Which factors most influence community college students to choose a particular university as their transfer destination?"). Students were first asked a set of questions designed to gain an understanding of their reasons for starting their educational pursuits at a two-year community college. They were presented with a list of potential reasons and asked to rank these reasons by importance. As seen in Figure 4.1, the main motivation for students to select a community college was cost/tuition. A large majority of students (80.4%) listed cost/tuition as very important or important in their decision making process. The availability of financial aid/scholarships was chosen as very important or important by 71.5% of the respondents. Programs offered was the third most common reason, with 68.9% respondents choosing this factor as very important or important.

Figure 4.1

Reasons to attend current community college

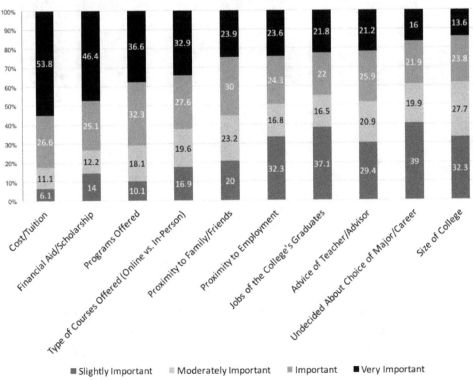

■ Slightly Important   ▨ Moderately Important   ▨ Important   ■ Very Important

Of the respondents who planned to transfer to a four-year college or university (90.1%), 38.4% planned to transfer to an in-state public institution, 8.3% to a private institution in the state, 24.5% to an out-of-state institution, and 28.8% were either undecided on their transfer destination or had other transfer plans (e.g. private for-profit). Students were asked about a variety of factors that influenced their decision to attend their intended transfer institution. The top factor influencing respondent choice to attend their chosen transfer institution was program offerings, followed by university academic reputation, financial aid/scholarships, and cost/tuition (see Figure 4.2).

Figure 4.2
Reasons to attend chosen transfer institution

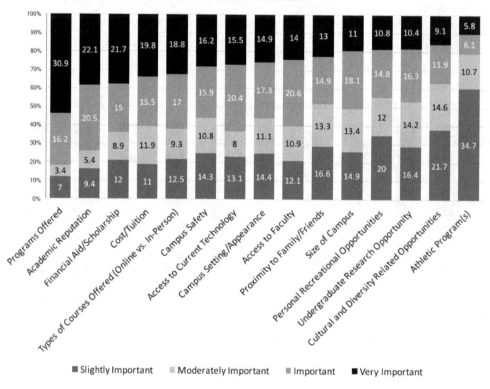

Preparation for transfer was measured by a series of questions designed to understand the activities that students complete prior to their transition from the community college to the four-year institution. As seen in Figure

4.3, only 22.6% of students have made sure that they are aware of the admission requirements at their intended transfer institution. In addition, 16.8% have interacted or spoken with academic counselors at their intended transfer school. Finally, 15.9% have researched the academic expectations at their transfer institution.

Figure 4.3

Transfer preparation activities

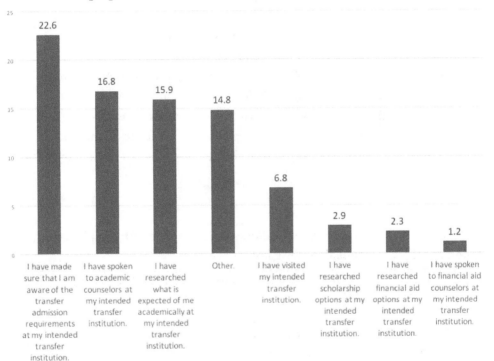

Exploratory factor analysis. In preparation for the regression analysis, an exploratory factor analysis was conducted to further reduce the college choice items into factors. After a thorough examination of all potential factors, one was chosen as an independent variable in the analysis (see Table 4.1). This factor is related to active exploration, and involves a student visiting their intended transfer campus, conducting active research on the intended transfer institution, and meeting with an advisor at the intended institution ($\alpha = 86$). Any other factors that emerged in this analysis did not have the necessary reliability levels to be included in the regression analysis.

Table 4.1

Factor Analysis Construct

Construct	α	Sample items
Active Exploration	.86	I have visited the admissions office at my intended transfer institution.
		I have met with an advisor at my intended transfer institution to plan my transfer.
		I have visited my intended transfer campus.

Regression analysis. A regression analysis was conducted to examine the impact of preparation for transfer on college choice. Active exploration was a significant predictor of community college student choice to attend in-state public universities ($\beta = .310$, $p < .001$), but not in-state private institutions ($\beta = .002$, $p = .428$). Active exploration was a significant negative predictor of community college student choice to attend out-of-state universities ($\beta = -.014$, $p < .01$). See Table 4.2 for the details of the regression analysis.

Table 4.2

Hierarchical Multiple Regression Analysis: Impact of Active Exploration on Public Institution Transfer Choice

	In-State Public β	In-State Private β	Out-of-State β
Active Exploration	.310	.002	-.014
R^2	.038	.001	.020
Adjusted R^2	.036	-.001	.018
F	21.341	.628	12.117

Qualitative Analyses

In addressing the second research question ("How do students perceive four-year institutions when making the decision to transfer?"), interviews explored educational choices, transfer process experiences and perceptions of select schools. Community college transfer students participating in the interviews recognized the power of education to expand their economic opportunities and to contribute to a meaningful life. Students expressed how much is "riding on" their education, particularly for those who see a return to college as a second chance after breaks in schooling due to military service, personal struggles, or raising a family. Many students viewed community college as a "jumping off" point and as a place to gain confidence and experience before transferring to a four-year institution. However, despite their stated desire to transfer, findings show most students are not actively engaging in behaviors to help them effectively navigate this transition.

A thread throughout the interviews was the desire for an educational experience and transfer process that is familiar, straightforward, supportive, comfortable, and approachable. Students understand the benefits of furthering their education, and they expressed the desire for support and guidance throughout a transfer exploration and application process perceived to be overwhelming and confusing. In our analysis of student interviews this was represented with themes of *reliance on confidants* and *personalized transfer process*.

Reliance on confidants. While students acknowledged they should conduct personal research—and some had engaged in initial fact-finding— they trusted the opinions of key confidants such as parents, siblings, classmates, and friends the most when considering transfer options. These opinions were impactful in gathering information about potential institutions, and some students identified their eventual transfer institution primarily from the input and feedback provided by these key confidants. A student who saw a lot of her peers depend on the input of others articulated this concept. April, who grew up in Korea, said "*. . . I guess they want to go to schools because they hear it from other people, it's like word of mouth. 'Oh, University of [name omitted]'s really good. You should go there.' And then they don't even think about looking into anything else.*" Comments such as these illustrate the idea that students rely on the guidance of peers and other trusted individuals to validate their choices and to simplify their decision-making process.

The assurance of going where they will know people also appears to provide the additional reassurance of a support system to guide them once they transfer. Bobby, a first-generation college student who never dreamed it would be possible for him to get a degree, said "*They are kind of helping me on what I should do, so that I will feel comfortable going there, because I already have friends there. For what I am doing, they tell me advice.*" During the course of our interviews it became apparent that students value personal sources more fully than the official information or established reputation of an institution, and that their depth of knowledge regarding cost, reputation, and programs was very incomplete.

In some cases, a dependence on a strong support system resulted in students limiting their college choice options in order to stay closer to their home. When asking students about why they chose to attend a specific community college, Dalton reflected, *"Because it's where I live. It's where my family is. The whole reason I got out of the military was to be back with my family, not to leave to go away to college."* Identifying with this, Sally shared that she had not looked too far from home to transfer because *"My connections are in this area. That's everything to me right now. Who I know and who can give me information and who can help me out the most. . . ."* Students want to stay close to home where they have a safety net in place rather than uprooting themselves and starting over in a new location.

Personalized transfer process. Participants were consistent in their definition of an ideal transfer institution as one in which transfer is easy, clear, and with personalized advising. Students consistently noted their desire for individualized guidance from both their current academic advisors and their transfer admission counselors, thus assuring consistent, tailored information. Pedro, a teaching major, reflected on the type of assistance he looks for from his advisor, *". . . instead of* [the advisor] *going like, 'You do this yourself and if you have any questions, just come talk to me,' I would like them to sit down and be like, 'Okay, these are your options. This is what you can do. This is what I can help you with.'"*

Students expressed a desire to be presented with clear information that outlined each step of the transfer process. Despite realizing there were resources available such as websites and college representatives, they seemed hesitant to gather information themselves. Johnny noted, *"Just the ease of the process. I don't want it to be a big pain in the ass. Sorry. I just want the process to be a smooth transition from one place to the other."*

Even more significant was student perception that institutions that make it easiest to transfer are those that will take the largest number of transfer credits. Many references were made to credit transfer in relation to time and money spent on education. When Bobby was asked his thoughts on an institution that makes it easy to transfer he said, *"I am trying to look at most of the schools that will take most of my credits, because I don't want to do them over again, because that would be a hassle."*

Students who were involved in TRiO, the federally-funded academic support program, expressed an advantage in their understanding of the transfer process due to access to a dedicated advisor and activities that provide personalized transfer information and options. Yvette, while raising three children and pursuing a goal of a law degree, has already committed to a school after receiving counseling and participating in university visits, *"I'm in TRiO, and they really try to match your credits to what you're trying to transfer to for your classes. They also will take you on campus visits and invite the college staff to talk to you. They have, like, study programs, so the transition to a four-year has been pretty simple for me because of TRiO."*

In addition to wanting credit transfer policies to be clearly articulated (and generous in their acceptance of previously completed work) by the receiving school, personalizing outreach during the decision process was also favorably received. Sally made several campus visits and detailed an experience at a school where the advisor was *"very open"* and gave his email address, and encouraged her to contact him anytime with any questions. As a result, she felt that she *"had a good experience with them with the whole transfer."* Another student, Tyra, described her struggle between choosing a moderately-priced public institution with a strong program in her major and a more expensive private college that has been courting her. In describing the smaller private college that had repeatedly reached out with information and interest, she said *"They're just very helpful in making sure that I don't feel too overwhelmed wherever I go. It's still a big college and I've been there a few times and I just like that they still seem, you know, I mean it's going to be costly but they make it seem like it's doable which is good."* Tyra's experience exemplifies the impact proactive and personal recruitment strategies have on student perception of prospective transfer institutions.

DISCUSSION

This study suggests many of the tools being utilized by institutions for transfer recruitment are ineffective and underutilized by students. The importance of active exploration during the college choice process combined with the disconnect between limited student use of institutional transfer resources in favor of a reliance on protective agents such as family and community networks (Stanton-Salazar, 1997) present a critical issue for both students and institutions. An understanding of this dynamic can help four-year colleges and universities redefine their recruitment strategies to be more effective in reaching students.

It is not surprising that active exploration (visiting admissions office, meeting with advisor, and visiting intended transfer institution) has a significant impact on student choice. The more important take-away is how few students engage in this process. As seen in Figure 4.3, only 16.8% of potential transfer students have spoken to an advisor at their intended transfer institutions. Even fewer, 15.9%, have researched academic expectations and requirements at their intended transfer institution. An even smaller proportion of students (6.8%) have visited the campus where they intend to transfer. This is despite the significant investments by institutions to facilitate exploration through services such as online transfer resources, articulation agreements, campus visits, and counseling.

Institutional agents need to understand a disconnect exists between what students say is important and what they do. For example, students say finances are a leading factor in their transfer choice, yet only 2.9% of respondents reported researching scholarship opportunities. Johnny's comments capture the contradiction between the awareness of institutional resources with a reluctance to engage in proactive activities to discover the resources in place to ease the transfer process. In the end, student behavior is not consistent with their understanding of how best to navigate the transfer process.

Instead of using tools and processes provided by four-year universities, students who begin at community colleges gather college choice information from family, friends, and other confidants. This is concerning given that many community college students have limited family experience with higher education (Ceja, 2006). Ultimately, traditional institutional choice factors are less important than personal influences when students arrive at the point of transfer decision-making.

Low levels of what we have termed active exploration are a concern from the institutional perspective, particularly on the part of public universities seeking to recruit in-state students. Transfer students are visiting admission counselors, researching financial aid options, and visiting campus at very low rates. Results in the current study suggest that incentivizing the increase of active exploration behaviors such as these would lead more students to choose in-state public universities as their transfer institutions.

University faculty and staff understand active exploration from an institutional perspective, while students explore via family, friends, and other personal connections. Qualitative findings demonstrated that students are seeking a straightforward, responsive, and personalized transfer process. Institutions have the option of either more effectively engaging students within existing transfer exploration tools, or designing new strategies that align with how students are telling us they gather information.

IMPLICATIONS

Since active exploration is a significant predictor of choosing a public, in-state four-year university, these institutions should find innovative ways to engage students in active research or introduce new methods or tactics to do so. Students' call for personalized, proactive support in preparation for transfer decision-making highlights the inadequacy of institutional reliance on passive information from websites, student-initiated campus visits, and information tables that require students to approach and ask questions. Instead, recruitment models must focus on active and individualized outreach such as home visits and personal contacts in face-to-face and social media formats. Institutions should involve prospective students in targeted campus events or localized programming to connect with their individualized interests and motivations. Examples range from providing transportation to the transfer institution to attend a theater performance to sponsoring a robotics competition on the community college campus.

Several students spoke about the importance of TRiO advising programs as an important vehicle for building understanding of transfer options, facilitating campus visits beyond where they would have otherwise looked when considering transfer options, and answering questions about application and financial aid processes. While this intrusive advising approach may be costly at scale, it may ultimately increase transfer rates and enrollments by broadening students' postsecondary options through facilitated exploration, and by providing personalized assistance in navigating a process that may seem confusing and overwhelming.

This study emphasizes the importance of family and friends in the college choice process for community college students. This adds to the body of existing research demonstrating parents and siblings provide significant emotional and financial support, particularly for first-generation and traditionally underrepresented students (Ceja, 2006) and therefore play an important role in educational decisions (Bers & Galowich, 2002). Given this reliance on family and friends, transfer recruitment efforts should include community and family-focused programming. Communications should highlight the experiences and testimony of siblings, parents, and peers who have attended the institution. College information sessions should be held in accessible settings like churches and community centers that encourage the involvement of family members.

Students in this study cited academic programs and academic reputation as the top two reasons for selecting their transfer institution. Given the primacy of academic factors in transfer college choice, creative approaches that connect with students' existing academic requirements could make exploration more feasible. For example, collaboration between two-year and four-year faculty members could result in course-related connections such as curriculum exchange and campus visits to work on joint projects. Such partnerships inspire personal relationships, provide course-specific visits to the four-year campus, and encourage engagement with academic departments and faculty prior to transfer. Admissions staff members could partner in these classroom collaborations to participate in activities and to provide transfer information for visiting students.

FUTURE RESEARCH AND CONCLUSIONS

Examining transfer rates and average student use of institutional resources reveals current strategies for supporting transfer choice are not delivering the results sought by public baccalaureate-granting schools and our nation. A deeper investigation of new and innovative recruitment and transfer support systems based on data on how students learn about transfer options is needed to develop a refined set of best practices.

Engaging families and confidants in the choice process—while resource intensive—may prove to be a sound investment. Future studies should seek to increase our understanding of potential community college transfers and their family structures, lives, and commitments outside of education, in order to inform new recruitment strategies. In addition, innovative academic partnership models are ripe for investigation. Future research should determine if two- and four-year faculty and curriculum exchanges and joint classroom-based initiatives would encourage higher rates of active exploration. Finally, while this study looked at the general community college population, future studies should further examine the impact of various demographic characteristics on perception and choice.

This study demonstrates that students are underutilizing traditional institutional resources in the college search, and are instead relying on personal and family influences. If four-year institutions are to better serve students with a wiser investment of resources, they need to expand institutional understanding of what drives transfer student choice. With this insight, institutions should adjust their approaches to community college engagement to encourage meaningful active exploration.

REFERENCES

Adelman, C. (2005). *Moving into town – and moving on: The community college in the lives of traditional-age students.* U.S. Department of Education Report. Retrieved from http://www2.ed.gov/rschstat/research/pubs/comcollege/index.html

Altbach, P. G. (2010). Competition's impact on higher education. *Forbes.* Retrieved from http://www.forbes.com/2010/08/01/higher-education-competition-opinions-best-colleges-10-altbach.html

American Association of Community College Students. (2013). *Fast facts from our fact sheet.* Retrieved from http://www.aacc.nche.edu/AboutCC/Pages/fastfactsfactsheet.aspx

Aud, S., Hussar, W., Johnson, Fl, Kena, G., Roth, E., Manning, E., Wang, Xl, & Zhang, J. (2012). *The condition of education 2012* (NCES 2012-045). Washington, D.C.: U.S. Department of Education, National Center for Education Statistics. Retrieved from http://nces.ed.gove/pubsearch

Bailey, T., Calcagno, J. C., Jenkins, D., Leinbach, T., & Kienzl, G. (2006). Is student-right-to-know all you should know? An analysis of community college graduation rates. *Research in Higher Education, 47*(5), 491–519.

Baum, S., Ma, J. & Payea, K. (2013). Education pays 2013: The benefits of higher education for individuals and society. Trends in Higher Education series. Retrieved from http://trends.collegeboard.org/sites/default/files/education-pays-2013-full-report.pdf

Bergerson, A. A. (2009). Special issue: College choice and access to college: Moving policy, research, and practice to the 21st century. *ASHE Higher Education Report, 35*(4), 1–141. doi: 10.1002/aehe.3504

Bers, T. H., & Galowich, P. M. (2002). Using survey and focus group research to learn about parents' roles in the community college choice process. *Community College Review, 29*(4), 67–82. doi: 10.1177/009155210202900404

Bradburn, E. M., Hurst, D. G., & Peng, S. (2001). Community college transfer rates to 4-year institutions using alternative definitions of transfer (NCES 2001-197). Washington, D.C.: U.S. Department of Education, National Center for Education Statistics. Retrieved from http://nces.ed.gov/pubs2001/2001197.pdf

Cabrera, A. F., & La Nasa, S. M. (2000). Overcoming the tasks on the path to college for America's disadvantaged. *New Directions for Institutional Research, 2000*(107), 31–43.

Cabrera, A. F., & La Nasa, S. M. (2001). On the path to college: Three critical tasks facing America's disadvantaged. *Research in Higher Education, 42*(2), 119–149.

Ceja, M. (2006). Understanding the role of parents and siblings as information sources in the college choice process of Chicana students. *Journal of College Student Development, 47*(1), 87–104.

Cohen, A. M., & Brawer, F. B. (2008). *The American community college* (5th ed.). San Francisco, CA: Jossey-Bass.

Dowd, A. C., Pak, J. H., & Bensimon, E. M. (2013). The role of institutional agents in promoting transfer access. *Education Policy Analysis Archives, 21*(15). Retrieved from http:/epaa.asu.edu/ojs/article/view/1187

Hossler, D., & Gallagher, K. S. (1987). Studying student college choice: A three-phase model and the implications for policymakers. *College and University, 62*(3), 207–221.

Hossler, D., Schmit, J., & Vespter, N. (1998). *Going to college: How social, economic, and educational factors influence the decisions students make.* Baltimore, MA: Johns Hopkins University Press.

Hossler, D., & Stage, F. K. (1992). Family and high school experience influences on the postsecondary educational plans of ninth-grade students. *American Educational Research Journal, 29*(2), 425–451. doi: 10.3102/00028312029002425

Iowa Department of Education. (1992). *Iowa's community colleges: A silver anniversary report.* Des Moines, IA: Author.

Johnson, M. R. (1973). *A history of the public two-year college movement in Iowa: 1918–1965.* (Doctoral dissertation). Ann Arbor, MI: University of Northern Iowa Rod Library. Retrieved from photocopy of typescript, University Microfilms.

Juszkiewicz, J. (2014). *Recent national community college enrollment and award completion data.* Washington, D. C.: American Association of Community Colleges.

Kirp, D. L. (2009). *Shakespeare, Einstein, and the bottom line: The marketing of higher education.* Harvard University Press.

Kurlaender, M. (2006). Choosing community college: Factors affecting Latino college choice. *New Directions for Community Colleges, 2006*(133), 7–16. doi: 10.1002/cc.223

Long, B. T., & Kurlaender, M. (2009). Do community colleges provide a viable pathway to a baccalaureate degree? *Educational Evaluation and Policy Analysis, 31*(1), 30–53.

Lopez Turley, R. N. (2009). College proximity: Mapping access to opportunity. *Sociology of Education, 82*(2), 126–146. doi: 10.1177/003804070908200202

National Center for Education Statistics. (2011). *Community college student outcomes: 1994–2009* (NCES 2012-253). Washington, D.C.: U.S. Department of Education. Retrieved from http://nces.ed.gov/pubs2012/2012253.pdf

Nora, A., & Rendón, L. I. (1990). Determinants of predisposition to transfer among community college students: A structural model. *Research in Higher Education, 31*(3), 235–255.

Organization for Economic Co-operation and Development. (2008). OECD factbook 2008: Economic, environmental and social statistics. Retrieved from http://www.oecd-ilibrary.org/education/education-at-a-glance-2008_eag-2008-en

Pérez, P., & McDonough, P. (2008). Understanding Latina and Latino college choice: A social capital and chain migration analysis. *Journal of Hispanic Higher Education, 7*(3), 249–265. doi: 10.1177/1538192708317620

Reindl, T. (2007). *Hitting home: quality, cost, and access challenges confronting higher education today.* Indianapolis, IN: Lumina Foundation for Education.

Selingo, J. (2012, October 4). Is Competition Really Good for Higher Education? *The Chronicle of Higher Education.* Retrieved from http://chronicle.com/blogs/next/2012/10/04/is-more-competition-really-good-for-higher-education/

Stanton-Salazar, R. D. (1997). A social capital framework for understanding the socialization of racial minority children and youths. *Harvard Educational Review, 67*(1), 1–41.

Terenzini, P. T., Cabrera, A. F., & Bernal, E. M. (2001). *Swimming against the tide: The poor in American higher education.* College Board Research Report No. 2001-1. Washington, D.C.: The College Board. Retrieved from http://research.collegeboard.org/sites/default/files/publications/2012/7/researchreport-2001-1-swimming-against-tide-the-poor-american-higher-education.pdf

Vultaggio, J., & Friedfeld, S. (2013). Stressors in college choice, application and decision-making—and how to reduce them. *Journal of College Admission.* Retrieved from http://acceptu.com/library/uploads/2013/12/Stressors-in-College-Choice.pdf

White House. (2009). Remarks of President Barack Obama—As prepared for delivery address to joint session of Congress, Tuesday, February 24th, 2009. Retrieved from http://www.whitehouse.gov/the_press_office/Remarks-of-President-Barack-Obama-Address-to-Joint-Session-of-Congress

Witt, A. A., Wattenbarger, J. L., Gollattscheck, J. F., & Suppiger, J. E. (1994). *America's community colleges: The 1st century.* Washington, D.C.: Community College Press.

Jessica Moon Asa *is the Director of the University Honors Program at the University of Northern Iowa.*

Steve Carignan *is the Associate Dean and Executive Director of the Gallagher Bluedorn Performing Arts Center at the University of Northern Iowan*

Kristi Marchesani *is the Director of the International Recruitment and Admissions at the University of Northern Iowa.*

Kristin Moser *is the Director of the Institutional Research and Effectiveness at the University of Northern Iowa.*

Kristin Woods *is the Director of the Student Success and Retention at the University of Northern Iowa.*

5

Policy Implementation From a Critical Perspective: Analyzing Transfer Policy Within an Urban Technical College

Megan M. Chase, Ph.D.

Abstract

This study contributes to the limited research on transfer policy implementation in higher education. Using case study research design and drawing on the tenets of critical policy analysis, I examined how practitioners in one two-year college implement transfer policy. Approaching the research from a critical perspective, the findings demonstrate that transfer as a tertiary goal of the college is congruent with the lack of transfer policy visibility and implementation, which has implications for students of color. These implications are addressed and recommendations are made as to how institutions can implement policy in a culturally relevant manner to better meet the needs of minoritized students.

Established as an open access institution, the two-year college originated with the promise of a democratic education, a stepping-stone to new careers and new possibilities for its entrants. Currently enrolling over 10 million students, public two-year colleges are the critical entry points to higher education and economic opportunity for half of the nation's college students. However, two-year colleges do not bear the brunt of college enrollments by chance. Over the last 50 years, state and federal higher education policymakers have designated the two-year college to be the "main artery" for broadening higher education opportunity for all Americans. The two-year college is assigned the task of harboring a multitude of high school graduates until they are prepared to transfer to a four-year institution or to enter the job market. The philosophy behind the segmented higher education structure is one of integration, where policymakers envisioned a system where students "can move with relative ease from level to level and from one part of the system to another" (such as a two-year college to a four-year university). Within this higher education arrangement there are, in theory, "no blind alleys" and "one can always transfer from one level to another" (Ben-David, 1974, p. 7).

Since minority students are more likely to commence their education at two-year colleges, it is believed that these colleges provide underrepresented students a "gateway" to higher degrees. However, critics argue that rather than presenting an opportunity for underrepresented students, two-year colleges lead students into a "dead end"; what critics constitute as a "form of tracking."[1] While research suggests that 30% of vocational students plan to transfer, the majority of two-year vocational programs do not provide pathways to a four-year institution but rather prepare students for positions in the labor market that generally pay less and have fewer opportunities for advancement. This is particularly disadvantageous to minorities who are overrepresented at vocational institutions.

In recent years, transfer policies have been created in an attempt to ease the transition of vocational students from two-year colleges to four-year institutions. While policymakers, higher education organizations, and academic researchers have all given considerable attention to transfer issues in recent years, none have explored how a state transfer policy is implemented by practitioners, nor how transfer policy implementation can enable or inhibit transfer equity for vocational students. This in-depth case study of an urban two-year technical college in Wisconsin, focuses first on understanding how the transfer policy was implemented, and then on understanding the policy's implementation from a critical perspective. For example, in what ways do the implementing efforts by the institution and practitioners meet the needs of a minoritized[2] population? In what ways do the implementing efforts allow the policy to act as a tool for equity?

---

1   The concept of *tracking* has provided educational researchers an important tool for understanding stratification in education and has been applied to higher education by distinguishing between the two- and four-year institutions as well as between vocational and academic curricula in two-year colleges.

2   In this paper, *minoritized* refers to the objective outcome, experienced by "minority" racial-ethnic groups, of the exclusionary practices of more dominant groups resulting from historical and contemporary racism (Gillborn, 2005). The use of the expression "minoritized" in preference to "minority" reflects the ongoing social experience of marginalization, even when groups subject to racial-ethnic discrimination achieve a numerical majority in the population.

Relevant Literature

Traditional methods of policy analysis, referred to as *rational scientific approaches*, treat policy creation and implementation as a logical step-by-step process in which facts are analyzed in order to arrive at the best policy solution. Traditional and other contemporary policy frameworks fail to capture the full complexity of policy environments and do not account for all the components that influence policy creation and implementation over time (Marshall, 1997b; Spillane, Reiser, & Reimer, 2002; Stein, 2004). Alternative models, such as *critical policy analysis* (CPA), "have been advanced to acknowledge policy as a political and value-laden process" (Allan, et al., 2010, p. 22.) Applying a critical policy analysis frame to implementation requires policy analysts to assess policy implementation by asking a unique set of questions such as: Who benefits? Who loses? How do low-income and racial minorities fare as a result of the policy's implementation? How is power manifested through policy and its implementation or non-implementation? Due to the fact that critical policy analysis was derived from an array of social science techniques it can not be easily delineated in a "step-by-step" manner (Martinez-Aleman, 2010, p. 44). For the purposes of this study, a list of suggested analysis guidelines have been arranged to assess the policy and its implementation (see Table 5.1).

A critical analysis of policy implementation can also assist in uncovering unintentional *institutionalized racism,* defined as racism that occurs in structures and operations of the college (Jones, 2000). This notion emphasizes how large scale institutional structures and policies "operate to pass on and reinforce historic patterns of privilege and disadvantage," such as deciding which groups gain access to the baccalaureate and which do not (Chesler & Crowfoot, 1989, p. 441). In this light, racism does not have to be an individual act, but is found in the "structures that determine and cyclically remanufacture racial inequity; and the institutional norms that sustain White privilege and permit the ongoing subordination of minoritized persons" (Harper, 2012, p. 10). It is important to note that institutionalized racism in the form of policy is most often unintentional. Referred to as *indirect institutionalized discrimination,* this form of racism occurs with no prejudice or intent to harm, despite its negative and differential impacts on minoritized populations (Chesler & Crowfoot,

1989). Institutional racism does not suggest that individuals are racist, but rather that the organizational polices, rules, or in this case implementing efforts, may have an indirect discriminatory impact.

Table 5.1

Critical Analysis Guidelines

Critical Analysis Guideline	Type of Data Guideline was Applied to	Example
Attention to the difference between policy rhetoric and practiced reality (Marshall, 1999; Young, 1999).	Interview transcripts, observation notes, documents	What do the college and practitioners claim to be doing to implement the policy and what actually appears to be happening? For example, if the institution declares a commitment to transfer equity, do they mean it? Do they monitor their effectiveness in this commitment?
Attention to the distribution of power, resources, and knowledge (Young, 1999).	Interview transcripts, observation notes, documents	What does the distribution look like and how does it appear to impact transfer? How are structures in the institution creating opportunities for students to transfer? Are there "arenas of struggle" over resources and turf?
Attention to how the implementing practices of practitioners enable or hinder opportunity for students to transfer (Marshall, 1997a).	Interview transcripts, observation notes, documents	Policy can create equity, but does it? Do practitioners interpret the policy as a potential tool of equity? Is the policy implemented in a culturally responsive manner?
Attention to the policy's place on the list of institutional priorities (Marshall, 1997a).	Interview transcripts, observation notes, documents	How important is the policy compared to the other programs in the college? Where does the policy fit in on the agenda of the institution and that of individual practitioners?
Attention to "silences" or what could have been written or said or done that wasn't (Allan, et al., 2010; Martinez-Aleman, 2010).	Interview transcripts, observation notes, documents	What is left out of documents that the average reader would not notice its absence? What is missing from the website to inform students and students of color specifically about transfer opportunities?

A critical analysis is useful because it provides a lens that helps us see the ways in which everyday policies and practices, such as those having to do with transfer, may perpetuate racial and gender inequity. For example, is the policy visible on campus? Does the institution teach students what transfer is and then guide them through the process? Does the institution encourage relationship development between students and practitioners to facilitate the transfer process? From this perspective the transfer policy can be argued to be an instrument of equity, a possible tool in reducing educational disparities in the state.

METHOD

In this case study, multiple methods were used to collect data, including interviews, relevant documents, and observation, which are customary in case study research (Stake, 1995). Purposive sampling was used to identify the college under study and the participants. I selected the case based on three characteristics. The college is a two-year technical college, has implemented a transfer policy, and has a high concentration of racial and ethnic minority students.[3]

Urban Technical College

Urban Technical College (UTC) is located in an area with high population density, is exceptionally racially diverse (see Table 5.2), is one of the poorest areas of the country, has a longstanding history of racial discrimination, and is one of the most segregated cities in the nation (Iceland, Weinberg, & Steinmetz, 2002; Lowe, 2011). The majority of UTC's programs provide (a) occupational education and training; and (b) customized training and technical assistance to business and industry (Merrifield, 2011). Other than the institution specific articulation agreements, the transfer policy—which is the focus of this study—is the only viable pathway for students to transfer to a public four-year institution.

As mentioned, UTC is exceptionally racially diverse. UTC has the highest concentration of minority students enrolled, enrolling approximately 70% of all students of color in the technical college system (Wisconsin Technical

---

3 At the time the research was conducted more than half (51%) of the student body were students of color (29.5% African American, 15.3% Hispanic, 4.6% Asian/Pacific Islander, 1.1% Native American.) Data are from 2008-2009 academic year. Data include all students pursuing an associate's degree, technical diploma, or who are enrolled in basic skills. Data exclude students enrolled in pre-collegiate vocational-adult and community service programs (Wisconsin Technical College System, 2008).

College System, 2012). In addition, UTC has a higher concentration of underrepresented minority students than any other institution of higher education in the state (Office of Policy Analysis and Research, 2012; Wisconsin Technical College System, 2012). Finally, if you combine all the students of color from all the public institutions of higher education in the state, UTC enrolls a higher number. This statistic underscores the idea that earning a bachelor's degree for students of color in the state is contingent upon transferring, and specifically transferring from this college. Figure 5.1 shows that when compared to the entire UWS, UTC enrolls more students of color.

Table 5.2

Demographic Profile of Urban Technical College

Profile	Urban Technical College
Total Student Population	36,973
Student Demographics	
Native American	1.1%
Asian/Pacific Islander	4.6%
Black	29.5%
Hispanic	15.3%
White	46.1%
Unknown	3.4%

Note: Data are from 2008–2009 academic year. Data includes all students pursuing an associate's degree, technical diploma, or who are enrolled in basic skills. Data excludes students enrolled in pre-collegiate vocational-adult and community service programs (Wisconsin Technical College System, 2008).

Figure 5.1

Number of Black, Hispanic, and Native American student enrollment at UTC and UWS, 2010. Figure illustrates that UTC has more students of color enrolled than all of the UWS added together.

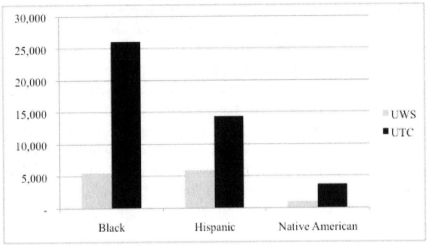

(Office of Policy Analysis and Research, 2012; Wisconsin Technical College System, 2012)

Note: The data includes students pursuing an associate's/bachelor's degree, diploma, or basic skills. Students enrolled in vocational adult or community service coursework were excluded.

Data Collection

I conducted semi-structured interviews as the centerpiece of my data collection efforts. To better understand how the policy was implemented, practitioners were asked to explain the visibility of the policy on campus, how they advise students on issues of transfer, and what programmatic efforts are in place to assist students with the transfer process. They were also asked to discuss the policy's place in the institutional agenda, and how they interact with the policy on a daily basis. I interviewed two levels of participants, external campus participants and internal campus participants, where external participants represented those not employed by the institution and internal participants were those who were either employed or previously employed by the case study institution. Participants ranged in their ethnic background and subgroup (i.e., campus board members, administrators, faculty, staff, WTCS and UWS level administrators, UW Regents, community activists, state lobbyist, and other pertinent stakeholders). At the conclusion of the study, I had conducted a total of 72 interviews. Interview length ranged from 45 minutes to two hours, and all but one interview was audio-taped and then transcribed.

To supplement interviews, I also analyzed documents at each phase of data collection. Documents included the transfer policy, transfer guides, the college catalog, campus newspaper, as well as posters and flyers related to transfer events. Select observations were also conducted over the time frame of a month-long site visit. The goal of the observations was to better understand the campus culture, how the transfer policy is enacted, as well as the saliency of race in transfer. I observed counseling sessions between students and counseling staff (with consent of both parties) as well as administrative meetings pertaining to transfer.[4]

Critical Data Analysis

Data collection and analysis occurred simultaneously. As a first step in data analysis, after each interview and document review, I took reflective notes in the margins of the text, noting possible major themes as well as topics for further research and questioning. After data collection was complete, all interviews were transcribed and the interview transcripts and observation field notes were uploaded into ATLAS.ti, where they were organized following techniques for thematic analysis (Luker, 2008). As mentioned previously, I used a set of unique questions and guidelines to analyze the data from a critical perspective and organize the data into larger themes (Table 5.1).

Trustworthiness

To increase confidence in my interpretations, I included several methodological safeguards throughout my research design. For example, I triangulated my findings by using multiple sources of data (interviews, document review, observations) to confirm emergent findings (Fielding & Fielding, 1986; Stake, 1995). I spent approximately three years charting the history of transfer policy in the state and learning about the institutional

---

4   I observed the Advising Center, the Welcome Center, and the Student Union. I attended two transfer events, one transfer information workshop, and the Transfer Day, where four-year partners came to UTC to talk to prospective transfer students. Finally, I also attended a daylong meeting for the Joint UWS and WTCS transfer meeting.

context via joint system level meetings at the state level, something Becker and Geer (1957, p. 126) refer to as "intensive, long-term involvement."

FINDINGS

The findings of this study provide insight into transfer policy implementation when analyzed from a critical perspective. When considering how the transfer policy is implemented, I chose a broad definition of implementation by including institutional and individual efforts directed at transfer as evidence of policy implementation. I approached learning about transfer implementation by attempting to understand how the institution and practitioners teach their students about transfer. What policies, programs, or other efforts are in place to help students learn about transfer and the transfer process? In answering this question, I found two levels of policy implementation. First, the policy was implemented at the *structural level*, which includes the formal implementing efforts taken by practitioners. This level includes all formal actions taken by the institution to implement transfer, including the creation of transfer policies and programs aimed at increasing the ease by which students transfer. The structural implementation efforts are divided into actions at the physical, documentation, and digital levels of implementation (see Table 5.3.) Second, the policy was also implemented at the *informal level*, which includes actions taken by individual practitioners to promote the transfer function and aid in the successful transfer of their students. In the following section I provide a composite of the policy implementation environment based on both the structural and informal levels of policy implementation.

Table 5.3

Structural Level of Policy Implementation

Physical Level of Implementation		
Programs/Events	**Human Resources**	**Print/Promotional Materials**
• Transfer Days (2 times a year) • Transfer Workshops (2 times a year) • General UTC Open House	• Counselors • Faculty Advisors • Student Service Specialists • Specific Four-Year Partner Transfer Specialist	• UTC Transfer Guide • Catalog • Posters/flyers to advertise programs and events
Digital Level of Implementation		

• Transfer Website
  • Curricular requirements for the primary and new online accelerated transfer degrees
  • Transfer contacts at nearby four-year institutions
  • *Articulation agreements (>435 agreements, 2 guaranteed transfer agreements)*
  • *Guaranteed transfer contracts and information*
  • Link to the Transfer Information System
• Email blasts to liberal arts and sciences students
• Other online transfer resources		

Note: Articulation agreements and the guaranteed transfer contract information are italicized because both are part of the documentation level of transfer. The agreements and contract are included on the Transfer Website list because students gain access to them via the website.

The Shadow College

In the process of documenting the structural and informal implementation efforts at the campus, select practitioners described the transfer function as a "shadow college," "hidden college," or "under the radar" within UTC. When practitioners were asked what led them to characterize the transfer function in this manner, one faculty member said, "it is because transfer is not embedded in what the college does on a daily basis." Similar comments were expressed by other practitioners, who said, "transfer happens in bursts, like the Transfer Days, but then goes away and is otherwise is not really talked about." Based on these conversations, I'm using the term *shadow college* to capture the invisibility and lack of presence of transfer at UTC. In this section, I describe aspects of UTC that have contributed to a shadow college characterization of the transfer function. This includes a lack of transfer visibility on campus, a community perception that transfer is not offered at the college, and the outsourcing of transfer resources. Finally, I discuss the informal implementation efforts that "happen under the radar," and while valuable to student transfer, are not institutionalized or a common practice.

A Lack of Transfer Visibility

To understand how UTC students learn about transfer, I spent time at UTC observing student service offices, such as the Help Desk, the Welcome Center, and the Advising Center. There was a lack of knowledge and general confusion regarding transfer in each of these settings. For example, at the Help Desk the student workers available to provide information to students did not know where to send a student with transfer questions and when they phoned their supervisor for assistance he could not be located to provide further information. This observation was common across the campus and provides evidence that transfer is not visible on the UTC campus, nor is it easy to find out information regarding transfer. In conversations with practitioners, one of the questions consistently asked was, "If I was a student and I wanted to learn about transfer options, would I know where to go if I was walking around campus?" The majority of responses were similar to an administrator's comment, "I don't think so."

Additionally, there is not a central location dedicated to transfer. A student service specialist expressed frustration over the lack of a transfer center.

> The other thing we are requesting is a transfer center. It really alarms me that with all the contact and all the articulation, all the share programs, all the transfer agreements that we have with all those universities and colleges, we don't even have a transfer center where students could go sit down, do their research, talk to somebody that is knowledgeable.

A staff member speculates that UTC does not have a center because it is not an administrative priority because they are concentrated on other areas, like enrollment and student retention.

To understand transfer visibility from a student's perspective, I walked around the main campus looking for the word "transfer" or related words, like "four-year institution" or "articulation." The only place on the main campus that displayed the words "transfer" or "articulation" was a small placard on the wall outside of the previous office of articulation. Currently, the person occupying this office is the administrative assistant to the Associate Provost. This illustrates that if students walk around campus looking for transfer information, it is not easily located by the signage posted; and, if students did locate the transfer and articulation office placard, the office lacks an advisor to assist them.

In addition, it is not apparent whom to approach with transfer related questions. Similar to the students I spoke with at the Help Desk, practitioners report that students generally find it difficult to identify a practitioner to speak with regarding transfer. Students with transfer questions can seek out one of four practitioners: a counselor, faculty advisor, student service specialist, or the transfer specialist from the local four-year institution (see Figure 5.2.) When practitioners were asked where to send students with transfer questions, they gave various responses. The most common response included referring the student to the receiving institution for advising.

According to an administrator, campus leadership is aware that there is "confusion" in the area of advising and counseling. He said that there is a disconnect between the counselors and faculty advisors. For example, when students initially enroll they see a counselor and then they are assigned a faculty advisor. However, if the student has transfer questions, the student needs to go back to the counselor because "typically faculty advisors are not knowledgeable about transfer." Although there are some faculty members that are very knowledgeable about transfer, according to one administrator, the general consensus is that there is "a big gap and weakness in that whole faculty advising thing." Practitioners mentioned two reasons that faculty members do not advise students well in terms of transfer: faculty members are not trained in the area of transfer and many "faculty advisors don't want to do that job."

Throughout conversations with practitioners I learned that the "go to" person for transfer advising was a particular staff member. When asked, this specific staff member agreed that she is the person students should be referred to with regard to transferring in or out of UTC, although her title does not reflect an expertise with transfer students. She is also difficult for students to physically locate. Originally funded under a grant issued to the Registrar's Office, she was initially located in the records room. The door that lead to her office said "Authorized Personnel Only." She said, "So students can't even come and see me unless I go out there and bring them back."

Figure 5.2
UTC counseling and advising structure. Students may receive counseling or advising from UTC counselors, faculty advisors, or student service specialists. Students may receive specific transfer advising from the local public four-year institution advisor two days per week.

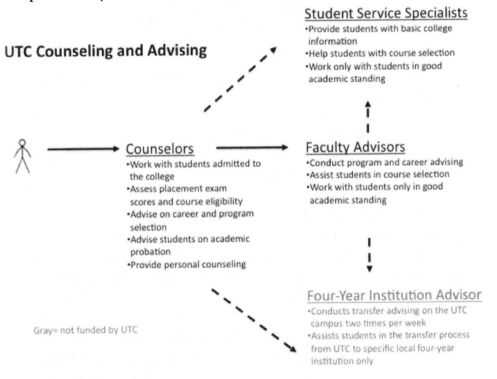

As outlined, transfer resources at UTC remain largely hidden because there is not a central location with transfer information or an easily located or identified UTC transfer staff member. In addition, most of the transfer resources reside in the digital realm. The data presented here does not suggest UTC lacks transfer information, but rather the resources are hidden from view or not readily apparent. To access transfer resources or guidance, students must be proactive by seeking the information out on their own, knowing *who* to ask, and *what* to ask.

An Enduring Technical Perception

Although transfer is a function of the college, UTC's history of "strong roots in vocational education" continues to be the dominant perception in the eyes of the community and students. According to practitioners, the UTC community is not aware UTC offers a transfer option. One of the contributing reasons the transfer function remains hidden is because the community continues to view UTC solely as a "trade school," or an extension of high school, rather than an academic college. As one administrator recounts, this perception is a result of the UTC history of technical education.

> Some people you talk to believe that we should only be a technical institution and deliver technical programs. That should be our focus. And those are the diehard, I want to say old-time people, but that's probably not an accurate way to say it. That has strong roots in our community and Wisconsin's foundation and in the roots of the technical college overall. Because that is where we came from and that is what they think we should continue to do.

A faculty member said "Most people would be very surprised to find out that you could do that [transfer]."

An enduring community perception of solely technical education is also evidenced in the name of the college, "Urban Technical College." As transfer opportunities were beginning to be given serious consideration in the early 2000s, there was a campaign to change the image of the institution from a technical college to a more comprehensive community college by changing the name of the institution to Urban Community and Technical College. There were practitioners who were in favor of the change and others who were adamantly opposed to it. Faculty and staff that were in favor of the name change believed that adding "community" to the name would accurately reflect the programs offered to students. Opponents thought that a name change would alter who they are as an institution and what they practice. These practitioners have a strong allegiance to their historical identity and believe that the institution should take pride in their technical mission. Practitioners viewed this change as an attempt by outsiders to change the purpose of the institution and, in the process, degrade the value of technical education and technical colleges.

The Outsourcing of Transfer Resources

Another reason that the transfer function at UTC is described as "hidden" or "in the shadows" is because external constituents provide the majority of transfer services. Resources such as transfer counseling, events, and publications provided to students are either created or funded by other institutions, illustrating that the responsibility for educating UTC students on transfer primarily resides with external institutions.

One of UTC's primary transfer resources is a transfer specialist from the local public four-year institution. The specialist spends two days a week on the UTC campus counseling prospective transfer students. The idea for the position was created in 2010, when UTC and the local public four-year institution were engaged in the Wisconsin Transfer Equity Study. As part of the project, focus groups were conducted with UTC students to augment the delivery of transfer resources.

> They wanted to make sure the students who want to transfer from a two-year to a four-year [institution] are successful in doing it. It came about from different kinds of student focus groups and surveys and things like that. They discovered that they needed somebody, a real live person on hand, to kind of help students in the process.

According to an administrator, one of the benefits of having this staff member on campus is that students can meet with her on campus instead of driving to the local four-year institution. Although the transfer specialist spends approximately half of her time at UTC, the transfer specialist position is entirely funded by the local four-year institution.

Although not readily apparent, there are "pockets where transfer happens." I found that transfer occurs by accident or informally, through the work of individual practitioners. For example, one faculty member in the Teacher Education Track collected her own transfer data to better understand how to support her students in the transfer process. Another faculty member ensures course alignment for students who plan to transfer by taking time from his own schedule to "sit in" on newly articulated math courses at other institutions to "double check" content alignment. These few examples provide evidence that transfer support does exist at UTC, however it is not common practice. As described by one practitioner, transfer support is "episodic" and tends to take place when practitioners go "above and beyond" their job responsibilities.

DISCUSSION

Critical policy studies in the past have focused on how a policy is developed or written and how the policy itself may marginalize racialized populations (Marshall, 1997b; Spillane, et al., 2002; Stein, 2004). This study is unique in that the focus is not on the policy alone, but how the act of implementing it may marginalize racialized students. The findings suggest that a policy can act as a tool of equity, but only if implemented in a manner that enhances the opportunities for the success of minority students. More important is how the non-implementing efforts of the institution and practitioners are interconnected to broader issues of power and prestige.

"Colorblind Transfer" Implementation

The findings of this study demonstrate a mismatch of implementing efforts and the population served. Currently, the implementing efforts at UTC support the ideology of hyper-individualism, where the primary transfer resources of articulation agreements are located in the digital realm and require proactive student engagement. Since it is not immediately clear where to learn about transfer or who is appointed to this role, students are charged with the responsibility of seeking out transfer resources and then knowing the right questions to ask. This is inherently troubling because an implementation strategy focused on an ideology of hyper-individualism or one that lacks the relational element is at odds with effective support strategies identified for students of color (Rendón, 1994, 2002; Swail, Cabrera, Lee, & Williams, 2004).

As mentioned previously, UTC enrolls more students of color than all public institutions in the state combined (Office of Policy Analysis and Research, 2012; Wisconsin Technical College System, 2012). Researchers have found that the success of students of color and first generation students in completing a course of study and transferring to a four-year college is supported when relationships with faculty, counselors, and other staff are established (Bensimon & Dowd, 2012; Dowd & Pak, 2013). Interactions with practitioners may help first generation students navigate complicated academic procedures, such as the transfer or application processes, as well as validate students' education aspirations and alleviate fears of isolation. Low income and racially diverse students are unlikely to possess a clear understanding of how to negotiate the college environment. As a result, when students encounter multiple academic options, they are often confused by the process (Alfonso, 2004; Person, Rosenbaum, & Deli-Amen, 2006). According to Rendón (2002), students from low-income backgrounds or who are first generation often do not know what questions to ask and are often reluctant due to a fear that they will appear "stupid or lazy" (p. 645).

According to a faculty member, UTC has "colorblind transfer," meaning that the manner in which the transfer policy is implemented at UTC is at odds with what the literature says supports students of color and first generation students. First, students at UTC that want to learn more about transfer have to know where to go and what questions to ask. If the student happens to find someone to speak with regarding transfer, he or she is then told to contact or visit the four-year institution they wish to attend for counseling.

Second, the online medium by which the majority of transfer resources are delivered is not conducive to promoting relationships. When students visit the UTC website they are confronted with a proliferation of articulation agreements. Although articulation agreements are an attempt by UTC to provide pathways for students to transfer, they have been found by researchers to "hamper" rather than assist student transfer due to a host of political issues and cause more confusion than clarity (CollegeBoard, July 2011). In addition, articulation agreements by themselves are not as useful as having a person-to-person conversation. According to Rose (2012) "information doesn't just flow and get processed in a vacuum. Information flow is embedded in human interaction and social networks" (p. 156). When students are provided opportunities to talk about information, it gets "elaborated, or legitimized" (Rose, 2012, p. 157).

This is not to say that transfer advising does not take place at UTC. As discussed, there are individual practitioners who take it upon themselves to implement transfer with their students, some specifically with regard to students of color. This finding shows that transfer happens at UTC by chance rather than by formal structural efforts. These findings echo previous research that select practitioners can act as "transfer agents" or individuals that work to facilitate the transfer of low income or racially diverse students (Bensimon & Dowd, 2009; Gabbard, et al., 2006). Borrowing from Dowd et al. (2006), I argue that transfer implementation at UTC has a "haphazard, or accidental quality" to it. The findings of this work do not proclaim that UTC does not provide transfer resources, but rather *how* the policy is implemented is not the best strategy given their student population. The results of this work demonstrate that a policy may be implemented, but in this case, the implementation is done without a strong awareness of serving a predominately African American student body. This research highlights the notion that policy may serve as a tool of equity, but only when implementation efforts are thoughtfully designed to meet specific student needs.

The Non-Implementation of Policy

The observations described provide insight into the non-implementation of the transfer policy and add to the literature on the critical policy analysis of implementation. Campus observations suggest a lack of information and visibility of transfer at UTC. Though these observations directly concern information and signage, they are representative of much larger issues. I argue that this non-implementation of transfer policy is a form of unintentional *institutionalized racism*. As mentioned, this form of racism emphasizes how large scale institutional structures and policies "operate to pass on and reinforce historic patterns of privilege and disadvantage," such as deciding which groups gain access to the baccalaureate and which do not (Chesler & Crowfoot, 1989, p. 441).

Indirect and unintentional institutional racism occurs in acts of omission, such as failing to have a transfer center, a designated person for transfer advising, and omitting required courses, such as math, from degree programs. Another example of omission is the resistance to including the word "community" in the name of the college. As observed at UTC and argued by Marshall (1997b), "policies will create arenas of struggle—sometimes just over resources or turf, but more often over ideology, over what is and what is not valuable and useful" (p. 7). Practitioners resisted the name change because it threatened the type of education they deliver and their livelihood, but also the ideology that UTC is first a vocational college. Although this is not overtly connected to opening opportunities to students of color, the omission of "community" has implications for the large number of students of color that UTC serves. The resistance and omission of "community" symbolizes a singular commitment to a culture that advocates vocational education. However, given the college demographics, excluding or diminishing the transfer function serves to foreclose opportunities that lead to higher levels of education. According to DuBois (1973), offering only a vocational education to the black community is a method for the continued subordination of that community.

Implications for Practice and Policy

This research provides evidence that how an institution implements a policy may be disadvantageous for the population served. These findings provide policymakers, practitioners, and researchers broader conclusions that may help educators understand the ways in which the everyday practices (or non-practices) of practitioners can indirectly contribute to the perpetuation of racial inequality. Based on these findings, I provide implications for practice and policy.

Transfer as an Expectation and a Mindset

Part of implementing transfer as an expectation involves creating a "transfer-going culture." Based on the literature showing the importance of high schools developing a "college-going culture" to increase the rates of their students that go on to attend college (see, for example, McDonough, 1997), it is argued that two-year colleges that advocate transfer tend to see increases in transfer rates (Handel & Herrera, 2003). Improving student awareness of transfer requirements may encourage students to transfer, as this increases interaction and relationship-building with practitioners, effective advising for students, and well-resourced transfer centers. It may also involve the creation of professional development opportunities for practitioners that demonstrate the value of a bachelor's degree. Also important to a vocationally-oriented campus are conversations surrounding how technical programs may coexist with academic ones.

Finally, to increase transfer opportunities for students, practitioners have to perceive it as an institutional priority. Creating a transfer "mindset" should be established by the campus leadership. Leadership among the president and the Board of Trustees is important in setting the atmosphere for the college. In order to have practitioners perceive the transfer policy as a priority, the board needs to establish an agenda that includes transfer. Prioritizing transfer requires reviewing practices to observe if they support transfer, building leadership-level (or presidential-level) relationships with four-year institutions, providing incentives for faculty to collaborate, and providing funding for resources such as a transfer center (Serban, et al., 2008).

Culturally Relevant Policy Implementation

Two-year colleges that serve a majority minority population should consider a culturally-relevant strategy to policy implementation. Research has suggested that faculty should alter their practices in the classroom to meet the needs of racially diverse students through what is called culturally-relevant or responsive pedagogy (Gay, 2000; Ladson-Billings, 1995). Gay (2000) argues that culturally-responsive teaching empowers racially diverse students by "cultivating their cultural integrity" and validates students' background by enacting deliberate teaching strategies tailored to the group of students (p. 43). I suggest that this idea expands to policy implementation. Institutions that serve a majority minority population should address the needs of that population. For instance, a culturally-relevant strategy to policy implementation would consider the student population when developing structures for counseling and advising, curriculum, and other student services. Culturally-relevant policy implementation may provide a strategy for institutions to allow a policy to act as a tool for equity. This approach to policy implementation would require institutional leaders and practitioners to regularly assess their own implementing efforts. For example, leaders and practitioners should ask themselves the questions, "Who does or does not benefit from our implementation of transfer policy? How does our implementation of transfer policy impact students of color?"

Recommendations for Future Critical Researchers

While the study findings provide valuable insights into transfer policy implementation from a critical perspective, the results highlight areas for future research. Goldrick-Rab and Shaw (2007) argue that more research is needed on higher education policy implementation. I argue that in addition to this idea, more higher education studies should emphasize policy implementation from a critical stance. Harper et al. (2009) argue that utilizing a critical approach to policy analysis is useful as it helps us observe how everyday practices or non-practices contribute to the perpetuation of racial inequality. This is important for multiple reasons, but most notably due to the population two-year colleges serve. The majority of students in two-year colleges are from low- to modest-income backgrounds, work part- or full-time, and did not benefit from attending high-performing high schools. Black and Hispanic students are more likely to be found at two-year public college campuses than at four-year public universities when compared to White and Asian undergraduate students, who enroll in two-year and four-year institutions in nearly equal numbers (Knapp, Kelly-Reid, & Ginder, 2012). These students depend on two-year colleges to implement transfer policies that will serve their unique needs. The first step for researchers is to select research designs that emphasize the relationships among educational policies and historical, cultural, political, economic, and racial contexts. Second, researchers should examine two-year college policy implementation critically by considering the student perspective on implementation. Researchers should ask questions such as:

1. How does the institution make students aware of the policy?

2. How does the institution teach students about the policy?

3. What physical signs on campus indicate the policy exists?

4. How are frontline staff and student staff educated about the policy?

5. Do the implementing efforts encourage interaction and relationship building?

6. How are the beneficiaries of the policy perceived? And, how does this perception influence interpretation and implementation?

7. How does the institution tailor policy implementation to the specific context or population served?

Addressing these questions will allow institutional leaders to assess and view their policies from the perspective of the student. Only after considering how well an institution's implementing efforts align with the population they serve will students begin to benefit from well-intentioned policy.

REFERENCES

Alfonso, M. (2004, November). *Community colleges and baccalaureate attainment: New insights into the democratization and diversion effects.* Paper presented at the Association for the Study of Higher Education, Kansas City, MO.

Allan, E. J., Iverson, S. V., & Ropers-Huilman, R. (Eds.). (2010). *Reconstructing policy in higher education: Feminist poststructural perspectives.* New York, NY: Routledge.

Bailey, D. S. (2003). "Swirling" changes to the traditional student path. *American Psychological Association Monitor on Psychology, 34*(11), 36.

Becker, H. S., & Geer, B. (1957). Participant observation and interviewing: A comparison. *Human Organization, 16*(3), 28–32.

Ben-David, J. (1974). Trends in American higher education. Chicago, IL: The University of Chicago Press.

Bensimon, E. M., & Dowd, A., C. (2009). Dimensions of the 'transfer choice' gap: Experiences of latina and latino students who navigated transfer pathways. *Harvard Educational Review, 7*(4), 632–658.

Bensimon, E. M., & Dowd, A. C. (2012). *Developing the capacity of faculty to become institutional agents for latinos in STEM.* Los Angeles, CA: University of Southern California.

Bogdan, R. C., & Biklen, S. K. (1998). *Qualitative research for education: An introduction to theories and methods* (Vol. 3). Boston, MA: Allyn & Bacon.

Boyatzis, R. E. (1998). *Transforming qualitative information: Thematic analysis and code development.* Thousand Oaks, CA: SAGE Publications, Inc.

Bragg, D. D. (2001). Opportunities and challenges for the new vocationalism in American community colleges. *New Directions for Community Colleges, 2001*(115), 5–15.

Charmaz, K. (2006). *Constructing grounded theory: A practical guide through qualitative analysis.* Thousand Oaks, CA: SAGE Publications, Inc.

Chesler, M. A., & Crowfoot, J. (1989). An organizational analysis of racism in higher education. *ASHE Reader on Organization and Governance in Higher Education*, 436–469.

Cohen, A., & Ignash, J. M. (1994). An overview of the total credit curriculum. In A. M. Cohen (Ed.), *Relating Curriculum and Transfer. New Directions for Community Colleges* (Vol. 86). San Francisco, CA: Jossey-Bass.

CollegeBoard. (July 2011). *Improving student transfer from community colleges to four-year institutions—The perspective of leaders from baccalaureate-granting institutions*. New York, NY: Author.

Creswell, J. W. (2007). *Qualitative inquiry and research design: Choosing among five approaches* (2nd ed.). Thousand Oaks, CA: SAGE Publications, Inc.

Crotty, M. (2003). *The foundations of social research: Meaning and Perspective in the Research Process*. Thousand Oaks, CA: Sage Publications, Inc.

Dougherty, K. J. (1994). *The contradictory college: The conflicting origins, impacts, and futures of the community college*. Albany, NY: State University of New York Press.

Dowd, A. C., Bensimon, E. M., Gabbard, G., Singleton, S., Macias, E., Dee, J. R., . . . Giles, D. (2006). Transfer access to elite colleges and universities in the United States: Threading the needle of the American dream. Retrieved from www.jackkentcookefoundation.org

Dowd, A. C., & Pak, J. H, Bensimon, E. M. (2013). The role of institutional agents in promoting transfer access. *Education Policy Analysis Archives, 21*(15). Retrieved from http://epaa.asu.edu/ojs/article/view/1187

DuBois, W. E. B. (1973). *The education of black people: Ten critiques 1906–1960*. Amherst, MA: University of Massachusetts Press.

Dumas, M. J., & Anyon, J. (2006). Toward a critical approach to education policy implementation. Implications for the (battle)field. In M. I. Honig (Ed.), *New Directions in Education Policy Implementation* (149–168). New York, NY: State University of New York Press.

Fielding, N., & Fielding, J. (1986). *Linking data*. Beverly Hills, CA: SAGE Publications, Inc.

Gabbard, G., Singleton, S., Macias, E., Dee, J., Bensimon, E. M., Dowd, A. C., et al. (2006). *Practices supporting transfer of low-income community college transfer students to selective institutions: Case study findings*. Boston, MA and Los Angeles, CA: University of Massachusetts Boston and University of Southern California.

Gay, G. (2000). *Culturally responsive teaching: Theory, research, and practice*. New York, NY: Teachers College Press.

Gillborn, D. (2005). Education Policy as an act of white supremacy: whiteness, critical race theory and education reform. *Journal of Education Policy, 20*(4), 485–505.

Goldrick-Rab, S. (2007). *Promoting academic momentum at community colleges: Challenges and opportunities.* New York, NY: Community College Research Center.

Handel, S., J. (2006, Fall). New math, tutoring trustees. *Community College Trustee Quarterly.*

Handel, S., J., & Herrera, A. (2003). Access and retention of students from educationally disadvantaged backgrounds: Insights from the University of California. In L. Thomas, M. Cooper & J. Quinn (Eds.), *Improving Completion Rates Among Disadvantaged Students.* Sterling, VA: Trentham Books Limited.

Harper, S. R. (2012). Race without racism: How higher education researchers minimize racist institutional norms. *The Review of Higher Education, 36*(1, Supplement), 9–29.

Heck, R. H. (2004). *Studying educational and social policy: Theoretical concepts and research methods.* Mahwah, NJ: Lawrence Erlbaum Associates, Inc.

Iceland, J., Weinberg, D. H., & Steinmetz, E. (2002). *Racial and ethnic residential segregation in the United States: 1980–2000.* Washington, D.C.: U.S. Government Printing Office.

Ignash, J. M., & Kotun, D. (2005). Results of a national study of transfer in occupational/technical degrees: Policies and practices. *Journal of Applied Research in the Community College, 12*(2), 109–120.

Jones, C. P. (2000). Levels of racism: A theoretic framework and a gardener's tale. *American Journal of Public Health, 90*(8), 1212–1215.

Knapp, L. G., Kelly-Reid, J. E., & Ginder, S. A. (2012). *Enrollment in postsecondary institutions, fall 2011; Financial statistics, fiscal year 2011; and graduation rates, selected cohorts, 2003–2008: First look (preliminary data).* Washington, D.C.: U.S. Department of Education, National Center for Education Statistics.

Ladson-Billings, G. (1995). Toward a theory of culturally relevant pedagogy. *American Educational Research Journal, 32*(3), 465–491.

Lincoln, Y. S., & Guba, E. G. (1985). *Naturalistic inquiry.* Beverly Hills, CA: SAGE Publications, Inc.

Lowe, M. (2011). Lanchester earns dubious distinction of most segregated city in America. Retrieved from website.

Luker, K. (2008). *Salsa dancing into the social sciences: Research in an age of info-glut.* Cambridge, MA: Harvard University Press.

Lynch, R. (1994). *Seamless education: A regional view of postsecondary transfer policy and practice.* Athens, GA: Georgia University, Department of Occupational Studies.

Marshall, C. (1999). Researching the margins: Feminist critical policy analysis. *Educational Policy, 13*(1), 59–76.

Marshall, C. (Ed.). (1997a). *Feminist critical policy analysis: A perspective from post-secondary education.* London: Falmer Press.

Marshall, C. (Ed.). (1997b). *Feminist critical policy analysis: A perspective from primary and secondary schooling.* Washington, D.C.: The Falmer Press.

Martinez-Aleman, A. M. (2010). Critical discourse analysis in higher education policy research. Boston College. Paper commissioned by the Association for the Study of Higher Education in collaboration with the Center for Urban Education for the Critical Policy Institute.

McCormick, A. C. (2003). Swirling and double-dipping: New patterns of student attendance and their implications for higher education. *New Directions for Higher Education, 121,* 13–24.

McDonough, P. M. (1997). *Choosing colleges: How social class and schools structure opportunity.* Albany, NY: State University of New York Press.

Merriam, S. B. (1998). *Qualitative research and case study applications in education.* San Francisco: Jossey-Bass.

Merrifield, L. (2011). *Wisconsin Technical College System.* No. Information Paper 34. Madison, WI: Wisconsin Legislative Fiscal Bureau.

Miles, M. B., & Huberman, A. M. (1994). *Qualitative data analysis: An expanded sourcebook*. Thousand Oaks: SAGE Publications, Inc.

Office of Policy Analysis and Research University of Wisconsin. (2010). *Headcount enrollment 2008–2009*. Retrieved from http://www.uwsa. edu/opar/ssb/2010-11/pdf/r_v103_tot.pdf

Office of Policy Analysis and Research, U. o. W. (2012). *Student enrollment fall 2010*. Retrieved from http://www.uwsa.edu/opar/ssb/

Person, A. E., Rosenbaum, J. E., & Deil-Amen, R. (2006). Student planning and information problems in different college structures. *Teachers College Record, 108*(3), 374–396.

Prager, C. (2001). Accrediting for curricular coherence. *General education in an age of student mobility*. Washington, D.C.: Association of American Colleges and Universities.

Rendón, L. (1994). Validating culturally diverse students: Toward a new model of learning and student development. *Innovative Higher Education, 19*(1), 33–51.

Rendón, L. (2002). Community college puente: A validating model of education. *Educational Policy, 16*(4), 642–667.

Rist, R. (1994). Influencing the policy process with qualitative research. In N. Denzin & Y. S. Lincoln (Eds.), *Handbook of qualitative research*. Thousand Oaks, CA: SAGE Publications, Inc.

Rose, M. (2012). *Back to school: Why everyone deserves a second chance at education, An argument for democratizing knowledge in America*. New York, NY: The New Press.

Sandelowski, M. (2008). Member check. In L. Given (Ed.), *The SAGE encyclopedia of qualitative research methods* (501-502). Thousand Oaks, CA: SAGE Publication, Inc.

Schein, E. H. (1991). *Organizational culture and leadership*. San Francisco, CA: Jossey-Bass.

Serban, A., Kozeracki, C., Boroch, D., Over, L., Malmgren, I., & Smith, B. (2008). *Transfer issues and effective practices: A review of the literature.* Sacramento, CA: State Chancellor's Office of the California Community Colleges.

Spillane, J. P., Reiser, B. J., & Reimer, T. (2002). Policy implementation and cognition: Reframing and refocusing implementation research. *Review of Educational Research, 72*(3), 387–431.

Stake, R. E. (1995). *The art of case study research.* Thousand Oaks: SAGE Publications, Inc.

Stein, S. J. (2004). *The culture of education policy.* New York, NY: Teachers College Press.

Swail, W. S., Cabrera, A. F., Lee, C., & Williams, A. (2004). *Pathways to the bachelor's degree for Latino students.* Stafford, VA: Educational Policy Institute.

Townsend, B. K. (2001). Blurring the lines: Transforming terminal education to transfer education. *New Directions for Community Colleges, 2001*(115), 63–71.

Wisconsin Technical College System. (2004). Progress Report on Credit Transfer. Retrieved from www.wha.org/workForce/pdf/ wtcsprogressreport3-04.pdf

Wisconsin Technical College System. (2008). Student enrollment fall 2008. Unpublished raw data.

Wisconsin Technical College System. (2010). System-wide enrollment by sex and race/ethnicity. Retrieved from http://www.wtcsystem.edu/ reports/data/factbook/index.htm

Wisconsin Technical College System. (2012). Student enrollment fall 2010. Unpublished raw data.

Young, M. D. (1999). Multifocal educational policy research: Toward a method for enhancing traditional educational policy studies. *American Educational Researcher, 36*(4), 677–714.

6

TRANSITIONING: EXPERIENCES OF TRANSFER STUDENTS

Dalinda Lou Martínez, Ph.D.

ABSTRACT

Although there are more transfer students enrolled in institutions of higher education than before, very little research has been done on the persistence of transfer students at the receiving institution. The persistence literature focuses on native students and overlooks transfer students who move from one institution to another. Many colleges and universities do not track transfer student movement. Worse, many institutions do not identify or serve transfer students after they matriculate at the receiving institution. The purpose of this study is to examine the experiences of transfer students following their transition to a new institution whose academic environment has been normed around the needs of first-year students. Findings from this study provide insight into how institutions can respond to the unique needs of transfer students.

INTRODUCTION

The need for more Americans to earn postsecondary degrees is almost universally agreed upon as a national imperative. President Obama argued that increasing the number of educated citizens within the United States is important to maintain global competitiveness for the nation's economy (2014). Additionally, Carnevale and Rose (2011) reported that the United States needs an additional 20 million postsecondary-educated workers by 2025, requiring 15 million individuals to earn their bachelor's degrees in order to compete in the global market.

Bachelor's degree recipients include "native" students (i.e., students who begin and finish their undergraduate degree at the same four-year institution) and transfer students (i.e., students who attend multiple two- or four-year institutions before completing the baccalaureate degree), (Adelman, 2006; Tinto, 1993). While bachelor's degree recipients are typically assumed to be native students, the increasing number of students attending multiple institutions on their path to a four-year degree is often overlooked (McGlynn, 2013; Hagedorn, 2006; Nunez and Elizondo, 2013; Shapiro et al., 2013). The U.S. will require that more students transfer successfully and earn a four-year degree to reach college completion goals and to remain globally competitive (McGlynn, 2013).

Students attending community colleges are the largest source of transfer students (Carnevale & Rose, 2011). Community colleges play a unique role in providing access to higher education for students, especially for students of color and students from other traditionally underrepresented groups, such as first-generation college and low-income students. These underserved students have already faced difficult circumstances and view community colleges as an affordable pathway for earning a bachelor's degree.

Unfortunately, not all students who transfer to four-year institutions achieve a bachelor's degree. The National Student Clearinghouse Research Center found that students who started their college careers at community colleges had a bachelor's degree completion rate of 16.2%, while students who started at four-year public institutions had a completion rate of 62.8% (Shapiro et al., 2013; Shapiro, Dundar, Yuan, Harrell, & Wakhungu, 2014). The disparity in degree completion—based on where students started college—perpetuates the negative stratification of postsecondary opportunity for students from underrepresented communities (Bensimon & Dowd, 2009; Shapiro et al., 2013). Although there are many students from underserved groups enrolled in community colleges, it is not sufficient that they gain access to four-year institutions; they must complete their bachelor's degree to change the stratification of opportunity (Carnevale & Rose, 2011). However, what is less clear in the current discourse is how to better serve transfer students following their transition to the bachelor's degree-granting institution. What is the experience of these students post-transfer and how can we serve them more effectively? What is the experience of transfer students within an environment designed to serve native students? These are the questions posed in this study.

Purpose of Study

Although there are more transfer students enrolled in institutions of higher education than before (Handel & Williams, 2012; Normyle, 2014), very little research has been done on the persistence of transfer students at the receiving institution. The persistence literature focuses on native students and overlooks transfer students who move from one institution to another (Tuttle & Musoba, 2013). Many colleges and universities do not track transfer student movement. Worse, many institutions do not identify or serve transfer students after they matriculate at the receiving institution (Jenkins & Fink, 2016). The purpose of this study is to examine the experiences of transfer students following their transition to a new institution whose academic environment has been normed around the needs of first-year students (Handel, 2012; Laanan, 2007; Tinto, 1993). Findings from this study provide insight into how institutions can respond to the unique needs of transfer students. The specific research questions that guided this study were: What are the post-transfer experiences of students? What challenges do these students encounter? What strategies do they employ to mitigate those challenges?

Significance

There are several important reasons to study the post-transfer experiences of students to better understand what contributes to their persistence at the receiving institution. First, many universities claim that one of their goals is to help prepare individuals to contribute to society as educated leaders (Altbach, Gumport, & Johnstone, 2001). However, if universities fail to understand the needs of their undergraduate transfer students, they will fail to adequately support these students towards graduation and success.

Second, understanding the post-transfer experience of students may help universities create policies and programs that may boost degree completion of students, especially students from underserved groups. Knowing what transfer students need as well as what resources they draw upon is an important and understudied aspect towards meeting the goal of increased degree attainment for all students, including those who transfer. In answering these questions qualitatively, a deeper understanding of the post-transfer experiences of transfer students may offer a way for the university to better assist transfer students' adjustment and address any difficulty in the students' persistence at the new institution.

Third, there is broad national and state interest in ensuring that more students earn postsecondary degrees and credentials (Complete College America, 2011). Increasing use of student retention rates as a performance indicator for higher education is an important benchmark in assessing the number of students who actually earned degrees in a timely manner (Porter, 1999; Strauss & Volkwein, 2004). Thus, states are beginning to use student persistence and graduation rates as performance indicators for both institutional accountability and budgeting (Strauss & Volkwein, 2004; Zhu, 2005).

Finally, understanding the post-transfer experience of transfer students may inform and influence university administrators' decisions about where to invest financial resources to support students. The results of this study may prove beneficial to individuals who work with transfer students, such as student affairs professionals, because university processes set up for native students may not be as beneficial to transfer students.

REVIEW OF THE LITERATURE

Transfer students are part of the undergraduate student population that enter and exist in the native student paradigm when they arrive at the receiving institution (Laanan, Starobin, & Eggleston, 2011). The university assumes that the challenges transfer students face may be addressed with the same policies and practices that are in place for native students (Lazarowicz, 2015). I argue that the post-transfer experience of students is best understood utilizing Schlossberg's (1981) transition theory, modified to include the native student paradigm (Figure 6.1).

Given that this study focuses on the experiences of transfer students after they transition to a four-year university, I hypothesize that their experiences will be significantly different when compared to students who began as native students because they had previously attended another postsecondary institution. Schlossberg's (1981) transition theory— described in the next section—proved useful to me in examining the transfer student experience.

CONCEPTUAL FRAMEWORK

Figure 6.1

Adapted from Schlossberg's Transition Model

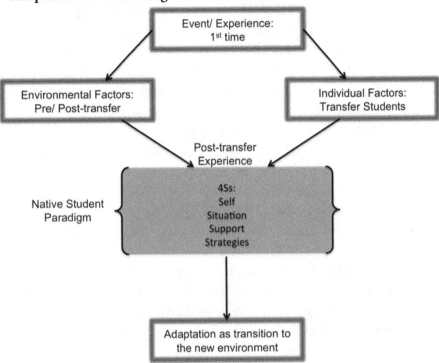

FRAMEWORK: SCHLOSSBERG'S TRANSITION THEORY

Schlossberg's (1981, 1984) transition theory derived from her model for analyzing human adaptation to transition. All students who begin their postsecondary education experience a transition. Schlossberg (1981) postulated three major sets of factors that influenced adaptation to transition: (1) the characteristics of the particular transition; (2) the characteristics of the pre- and post-transition environments; and (3) the characteristics of the individual experiencing the transition. According to Schlossberg (1981), all three sets of factors interact to produce a discernable outcome resulting from the transition, either an adaption to that transition or a failure to adapt to the transition. I apply this theory as it provides actionable steps for supporting the transition of transfer students and for improving their persistence at the receiving institution. Anderson et al.

(2012) and Goodman et al. (2006) advanced the model through the use of the 4S system: situation, self, support, and strategies (see Figure 6.1). These "4Ss" are the resources and assets that individuals use to transition towards adaptation. I describe each of these particular factors as they pertain to transfer students within a native student paradigm (Laanan et al., 2011).

In a native student paradigm, first-year students are embraced by their institution as "traditional" or "residential" students, categories that come with specific assumptions about college-going (Quaye & Harper, 2015). The four-year institutional environment was intentionally established to serve the needs of native students. Yet this may be problematic for transfer students who are new to the receiving institution—yet familiar with postsecondary education—who are asked to adapt to programs and services that were not designed for their unique needs (Quaye & Harper, 2015).

Schlossberg (1981) described a "trigger" as a transition that an individual experiences. For this study, I argue that the trigger is the student's transfer to a new institution. Although transfer students already experienced postsecondary education elsewhere, they were in essence having another "first-year" experience after enrolling at the receiving institution. Schlossberg (1981) emphasized that the student's perception of the transition was key to the way in which an individual experienced and adapted to that event.

Attending college within a native student paradigm is part of the transition that transfer students have to manage upon their arrival at the receiving institution. University policies and programs are often built around the needs of native students. According to Manning, Kinzie, and Schuh (2014), "Most institutions pay far more attention to new first-time first-year than transfer students" (p. 136). Nevertheless, when 41% of students completing degrees at four-year institutions are transfer students, it is essential that we understand and respond to transfer students' unique experiences and challenges (Baker, 2014).

Institutions dedicate significant resources to help undergraduates persist and complete their degrees (Renn & Reason, 2013). The first year of college is considered a precarious time, and institutions make substantial efforts to intervene at this critical period to increase persistence (Carter, Locks, & Winkle-Wagner, 2013). Most student services, such as orientation, advising, and first-year programs generally focus on the native student experience (Renn & Reason, 2013). Moreover, student success programs typically emphasize first-year student needs over the needs of transfer students attending the university for the first time. Understanding the experience of transfer students may give universities a better perspective on how to utilize resources to bolster transfer student persistence and graduation.

Postsecondary education persistence literature often does not distinguish between the needs of native and transfer students. Failing to disaggregate the data between these two distinct student populations may ignore the fact that these student constituencies experience the institution differently based on their previous postsecondary history. Quantitative research on transfer students tends to focus only on graduation and time to degree completion rates rather than on the transfer experience itself at the receiving institution (Allen, Robbins, Casillas, & Oh, 2008; Blecher, 2006; Dougherty & Kienzl, 2006; Ishitani, 2008).

Schlossberg (1981) provides a framework within which we can describe the characteristics of pre-transition and post-transition environments as internal support systems, institutional supports, and physical setting—all relevant to the transfer student's experience. Despite that fact that much of the pre-transfer literature focuses on pre-college factors that influence college-going and success (Adelman, 2006; Crisp & Nora, 2010; Dougherty & Kienzl, 2006; Strauss & Volkwein, 2004), other researchers have emphasized students' experiences prior to attending their new institution as having an influence on transition and persistence (Bensimon & Dowd, 2009; Crisp & Nora, 2010; Crisp & Nunez, 2014; Dougherty & Kienzl, 2006; Dowd, Cheslock, & Melguizo, 2008). It is critical—for students and researchers—to acknowledge the centrality of the pre-transfer experience as key to effective understanding of students' adaptation to their transfer transition.

Important studies provide insight into what community colleges have accomplished to improve the transfer process, support their students, and improve retention and success rates (Adelman, 2006; Bensimon & Dowd, 2009; Doughtery & Kienzl, 2006; Gilroy, 2013; Laanan et al., 2011; Li, 2010; Whitfield, 2005; Crisp & Nora, 2010; Dowd, et al., 2006; Miller, 2013). These improvements affect transfer students, and are connected to the internal institutional supports at both the sending and the receiving institutions.

Several reports point to the success of transfer students at receiving institutions; however, data also indicate that 40%, on average, of two-year to four-year transfer students do not graduate in four years (Shapiro et al.,

2013). Cheslock (2005) noted, "The percentage of an institution's incoming class that is transfer students depends on the institution's selectivity level, institutional type, attrition rate, number of majors, financial resources, tuition level, proximity to potential transfer students and direct attendees, and convenience for commuting students" (p. 256). These multiple factors influenced the transfer student experience.

I argue that it is not only the responsibility of the higher education system to admit transfer students but also to support them through degree attainment. Understanding transfer students have different experiences from native students, it is imperative that universities utilize transfer student capital (Laanan et al., 2011). When transfer students recognize this capital, they are more able to navigate the institutional processes. Wang (2009) concludes:

> The positive association between college involvement and baccalaureate attainment lends empirical evidence to the notion that more involved community college transfer students are likely to have more gains academically from the educational experience at their new home institutions. Institutional policies and student affairs practices should aim at developing programs and activities that involve more students, especially community college transfer students who arrive in the new college environment later than their native counterpart (p. 584).

An institution's mission influences the experiences of transfer students to persistence. Strauss and Volkwein (2004) wrote, "Retention research on four-year institutions cannot automatically be generalized to community colleges" (p. 204), and the reverse is also not generalizable. This may be due to different institutional types and missions. Moreover, transfer student research generally focuses on the process itself and much less on the role the receiving institution plays in advancing transfer student success.

Adaptation as Transition to the New Environment

For the purposes of this study, I interpret adaptation, as conceptualized by Schlossberg (1981), as a transition to a new academic environment and apply it specifically to the transfer student experience. In adapting to their new environment, I question whether we know if transfer students persist and thrive or if they are merely "getting by." Based on the current scholarship, I argue transfer students' adaption within the receiving institution has not been sufficiently examined. According to Schlossberg (1981), adaptation is dependent on a balance between an individual's available "resources and deficits" and the substantive differences between the "pre- and post-transition environments" (p. 5). Understanding the personal resources that transfer students bring to help themselves adapt to the new environment helps the receiving institutions understand more deeply the challenges that transfer students face and guides these institutions in developing transfer-appropriate programs and services.

METHODS

This study was conducted to understand the transition experience of transfer students at the receiving institution. Applying a qualitative framework, my central research questions are: What are the post-transfer experiences of students from underserved groups? What challenges do these students encounter? What strategies do they employ to mitigate those challenges?

Case Study Approach

A qualitative methodology was the most appropriate methodology strategy for this study because it allowed me to know more about the meanings that transfer students made of their post-transfer experiences (Maxwell, 2013). I used an exploratory, holistic case study approach because it provided an opportunity for me to conduct "an in-depth description and analysis of a bounded system" (Merriam, 2009, p. 40). I defined exploratory as an investigation into the phenomenon of the transfer student experience at the receiving institution. I saw this as a holistic case study as I looked at the various factors that contributed to the post-transfer experience of students, with a special interest in aspects of the institution. This was also a bounded system because my unit of analysis was transfer students' experiences at one receiving institution (Merriam, 2009). With a case study approach, I was able to obtain a deeper understanding of what challenges transfer students identified and ways that they addressed those challenges within the context of the receiving institution. I hoped this approach would illuminate their experiences and, in turn, help receiving institutions gain a deeper understanding of the needs of transfer students.

In this study, I positioned myself as a constructivist/pragmatist researcher. I believe that reality is socially constructed, and as such, I wanted to understand the lived realities of transfer students (Merriam, 2009). Transfer students entered into a native student paradigm at the university and their experiences are their reality. As a pragmatist, I was interested in finding practical solutions to this problem by conducting my research with appropriate methods (Patton, 2002). As I continued with my research, I engaged in a research-to-practice mindset that would provide universities with an opportunity to make a more welcoming environment for transfer students.

Research Site and Location

This exploratory case study took place at Liberty State University (pseudonym), a large, public, predominantly white institution (PWI) in the Midwest. This university was one of over a dozen public universities in a state that also had over two dozen community colleges. At the case institution, there were over 35,000 undergraduate students, with approximately 7,000 first-year students enrolled every year; about 1,500 were transfer students. I chose a single institution because I wanted to obtain an in-depth understanding of the experiences of transfer students at a research-intensive institution (Stake, 2000). While this decision limited the generalizability of this study's results, it nevertheless allowed me to gain a more holistic understanding of post-transfer experiences at receiving research-intensive institutions.

Sampling

The research sample for this study included transfer students who had been enrolled at the receiving institution for a minimum of one academic year, meaning both fall and spring semesters. Purposely selecting these students was necessary so that transfer students had time to experience the university. Having spent more time at the university, transfer students had more opportunities to make connections with university officials, faculty, and other individuals who affected their post-transfer experiences on campus and had more information to offer for the study (Patton, 2002). Participants shared their experiences, perceptions, and attitudes concerning their transfer student experience at the receiving institution.

In order to answer this study's research questions, I interviewed transfer students to understand their transfer experiences, the challenges they faced, and the strategies they enacted to overcome those challenges. Prior to the face-to-face interview, participants completed a consent form which requested permission to audio record the interviews and to take notes during the interview (Glesne, 2011). Taking notes allowed me to stay engaged and keep myself focused on the interviewee. It also guided me to probe further on the open-ended questions (Glesne, 2011). I was able to reflect on these notes and write down my speculations of what was occurring (Creswell, 2009). At the conclusion of the interview, participants received a $10 Amazon gift card for their participation and time.

I conducted semi-structured interviews with participants for approximately 60 minutes. Semi-structured interviews allowed me to ensure I had covered basic questions consistently with all participants while still exploring more points made by individual participants in their responses (Merriam, 2009). I was also able to ask additional questions in order to explore more of the student's particular experience. I utilized questions that were both targeted and open-ended, which I developed based on the literature reviewed and from what scholars noted as areas for further research related to the topic of this study. I also used my framework to design the protocol. All of the interviews were audio recorded. They were also transcribed to allow deeper analysis of the data collected to gain a better understanding of the themes that emerged (Glesne, 2011). The notes and initial interviews provided rich data for analysis.

Before I began interviewing any participants, I conducted three pilot interviews with transfer students from other universities to test my protocol. I included their feedback to clarify the interview questions and to elicit responses that allowed for participants to share their story. After conducting the pilot tests, I updated the interview protocol.

I examined university documents that shed light on institutional policies and practices regarding transfer. Such document data is beneficial "because of what can be learned directly from them but also as stimulus for paths of inquiry that can be pursued only through direct observation and interviewing" (Patton, 2002, p. 294). I also reviewed the institutional website. These sources of information helped me gain an understanding of what the institution claimed it provided for transfer students so that I could compare those claims with what transfer students actually experienced. I spoke to ten staff members who served in administrative roles at the university to gain a deeper understanding of the institutional context concerning transfer students. These individuals interacted with transfer students in a variety of ways, including admissions and student services. I used these conversations as background information to gain an appreciation for the complexity of the environment that transfer students needed to navigate at the institution. I did not analyze these interviews nor were they part of my formal data collection.

After receiving permission to begin my research, I contacted the university registrar's office at Liberty State University (LSU) and requested that they distribute an email letter from me inviting all transfer students who met the criteria to participate in this study. The letter outlined the nature of my study and the criteria for participation (i.e., previous enrollment at the receiving institution for at least one academic year, a first-generation college student or Pell-eligible student, and not be a student athlete). Finally, the letter invited interested students to click on the embedded link in the letter and to complete an online profile questionnaire. I used this as a tool to obtain a diverse group of transfer students. I wanted to recruit a transfer student mix of race/ethnicity, areas of study, gender, and age, if possible. The diversity of student profiles was important to obtain a wide representation of lived experiences. Selected students were sent a confirmation email, instructed where the interview would take place, and promised an Amazon gift card if they chose to participate. I expected to identify and interview ten to fifteen individuals who fit the criteria of this study, which is not atypical for qualitative studies (Remler & Van Ryzin, 2011, p. 156). Surprisingly, 149 students expressed interest in participating in the study. I invited close to sixty students to be interviewed who fit the criteria and ended up interviewing 27 transfer students. I rejected 39 individuals because they did not fulfill the requirements of the study. I notified the remaining 83 individuals who expressed interest in this study that I had acquired enough participants. Table 6.1 provides additional details about the characteristics of the participants I interview for this study.

Table 6.1

Demographic Summary of Participants

Interviews	27	**Race/Ethnicity**	
Female	14	Arab-American	1
Male	13	Asian	2
		Black or African-American	2
Underserved markers		Hispanic or Latino	5
First-generation college student only	7	Multiracial	4
Pell Grant-eligible only	9	White (Not Hispanic/Not Latino)	12
Both first-generation and Pell Grant-eligible	11	Member of race not listed above	1

DATA ANALYSIS

After the interviews, I wrote down my initial observations, read the transcribed interviews and kept organized notes from all of the interviews (Glesne, 2011). Analysis began immediately after finishing the first interview and continued throughout the study (Maxwell, 2013), using my theoretical framework as a guide for grouping data into large categories and looking for patterns, themes, and issues in the analysis (Miles, Huberman, & Saldaña, 2014).

Coding is a way to organize and prepare the data, to become familiar with it, and to understand what the student participants stated (Creswell, 2009). While listening again to the interviews, I read through the data, obtained a general sense of the material, then segmented the text before assigning meaning (Creswell, 2009). I looked for themes in the data based on the insights gleaned from the research literature, Schlossberg's transition theory framework (1984) and conversations with my peer coder and advisor. I kept a record of the themes that I identified immediately after collecting my data to help me as analysis continued (Glesne, 2011). I remained open to inductive coding, which allowed for other codes to emerge from the data. I coded the transcripts by hand and then entered this information into MAXQDA12 qualitative data analysis software for further analysis. I asked a peer to review and critique the codes I developed, paying close attention to any bias or assumptions that I may have made. I did this to help ensure reliability (Creswell, 2009).

RESULTS

Transfer Student Challenges

Although the experiences detailed by the participants in this study are not unique in the literature (see, for example, Adelman, 2006; Goldrick-Rab & Pfeffer, 2009; Moodie, 2007), the main finding from my interviews indicate the academic and social challenges that transfer students encounter within a strong native student paradigm is an "invisible identity." The participants in my study understand themselves as transfer students, despite the fact that the receiving institution does not explicitly recognize their status or honor their prior postsecondary experiences. As a result, their transfer student identity becomes invisible, creating a sense of isolation.

This invisible identity and sense of isolation contributes to transfer students' perception that they are not capable of completing the academic work at the receiving institution and that they did not deserve to be at the university. Moreover, it perpetuates the perception in the students' minds that their previous academic institutions were not as academically rigorous. Students, like Monzerad, felt that they did not belong at the receiving institution. She shared:

> Sometimes I do feel like when you tell people you're a transfer student, they look at you differently, especially when you tell them what college you came from. They think that you took the easy way. They're like, oh, those classes are easier.

Transfer students shared how experiences in the classroom also contributed to their sense of isolation and not fitting in, and that this lack of connection contributed to an invisible identity. Studies show that strong relationships with faculty contribute to student success (Barnett, 2011; Rendon, 1993). For example, participants in my study were eager to forge stronger relationships with faculty. But the reality is that transfer students' schedules may be more constrained and may not be aligned with a professor's office hours. Additionally, students felt that they were not recognized in class. The professors made no distinctions between transfer and native students and therefore, did not create space for transfer students to be appreciated for their previous experiences.

This invisible identity of transfer students may have substantive, negative effects, such as transfer shock (Laanan et al., 2011). While there are multiple reasons why students experience shock, the most common explanation is that students are ill-prepared for the academic rigor. My findings push this understanding further, in that the transfer students in this study identified the lack of informal academic support as an important component of their transfer shock. Students relied on their transitioning capital to accommodate for this lack of support. One way they did this was to create informal groups by obtaining classmate phone numbers to get help or taking the initiative to be a leader in the class.

Strategies

Transfer students employed various strategies to address the challenges they encountered, as they worked within the native student paradigm to create space for themselves. I identified six strategies that the transfer students utilized to maneuver within the receiving institution:

Transfer Networks. Transfer students' connection to other transfer students substantiates the need to have a network of individuals who share similar identities. The transfer students in this study spoke of feeling validated or rather not feeling as isolated when they met other transfer students.

School Spirit. Embracing school spirit means students were seeking a way to be a part of something and seeking connection to the institution. The students who mentioned being part of the LSU family also mentioned the benefits that were associated with being part of this university network. Transfer students felt that they were as much a part of the university as any other student and embraced the school spirit.

Housing Arrangements. A strategy transfer students used while at the university involved deciding where to live. Some students lived on campus, and others wished they had done so, but most importantly, the participants adjusted their living arrangements. Moving was mostly from on-campus to off-campus housing, but what students defined as off-campus housing may have been only across the street from the university. The proximity to the university provided students with both the benefits of campus and the freedom they wanted.

Work Experiences. Students identified work as a way to find a support network. In a native student paradigm, work has been found to provide structure and experience for students. Universities typically do not focus on work as a primary avenue for social integration (Perna, 2010). However, for transfer students, the purpose of their job was to have gainful employment in order to provide for themselves and their family. Some students worked full-time at banks and in government agencies, quite an alternate narrative to a more typical notion of a student holding a part-time work-study job on campus. Many transfer students held multiple jobs, so they were spending more time in those spaces than on campus.

Classroom Leadership. The participants in my study used classroom leadership as a strategy to find connection and decrease isolation. These strategies are similar to Strauss and Volkwein's (2004) study that argued classroom experiences are strong predictors of a student's commitment to the institution. My participants used their intentionality to stay focused on obtaining a degree. They recognized the need to take control of finding their own supports to learn in the classroom.

University Opportunities. The ways in which students were intentional in taking advantage of institutional opportunities and resources showed how they had maneuvered through the university. Transfer students did not feel that the university sought to integrate them; rather, it was more the student taking initiative. Quaye and Harper (2015) argued the university should intentionally provide ways to integrate students, and I agree that this continues to be an area for growth in serving transfer students. Universities tout student organizations as places where students can find social support networks (Tinto, 1993). For the most part, transfer students in this study were intentional and rarely participated in student organizations. They were strategic in how they spent their time and would not pursue a student organization merely for making friends. They saw being a part of a student organization as instrumental in furthering their career network.

DISCUSSION

The purpose of this study was to examine the post-transfer experiences of underserved transfer students at Liberty State University (LSU). The study highlighted the perceptions of students existing within a native student paradigm. I investigated how transfer students utilized different strategies to address challenges they encountered at the institution. Building upon Schlossberg's (1984) transition theory, I identified the internal resources and personal characteristics of the transfer students, their support networks, their understanding of their situation, and the strategies they employed in their post-transfer experience. This study contributes to the existing literature focused on transfer students as it extends the investigation past the initial transfer experience and into the transitioning process.

Transitioning Capital

Schlossberg's (1984) model is comprehensive, but the reality is that the complexity of everyday academic life for transfer students cannot be fully understood by reference to the 4Ss of self, situation, support, and strategy (Anderson et al., 2006). I replaced the fourth S (strategy) with a "transitioning capital" (TgC) schema. I conceptualize transitioning capital as the knowledge and nuanced understandings that transfer students gain while undergoing the transition at the receiving institution. I suggest that it is this context-specific capital that students acquire while navigating the new environment, even if they have acquired some capital while attending other institutions. Schlossberg and colleagues (Anderson et al., 2012; Goodman et al., 2006) posit that strategies are the individual behaviors used to undergo the transition, but this oversimplifies the transfer student reality. As a concept, strategies can be viewed as pedestrian, perfunctory and nicely-packaged solutions to the challenges transfer students face. However, the complex reality that transfer students experience in a native student paradigm requires students to employ strategies based on the students' personal characteristics or predispositions, their assessment of the new situation, and the availability of support. All these factors create transitioning capital that facilitates the selection of an appropriate strategy. Transfer students use transitioning capital to different degrees depending on their needs and the situation they are trying to navigate.

I modeled this concept of transitioning capital after Yosso's (2005) community cultural wealth framework. Community cultural wealth addresses the issues that communities of color face when they are marginalized. Yosso discussed community cultural wealth in six forms of capital: aspirational, social, linguistic, familial, resistant, and navigational. Similar to navigational capital, my concept of transitioning capital is the way in which transfer students maneuver through social institutions primarily focused on native student needs. Parallel to community cultural wealth, where the "various forms of capital are not mutually exclusive or static, but rather are dynamic processes that build on one another" (Yosso, 2005, p. 77), transitioning capital is a fluid development. The progression of TgC is dependent on the transfer student's varying needs. For example, if a student is self-aware, s/he may be more likely to take initiative and approach a professor or a classmate and recognize that meeting peers can make her/him successful in the classroom. Through the post-transfer experience, I argue that transitioning capital is a vehicle to transform the transfer student narrative from a deficit model to a narrative that highlights the strong characteristics of students that are beneficial to the success of students and the university.

Although I used Schlossberg's (1984) framework to understand adaptation as persistence, what is not emphasized in this framework is that through the transition experience, learning is happening along the way. I believe that this is a way of creating a positive narrative around the strength and tenacity needed for transfer students to exist in a collegiate environment that does not place them at the center of its policies and practices. Yet, in my study, the structure of a native student paradigm at the receiving institution continues to exist and creates a challenging environment for transfer students. Despite the fact that transfer students enter with transfer capital, the university overshadows those assets with the native paradigm embedded in various policies and practices. Transfer students know they will be entering a new space with which they are unfamiliar. When transfer students enter this context, I argue that they face isolation and stigma that they may internalize. Yet, the university perpetuates a native student paradigm for its own benefit. There is no impetus to change this orientation, because the majority of the student population remains native students.

A native student paradigm conceptualizes undergraduate students as those who matriculate at the university immediately after graduating from high school and are eager to enter a relationship with the university (Quaye & Harper, 2015). These students are assumed to live on campus and work part-time jobs that situate them as students first. While some universities predominantly enroll traditional students, it is important to recognize that the demographics of postsecondary institutions are changing. To oversimplify and use the native student paradigm as an all-encompassing perspective is misguided as it does not take into consideration the diverse student populations such as post-traditional-age returning students.

Universities make assumptions about the undergraduate student population and place the onus of fitting in and adjusting on students (Laanan et al., 2011). Many students in this study did not "fit the mold," and the native student paradigm did not mitigate the experience of transfer students in a way that assisted transfer students with the challenges inherent in making the transition to a new college or university. If universities are where knowledge and growth occur, then they need to foster a comprehensive approach for all students, including transfer students.

Implications for Practice and Policy

The findings of this study are important and may be helpful to students, faculty, student affairs professionals, and administrators. The transfer students' comments inform my recommendations in how to better serve transfer students. First, the concept that transfer students felt invisible should be concerning to institutional leaders (e.g., faculty, staff, administrators). Any initial communication with students through websites and personal interaction should reflect the experiences of transfer students. Once students are enrolled at the institution, faculty and staff should try to mitigate the invisible transfer student identity by providing information that is more inclusive of transfer students. Faculty could discuss the diverse pathways that students use to enter the university by making the entering class aware of different starting points.

Students suggested college or departments might provide a transfer student mentor that could be an ally and provide another avenue to learn about the university and institutional culture. These mentors would also be transfer students, thus ameliorating the invisible student identity for and with the newly transferred student.

During the interviews, transfer students mentioned orientation as an early interaction with the university. They wanted transfer student orientation leaders who could understand the challenges that were unique to transfer students. At orientation, transfer students also remarked the advising they received lacked a nuanced understanding of what they needed.

This study could prove helpful in highlighting the plight and unique experiences of transfer students. As noted in the study, faculty may not realize the diverse and unique needs that transfer students bring to the classroom environment. Faculty members at the receiving institution may also fail to make themselves available to transfer students in the way that students expect, given their experiences in their previous institutional setting, or at times that provide access for those commuting to campus. Faculty behaviors should take into account the transfer students in their classroom and make sure that the curriculum and class dynamics are more welcoming; for instance, they could invite transfer students to talk about their experiences, thus giving voice to transfer students (Rendón, 2006). Another example of how this could occur is for faculty to create small groups and encourage students to exchange phone numbers, emails or connect via social media. Whether the student is a transfer student or not, this would be a way to foster inclusion in the new environment.

When administrators are examining policies and practices about student success, the native student paradigm should be acknowledged. If the university accepts transfer as an ongoing learning activity, then merely providing a one-time orientation or a pamphlet is not sufficient. A more nuanced approach, such as a new student paradigm, would include all students who are new to the university. The Initiative on Transfer Policy and Practice (2011), in collaboration with the College Board's Advocacy and Policy Center, supports a continuous method of providing services, perhaps creating a transiton center for all students new to the receiving university.

The investment in higher education for traditionally underserved students continues to be an area of focus for policymakers. As more legislative and institutional policies are instituted to make student transfer less cumbersome, policymakers should keep in mind that credit transfer issues are not the only concern of students. Policies should also focus on the institutional resources of the receiving institution that can better serve transfer students. These policies should include equitable financial aid resources and reasonable credit transfer policies.

LIMITATIONS

The findings from this study are context-specific, and so are not meant to be generalizable, though there are likely lessons to be learned for those trying to support transfer students at similar receiving institutions. The participants were interviewed only once. Although the majority of interviews provided rich data for this study, a second interview would have provided students more time to reflect on their experience. The timing of the interview influenced the transfer students' experience. The point in the semester in which I interviewed the participant, life events, and the length of their tenure at the university influenced the description of their experience. None of these students had graduated, but all had a timeline and a plan to finish. Finally, this study only includes the perspectives of students who have persisted from one semester to the next and not of those who did not.

CONCLUSION

Findings from this study shed light on the challenges students face upon entering into an environment that does not prioritize transfer students but instead focuses on the needs of native students, thus leaving transfer students frequently feeling faceless and unrecognized. Transitioning capital allowed students to use their personal characteristics (perseverance, resilience, intentionality, and self-awareness) as resources to overcome feelings of isolation and stigma to exist and persist. The post-transfer experience is marked with continuous learning and knowledge production. The transitioning capital students gain continues to add to their strengths and success.

REFERENCES

Adelman, C. (2006). *The toolbox revisited: Paths to degree completion from high school through college.* Washington, D.C.: U.S. Department of Education, 2006.

Allen, J., Robbins, S. B., Casillas, A., & Oh, I. (2008). Third-year college retention and transfer: Effects of academic performance, motivation, and social connectedness. *Research in Higher Education, 49*(7), 647–664. http://doi.org/http://dx.doi.org.proxy2.cl.msu.edu.proxy1.cl.msu.edu/10.1007/s11162-008-9098-3

Altbach, P. G., Gumport, P. J., & Johnstone, D. B. (Eds.). (2001). *In defense of American higher education.* Baltimore, MA: Johns Hopkins University Press.

Anderson, G. M., Alfonso, M., & Sun, J. C. (2006). Effectiveness of statewide articulation agreements on the probability of transfer: A preliminary policy analysis. *Review of Higher Education, 29*(3), 261–291.

Anderson, M. L., Goodman, J., & Schlossberg, N. K. (2012). *Counseling adults in transition: Linking Schlossberg's theory with practice in a diverse world* (4th ed.). New York, NY: Springer Publishing Company. Retrieved from http://ezproxy.msu.edu:2047/login?url=http://search.ebscohost.com/login.aspx?direct=true&scope=site&db=e000xna&AN=450166

Baker, S. J. (2014). Role of transfer students in meeting college completion: Maryland state law library. Retrieved from http://cdm16064.contentdm.oclc.org/cdm/ref/collection/p266901coll7/id/4683

Barnett, E. A. (2011, Winter). Validation experiences and persistence among community college students. *The Review of Higher Education*, 34(2), 193–230. http://doi.org/10.1353/rhe.2010.0019

Bensimon, E. M., & Dowd, A. (2009). Dimensions of the 'transfer choice' gap: Experiences of latina and latino students who navigated transfer pathways. *Harvard Educational Review*, 79(4), 632–658, 780, 782.

Blecher, L. (2006). Persistence toward bachelor degree completion of students in family and consumer sciences. *College Student Journal*, 40(3), 469–484.

Carnevale, A. P., & Rose, S. J. (2011). The undereducated American. *Georgetown University Center on Education and the Workforce*. Retrieved from http://eric.ed.gov/?id=ED524302

Carter, D. F., Locks, A. M., & Winkle-Wagner, R. (2013). From when and where I enter: Theoretical and empirical considerations of minority students' transition to college. In M. B. Paulsen (Ed.), *Higher education: Handbook of theory and research*, 28, 93–149. Dordrecht: Springer Netherlands. Retrieved from http://link.springer.com/10.1007/978-94-007-5836-0_3

Cheslock, J. J. (2005). Differences between public and private institutions of higher education in the enrollment of transfer students. *Economics of Education Review*, 24(3), 263–274. http://doi.org/10.1016/j.econedurev.2004.06.002

CollegeBoard. (2011). The initiative on transfer policy and practice – For community colleges | Education Professionals – The College Board. Retrieved from https://professionals.collegeboard.org/higher-ed/community-colleges/initiative-transfer-policy-and-practice

Complete College America. (2011, September). *Time is the enemy: The surorising truth about why today's college students aren't graduating… and what needs to change.* Washington, D.C.: Author. Retrieved from http://www.completecollege.org/docs/Time_Is_the_Enemy_Summary.pdf

Creswell, J. W. (2009). *Research design: Qualitative, quantitative, and mixed methods approaches* (3rd ed.). Thousand Oaks, CA: SAGE Publications, Inc.

Crisp, G., & Nora, A. (2010, March). Hispanic student success: Factors influencing the persistence and transfer decisions of Latino community college students enrolled in developmental education. *Research in Higher Education, 51*(2), 175–194. http://doi.org/http://dx.doi.org.proxy2.cl.msu.edu/10.1007/s11162-009-9151-x

Crisp, G., & Núñez, A.M. (2014). Understanding the racial transfer gap: Modeling underrepresented minority and nonminority students' pathways from two-to four-year institutions. *The Review of Higher Education, 37*(3), 291–320.

Dougherty, K. J., & Kienzl, G. S. (2006). It's not enough to get through the open door: Inequalities by social background in transfer from community colleges to four-year colleges. *Teachers College Record, 108*(3), 452–487.

Dowd, A. C., Cheslock, J. J., & Melguizo, T. (2008). Transfer access from community colleges and the distribution of elite higher education. *The Journal of Higher Education, 79*(4), 442–472.

Dowd, A. C., Bensimon, E. M., Gabbard, G., Singleton, S., Macias, E., Dee, J. R., … Giles, D. (2006, August 14). Transfer access to elite colleges and universities in the United States: Threading the needle of the american dream. *The Hispanic Outlook in Higher Education, 16*(22), 41.

Gilroy, M. (2013). Taking the "shock" out of the transfer process. *The Hispanic Outlook in Higher Education, 23*(7), 26–28.

Glesne, C. (2011). *Becoming qualitative researchers: An introduction* (4th ed.). Boston, MA: Pearson.

Goldrick-Rab, S., & Pfeffer, F. T. (2009). Beyond access: Explaining socioeconomic differences in college transfer. *Sociology of Education, 82*(2), 101–125.

Goodman, J., Schlossberg, N. K., & Anderson, M. L. (2006). *Counseling adults in transition: Linking practice with theory* (3rd ed.). New York, NY: Springer Publishing Company. Retrieved from http://site.ebrary.com/lib/alltitles/docDetail.action?docID=10171371

Hagedorn, L. S. (2006). *How to define retention: A new look at an old problem.* Retrieved from http://eric.ed.gov/?id=ED493674

Handel, S. J. (2009). Transfer and the part-time student. *Change: The Magazine of Higher Learning, 41*(4), 48–53. http://doi.org/10.3200/CHNG.41.4.48-53

Handel, S. J. (2012). *Increasing higher education access and success using new pathways to the baccalaureate: The emergence of a transfer-affirming culture.* Retrieved from http://media.collegeboard.com/digitalServices/pdf/rd/StephenJHandel-IncreasingHigherEducationAccess.pdf

Handel, S. J. (2013). *Recurring trends persistent themes: A brief history of transfer* (A report for the initiative on transfer policy and practice). The College Board. Retrieved from http://media.collegeboard.com/digitalServices/pdf/advocacy/policycenter/recurring-trends-persistent-themes-history-transfer-brief.pdf

Handel, S. J., & Williams, R. A. (2012). The promise of the transfer pathway: Opportunity and challenge for community college students seeking the baccalaureate degree. *College Board Advocacy & Policy Center.* Retrieved from http://eric.ed.gov/?id=ED541969

Ishitani, T. T. (2008). How do transfers survive after "transfer shock"? A longitudinal study of transfer student departure at a four-year institution. *Research in Higher Education, 49*(5), 403–419. http://doi.org/http://dx.doi.org.proxy2.cl.msu.edu.proxy1.cl.msu.edu/10.1007/s11162-008-9091-x

Jenkins, D., & Fink, J. (2016). Tracking transfer: New measures of institutional and state effectiveness in helping community college students attain bachelor's degrees. *Community College Research Center, Teachers College, Columbia University.* Retrieved from http://eric.ed.gov/?id=ED563499

Laanan, F. S. (2007). Studying transfer students: Part II: Dimensions of transfer students' adjustment. *Community College Journal of Research and Practice, 31*(1), 37–59. http://doi.org/10.1080/10668920600859947

Laanan, F. S., Starobin, S. S., & Eggleston, L. E. (2011). Adjustment of community college students at a four-year university: Role and relevance of transfer student capital for student retention. *Journal of College Student Retention: Research, Theory & Practice, 12*(2), 175–209.

Lazarowicz, T. A. (2015). *Understanding the transition experience of community college transfer students to a 4-year university: Incorporating schlossberg's transition theory into higher education* (Order No. 3688491). Available from Dissertations & Theses at CIC Institutions; ProQuest Dissertations & Theses Global. (1673878331). Retrieved from http://ezproxy.msu.edu.proxy2.cl.msu.edu/login?url=http://search.proquest.com.proxy2.cl.msu.edu/docview/1673878331?accountid=12598

Li, D. (2010, Winter). They need help: Transfer students from four-year to four-year institutions. *The Review of Higher Education, 33*(2), 207–238.

Manning, K., Kinzie, J., & Schuh, J. H. (2014). *One size does not fit all: traditional and innovative models of student affairs practice* (2nd ed.). New York, NY: Routledge.

Maxwell, J. A. (2013). *Qualitative research design: An interactive approach* (3rd ed.). Thousand Oaks, CA: SAGE Publications, Inc.

McGlynn, A. P. (2013, September 23). Report shows community colleges separate and unequal. *The Hispanic Outlook in Higher Education, 23*(23), 13–14.

Merriam, S. B. (2009). *Qualitative research: A guide to design and implementation.* San Francisco, CA: Jossey-Bass.

Miles, M. B., Huberman, A. M., & Saldaña, J. (2014). *Qualitative data analysis: A methods sourcebook* (3rd ed.). Thousand Oaks, CA: SAGE Publications, Inc.

Miller, A. (2013). Institutional practices that facilitate bachelor's degree completion for transfer students. *New Directions for Higher Education, 2013*(162), 39–50. http://doi.org/10.1002/he.20055

Moodie, G. (2007). Do tiers affect student transfer? Examining the student admission ratio. *Community College Journal of Research and Practice, 31*(11), 847–861.

Normyle, M. (2014, April 24). *What the latest research tells us about serving college transfer students.* Retrieved from http://blog.noellevitz.com/2014/04/24/latest-research-tells-us-serving-college-transfer-students/

Núñez, A. M., & Elizondo, D. (2013, Spring). Closing the latino/a transfer gap: Creating pathways to the baccalaureate. *Perspectivas: Issues in Higher Education Policy and Practice, 2013*(2), 1–15.

Obama, B. (2014). *Building American skills through community colleges.* Retrieved from https://www.whitehouse.gov/node/177301

Patton, M. Q. (2002). *Qualitative research & evaluation methods* (3rd ed.). Thousand Oaks, CA: SAGE Publications, Inc.

Perna, L. W. (Ed.). (2010). *Understanding the working college student: New research and its implications for policy and practice.* Sterling, VA: Stylus Publishing, LLC.

Porter, S. (1999). Assessing transfer and native student performance at four-year institutions. *AIR Annual Form.* Retrieved from http://eric.ed.gov.proxy1.cl.msu.edu/?id=ED433790

Quaye, S. J., & Harper, S. R. (Eds.). (2015). *Student engagement in higher education: Theoretical perspectives and practical approaches for diverse populations* (2nd ed.). New York, NY: Routledge.

Remler, D. K., & Van Ryzin, G. G. (2011). *Research methods in practice: Strategies for description and causation.* Thousand Oaks, CA: SAGE Publications, Inc.

Rendón, L. I. (1993). Validating culturally diverse students: Toward a new model of learning and student development. *Innovative Higher Education, 19*(1), 29. Retrieved from http://search.proquest.com. proxy2.cl.msu.edu/docview/62790108/DD1B21E836734286PQ/1?

Rendón, L. I. (2006). Reconceptualizing success for underserved students in higher education. *National Postsecondary Education Cooperative.* Washington, D.C.: National Center for Education Studies. Retrieved from http://academics.uky.edu/UGE/PFW/Shared%20Documents/ Rendon_ReconceptualizingSuccess4UnderservedStudentsHigherEd_ NCES2006.pdf

Renn, K. A., & Reason, R. D. (2013). *College students in the United States: Characteristics, experiences, and outcomes.* San Francisco, CA: Jossey-Bass.

Schlossberg, N. K. (1981). A model for analyzing human adaptation to transition. *The Counseling Psychologist, 9*(2), 2–18. http://doi. org/10.1177/001100008100900202

Schlossberg, N. K. (1984). *Counseling adults in transition: Linking practice with theory.* New York, NY: Springer Publishing Company.

Shapiro, D., Dundar, A., Yuan, X., Harrell, A., & Wakhungu, P. K. (2014). *Completing college: A national view of student attainment rates–Fall 2008 cohort (Signature report no. 8).* National Student Clearinghouse Research Center. Retrieved from http://nscresearchcenter.org/signaturereport8/

Shapiro, D., Dundar, A., Ziskin, M., Chiang, Y., Chen, J., Torres, V., & Harrell, A. (2013). *Baccalaureate attainment: A national view of the postsecondary outcomes of students who transfer from two-year to four-year institutions (signature report no. 5).* Retrieved from http:// nscresearchcenter.org/signaturereport5/

Simmons, J. (2012). High cost of low grad rates. *The Hispanic Outlook in Higher Education, 22*(8), 10–12.

Stake, R. (2000). Case Studies. In N. K. Denzin & Y. S. Lincoln (Eds.), *Handbook of Qualitative Research* (2nd ed.), 435–454. Thousand Oaks, CA: SAGE Publications, Inc. Retrieved from http://eric. ed.gov/?id=ED477147

Strauss, L. C., & Volkwein, F. J. (2004). Predictors of student commitment at two-year and four-year institutions. *The Journal of Higher Education, 75*(2), 203.

Tinto, V. (1993). *Leaving college: Rethinking the causes and cures of student attrition* (2nd ed.). Chicago, IL: University of Chicago Press.

Tuttle, L. V., & Musoba, G. D. (2013). Transfer student persistence at a Hispanic-serving university. *Journal of Latinos and Education, 12*(1), 38–58. http://doi.org/10.1080/15348431.2013.734248

Wang, X. (2009). Baccalaureate attainment and college persistence of community college transfer students at four-year institutions. *Research in Higher Education, 50*(6), 570–588. http://doi.org/http://dx.doi.org.proxy1.cl.msu.edu/10.1007/s11162-009-9133-z

Whitfield, M. (2005). Transfer-student performance in upper-division chemistry courses: Implications for curricular reform and alignment. *Community College Journal of Research and Practice, 29*(7), 531–545.

Yosso, T. J. (2005). Whose culture has capital? A critical race theory discussion of community cultural wealth. *Race, Ethnicity and Education, 8*(1), 69–91.

Zhu, L. Y. (2005). *Transfer students' persistence and contribution to college graduation rate—A case of four-year public institution.* Paper presented at the Annual Forum of the Association for Institutional Research. Retrieved from http://eric.ed.gov/?id=ED491042

SECTION III

REFINING PUBLIC POLICIES TO SUPPORT
TRANSFER STUDENTS

7

THE COMPLETION AGENDA AND TRANSFER STUDENTS: DIVERGENT EXPECTATIONS

Kimberly Faris, Ph.D.

ABSTRACT

The perceptions of policymakers and their expectations for public institutions and transfer students were explored in a qualitative study. Policymakers play an important role in the formation of higher education policy, and this study identified the perceptions of legislators and other policymakers on the transfer pathway in Texas. Research questions pursued in this study included the following: 1) What experience do state-level policymakers have with transfer policy and the improvement of the pathway for community college students transferring to universities? 2) What are state-level policymakers' perceptions of the transfer pathway and their intended outcomes for transfer students? 3) How can the voices of policymakers help refine our understanding of transfer policy development and improve student persistence and educational experiences?

INTRODUCTION

Higher education in the United States is being held more accountable to the public for its outcomes (Cohen & Kisker, 2010; Schmidtlein & Berdahl, 2005; Dougherty, Jones, Lahr, Natow, Pheatt, & Reddy, 2013). Pressure from the public and policymakers are making the completion agenda a top priority (Brint, 2011; Hamilton, 2013a; Handel, 2013; Kiley, 2012; Mangan, 2013), with an accompanying sense that universities are not adequately focusing on outcomes (Brint, 2011; Cohen & Kisker, 2010; Mangan, 2013; Zusman, 2005). As accountability pressure increasingly focuses on student completion, policymakers assess the effectiveness of institutions based on outcome metrics including graduation rates (Texas Higher Education Coordinating Board [THECB], 2014c). Thus, degree completion has become a "true bottom line" for administrators, policymakers, parents, and students (Pascarella & Terenzini, 2005, p. 644).

Texas is not immune to the challenges of improving postsecondary participation and success. One opportunity lies with community college transfer students pursuing their baccalaureate. Of all undergraduate students pursuing degrees and certificates in Texas public institutions, 58.6% are attending two-year colleges (Complete College America [CCA], 2011). The rate of these community college students successfully transferring to universities continues to lag, as do the baccalaureate graduation rates of transfer students. Of the estimated 90,000 undergraduate students enrolled in Texas public universities in 2013, roughly 19,000 are transfer students, representing 21% of the total state undergraduate enrollment (THECB, 2014c, p. 9). However, these 19,000 transfer students do not have the same time-to-degree as native students at the public university; on average, they require two additional years to complete their baccalaureate degree (THECB, 2014c). Over half of all undergraduates attend public community colleges in Texas, but only 21% actually transfer to public four-year institutions (CCA, 2011; THECB, 2014c).

Texas public community college students are a diverse population. Hispanic students comprise 38.8% of the community college population; African American students represent 14.1% of enrollment; while White students comprise 37.2% of the community college population (THECB, 2014b). In Texas, the rate of students receiving a certificate or degree from Texas colleges and universities within six years of high school graduation is 19.4% (The Texas Tribune, 2013). The graduation rate for full-time Texas students pursuing associate's degrees at public institutions entering the fall of 2004 and finishing in four years was 11.2%, while the rate for bachelor's degree seekers entering in fall 2002, and graduating in eight years was 62.6% (CCA, 2011). These statistics illustrate the challenge Texas faces in increasing college completion rates, especially at the associate level. By the year 2020, there will be a 29% skills gap between the jobs requiring career certifications or college degrees and the Texas adults who are qualified to fill them, potentially jeopardizing the state economy (CCA, 2011).

THE ECONOMY DEPENDS ON REDUCING THE BACCALAUREATE GAP

Students who enter higher education through community colleges are less likely to receive a baccalaureate degree despite their aspirations or intentions to do so. This gap is critical as community colleges are the primary collegiate entry point for students with lower socioeconomic backgrounds and minority students (College Board, 2011; Council of Public University Presidents and Chancellors [CPUPC], 2010; Dougherty, 2003; Fann, 2013). Even with significant efforts to improve transfer pathways, students are frustrated with the barriers they face, including a complicated articulation and the transfer process (McGuinness, 2005). Policymakers are aware of the baccalaureate gap for transfer students. State legislators are addressing the baccalaureate gap with various policies intended to decrease the amount of time students stay in college while reducing the cost of higher education for the state and the student.

The transfer pathway remains important to community college students and to the economy in terms of producing a skilled workforce (Handel, 2013). Texas is a diverse state and its economy depends on producing educated citizens from all socioeconomic backgrounds. The in-state production rate of bachelor's degrees impacts the competitiveness of Texas both nationally and internationally.

Increasing graduation rates for all population groups increases social mobility, and supplies Texas with a competitive workforce. Altbach, Reisberg, and Rumbley (2010) stress degree completion:

Social equity will not be achieved through access to further education alone. In order to fully enjoy the benefits of higher education and to contribute to the society and economy in which they live, individuals need to complete their program of study. True progress depends on high levels of completion for all population groups. (p. 45)

Altbach et al. (2010) notes "mechanisms to support success are essential, yet they are rarely in place and where they do exist inadequately address the needs of the new diverse populations enrolling" (p. 45). Efforts have been made in Texas to serve the state's diverse, vulnerable student population by improving pathways for students transferring from community colleges to universities (CPUPC, 2008, 2010; THECB, 2014c). Policymakers have a stake in improving transfer success.

THE IMPORTANCE OF COMMUNITY COLLEGES AND THEIR STUDENTS

The College Board (2008) claims "American community colleges are the nation's overlooked asset. As the United States confronts the challenges of globalization, two-year institutions are indispensable to the American future" (p. 15). As an avenue for social mobility, community colleges provide an entry point to higher education for students (College Board, 2006; College Board, 2008; Trow, 2010). American community colleges "are the Ellis Island of American higher education, the crossroads at which K-12 education meets colleges and universities, and the institutions that give many students the tools to navigate the modern world" (College Board, 2008, p. 15). These tools include the knowledge and skills to obtain employment, to excel, and to pursue their aspirations.

Statistically, some of the most vulnerable college students in America are studying on community college campuses. Forty-two percent of first-time, first-year students enroll in community colleges and 36% are the first in their family to attend college (American Association of Community Colleges [AACC], 2014). Among all U.S. undergraduate students in 2012, 56% of Hispanic students, 48% of Black students, 44% of Asian/Pacific Islander students, and 59% of Native American students attend community colleges (AACC, 2014). One reason why community colleges are attractive is the cost. The average annual tuition and fees for a community college is $3,260, compared to an average annual cost of $8,890 at public, in-state four-year colleges (AACC, 2014).

Community colleges are a large sector of American higher education with access and equity as their mission (College Board, 2006; Trow, 2010). The College Board (2006) reveals that there are a variety of reasons why students choose a community college: to transfer to four-year colleges; technology; affordability; accessible faculty; class size; variety of programs; flexibility; support services; community service; student success and their commitment to diversity. Community colleges serve disadvantaged students, and the initiatives and intentional efforts of community colleges to facilitate a successful transfer process is an important strategy to advance access and equity in American higher education (Dowd, Cheslock, & Melguizo, 2008; Wang, 2012).

Community colleges play unique roles in producing more baccalaureate degrees in the United States (Trow, 2010), and community college faculty and administrators devote time building articulation agreements, aligning curricula and structuring advising to aid students planning to transfer (Flaga, 2006). Crafting articulation agreements is extremely complicated as well as time consuming for both two-year and four-year institutions. Articulations are less effective for students who change their major or who have not identified their receiving institution after attending community college (Bers, 2013; Handel, 2013). The students' ability to navigate the transfer pathway and gain transfer knowledge correlates with their ability to persevere (Fann, 2013). Handel (2007) claims "policymakers argue that seamless transfer means 100% transferability of all courses with no loss of credit, but community college faculty rarely warm to the notion of revising their courses to meet a generic threshold of acceptability" (p. 43).

ALIGNING PUBLIC PRIORITIES WITH POLICY

Policymakers balance broad state demands, market forces, shifts in societal priorities, and limited resources with the needs of the higher education system; and their policy decisions have short-term and long-term consequences for students (Richardson, Bracco, Callan, & Finney, 1999). The state determines the services institutions are expected to provide, and develops policies to align with the public's priorities, as explained by Richardson and Martinez (2009). Policymakers use a variety of strategies to influence institutional or student behavior, and these state policies shape the process for students to transition from community colleges to universities, but frequently additional consequences arise.

Wellman (2002) describes seven types of policy instruments that influence transfer: legislation, cooperative agreements, transfer data reporting, student incentives and rewards, statewide articulation, statewide common core curricula, and common course numbering systems. Kisker, Wagoner, & Cohen (2011) also cite legislation, statewide coordination, and alternative funding scenarios for implementing statewide transfer and articulation reforms. Legislators and policymakers share common objectives for higher education, hoping to demonstrate greater efficiency and cost effectiveness in the transfer pathway; increasing transfer and degree completion; developing the economy; and implementing degree programs deemed vital to state workforce needs (Kisker et al., 2011).

Large, Decentralized System of Autonomous Institutions

The higher education governance structure in Texas is characterized as a federal system. "Federal systems have a statewide board responsible for collecting and distributing information, advising on the budget, planning programs from a state-wide perspective, and encouraging articulation" (Richardson et al., 1999, p. 17). Texas also has a coordinating board that is a regulatory authority in a state with mixed single-campus and multi-campus institutions (Richardson et al., 1999).

In Texas, "legislators provide technical leadership and see themselves as watchdogs protecting institutions from excessive central dominance" (Richardson et al., 1999, p. 125). Articulation and collaboration in the Texas transfer pathway depends on institutional cooperation (Richardson et al., 1999). Richardson et al. (1999) emphasize that, "the state's strong emphasis on local control and local decision making creates a constant, dynamic tension among the institutions, the legislature, and the coordinating board" (p. 125). Transfer pathways are difficult to implement or to maintain in this shifting environment, and the transfer student is disadvantaged by the design of the Texas higher education system.

Statewide coordinating agencies "may be buffers or conduits for state influence" explains Zusman (2005, p. 149), while Richardson et al. (1999) characterizes the THECB as a "referee or scapegoat" that "must carry out its responsibilities in an environment that often involves antagonism from the legislature and from some of the sub-systems" (p. 126). A political environment that pits legislators against the Texas Higher Education Coordinating Board and, in turn, positions the Coordinating Board against institutions, complicates transfer policies and disadvantages students (Richardson et al., 1999).

Completion Agenda Versus Transfer Students

Politicians are not the only stakeholders at odds with one another. The college completion agenda also causes friction for transfer students and community colleges. The focus on completion frequently works against the community college transfer function (Mullin, 2012). Native students experience a more refined path to the baccalaureate as compared to transfer students, although Mullin (2012) claims that a transfer pathway to the baccalaureate is a core function. A report by the THECB states the graduation rates of Texas transfer students at public universities lag behind native students by 13% to 20% (THECB, 2014c).

Transfer students navigate a path filled with barriers. The transfer pathway contains barriers that hinder students' ability to graduate on time when compared to native students. Simone (2014) stated that when students transfer from one public institution to another they typically lose around 12 credits. Mangan (2014b) notes that the "pipeline between colleges is full of leaks." Many transfer students must retake courses already completed at a community college (Keierleber, 2014). Research predicts bachelor's degree attainment for community-college transfer students could increase from 45% to 54% if credit hours were not lost at the time of transfer (Keierleber, 2014). Community colleges are associated with low program-completion rates and thus have "become ground zero in the national completion movement" (Mangan, 2014a, para. 2).

Completion metrics do not adequately measure transfer student outcomes. Measuring degree completion disadvantages many institutions. Completion metrics heavily focus on native student progress at each institution, and generally do not consider enrolled transfer students. Institutions that enroll students without a strong intent to earn a degree; enroll students with plans to transfer; or students seeking employability skills rather than a credential maybe viewed as less effective (Habley, Bloom, & Robbins, 2012). "Institutions that serve a significant number of these students generally do not fare very well when retention and degree completion are the metrics to which they are held accountable" (Habley et al., 2012, p. 344). Habley et al. (2012) suggest "policymakers should reengineer the standard accountability metrics to focus on the percentage of students who enter higher education at *any* institution, the percentage of students who are retained in higher education at *any* institution, and the percentage of students who complete degrees or achieve their goals at *any* institution" (p. 347). Students who attend multiple institutions and graduate should be counted as completers.

The completion agenda impacts policymakers' expectations. Policymakers may have the best intentions for students or institutions, but many policies are ineffective and fail to reach their intended goal. "Policymakers believe that higher education is linked to the economic, social and cultural well-being of their state. Legislators are under pressure to show the results of their decisions, so it is no surprise that they frequently speak about the expectations they have of higher education" (Martinez,

2004, p. 91). Policymakers are pressured by the public to show positive results to their efforts. "Economic growth, degree attainment, and starting salaries are measurable and provide policymakers with figures and statistics that they can attribute to their efforts" (Martinez, 2004, p. 92). "Policy ideas that sound great in theory often fail under conditions of actual field implementation. The implementation process has a life of its own. It is acted out through large and inflexible administrative systems and is distorted by bureaucratic interests" (Bardach, 2009, p. 35). The policy infrastructure is generally less forgiving to transfer students compared to native students.

STUDY OF THE TEXAS TRANSFER PATHWAY

The perceptions of policymakers and their expectations for public institutions and transfer students were explored in a qualitative study. Policymakers play an important role in the formation of higher education policy, and this study identified the perceptions of the Texas transfer pathway of legislators and policy influencers. Policy influencers were identified as state coordinating board staff, professional association members, and higher education journalists. This study assessed policymakers' impressions of policy and infrastructure affecting transfer success. Policymakers' perceptions inform stakeholders of the expectations for students and public institutions; and illustrate policymakers' relationship to the state economy and their focus on developing a competitive workforce.

A qualitative research approach was used to bring meaning to the decision-making process for policymakers on transfer policy for Texas higher education. This study explored the phenomenon of transfer policy development in Texas higher education through the voice of state policymakers and their influencers. This study focuses on the complicated structure of the transfer pathway and the policies that orchestrate it. Participants were selected due to the accessibility of data and their experience with the phenomenon to be studied. They were chosen through purposeful sampling and snowball sampling.

The following research questions were addressed in this study:

1. What experience do state-level policymakers, coordinating board staff and influencers have with transfer policy and the improvement of the pathway for community college students transferring to universities?

2. What are state-level policymakers' perceptions of the transfer pathway and their intended outcomes for transfer students?

3. How can the voices of policymakers and their influencers help refine our understanding of transfer policy development and improve student persistence and educational experiences?

Data collection for this study included semi-structured individual interviews with four legislative staff from the Texas Senate Higher Education Committee and the Texas House of Representatives Higher Education Committee. Three additional interviews were held with staff from the THECB. Five professional association members and two higher education journalists were interviewed on their perspective of the transfer pathway and actions that would improve transfer success. Interviews were conducted in person or by phone with a typical duration of 30 to 90 minutes.

The population of policymakers was small and qualified by having responsibilities in enacting higher education policy. To increase the depth and meaning of the responses, a semi-structured, open-ended approach was utilized. The qualitative data was digitally recorded and transcribed from fourteen interviews. Transcripts were sent to participants for narrative accuracy checks. The transcripts were read multiple times before coding began. Analytical insights that occurred during data collection were recorded to track emergent themes and field-based analytical insights (Patton, 2002). Coding was used to identify the categories, patterns and themes reoccurring in the transcribed interviews, and NVivo computer software was used for this content analysis (Patton, 2002). Participants from each category reviewed the findings to provide a member check for the conclusions and implications developed.

The theoretical framework of the study was based on the Espoused Theories of Action (Argyris & Schon, 1996). The theory was developed to identify governing variables and action strategies that manage behavior to gain and to maintain the control others, and to set goals (Howell, 1999). This framework guided the development of interview questions and data analysis, and confirmed policymakers do attempt to influence the actions of institutions and students. Policymakers were strongly focused on reducing the time to degree through their policies.

Policymaker Expectations

The perceptions of Texas policymakers and those that influence transfer policy reveal that there is an expectations gap between policymakers and community college transfer students:

- Policymakers expect students to embark on a linear path from community colleges to universities, taking the specific courses that transfer directly into a baccalaureate degree.
- Policymakers expect students to earn credit within a finite length of time from start to finish.
- Policymakers expect students to know which baccalaureate degree they seek and to identify their desired transfer university at the time they enter community colleges.
- Policymakers expect advisors will individualize a degree plan and timeline for each student.

The perceptions of policymakers and those that influence policy in Texas revealed priorities and values that are at odds with the current functioning of the public higher education system and the actual behavior of transfer students.

Focus on time-to-degree. Participants stressed the need to reduce the time transfer students require to graduate with their baccalaureate degree. Current policies in the state are intended to curb costly excessive credit hours for undergraduate students. Leslie (2015) concludes that:

The cost to underwrite unnecessary courses to state taxpayers is $300 million annually. The total cost to Texas students and taxpayers of excess credit hour accrual is $490 million, almost half a billion dollars annually. (Negative Financial Impacts section, para. 4)

Participants stated that the primary focus of policymakers' work is to save money by reducing the time to degree for all students, including transfer students; these sentiments were illustrated by several participants.

The main goal is time to degree. If you focus on decreasing the time to degree, either to an associate's degree or a baccalaureate degree, you decrease costs to the institution, costs to the student and family; and you increase efficiency in higher education and the ability to move somebody through the system, so use of the resources can be for the next cohort of students. The real challenge as a state now is in completion. We've made great strides on access and enrollment, but fall short in completion.

—Legislative Staff Member

For the legislature, the overall goal is to save money and decrease the time to degree, which also saves the state money and saves the students some money and time. Students can go to work, start paying taxes and other good things can come out of this, right? What drives this is saving money, getting people into the workforce sooner, reducing the stress on state resources and [the] money that students need to borrow. They can then buy houses, spend money, and start investing.

—Coordinating Board Staff

For the legislature, the overall goal is to save money. It's not necessarily a bad thing because it's one of those things where you can actually have two different goals that actually converge on the same end results . . . The real question we have to ask ourselves is—and it's our responsibility to do that— "What's good for students? What is good for Texas students? Not what is good for our institution, but for the students?" The reality is that what's good for Texas students is also what's good for your institution's students.

—Coordinating Board Staff

Aligning with the theoretical framework, these findings demonstrate that Texas policymakers attempt to influence student behavior through punitive transfer policies, such as the Excess Credit Hour Tuition Limit, Six-Drop Limit and Three-Repeat Limit (Table 7.1). These policies carry significant financial consequences for students and hold formula funding consequences for institutions. (It is important to note that the federal government does the same by limiting financial aid to students at 150% of time to degree.)

Policymakers assume students are savvy navigators of higher education with sophisticated knowledge about their future career interests. Policymakers stress graduating on time as important, seeing students as filling workforce needs and growing the economy by "buying cars and houses" and "getting off state support." Policymakers assume that students are sophisticated and savvy, and that they enter college with the preparation and social capital necessary to succeed. This is not realistic or accurate.

Table 7.1

List of Texas Transfer Policies and Initiatives that Penalize Student Behaviors

Name	Purpose	Student Impact	Statute or Rule
Excess Credit Hour Surcharge	Institutions do not receive formula funding for 30 or more excess credit hours attempted towards an undergraduate degree. (Tuition for Repeated or Excessive Undergraduate Hours, 2005)	Students may face tuition surcharges once they attempt 30 or more credit hours over the credit hours required for their undergraduate degree at public institutions.	Texas Administrative Code, Title 19, Part 1, Chapter 13, Subchapter F, §13.100-13.109
Six-Drop Limitations	Institutions may not permit an undergraduate student a total of more than six dropped courses, including transfer work.	Unless students meet specific exceptions, undergraduates cannot drop more than six courses during their career while attending public institutions.	Texas Administrative Code, Title 19, Part 1, Chapter 4, Subchapter A, Rule §4.10
Three Repeat Limitations	Institutions do not receive formula funding for a course attempted more than two times. (Tuition for Repeated or Excessive Undergraduate Hours, 2005)	Students may face surcharges once they attempt the same course more than two times. The surcharge may occur on the third attempt.	Texas Administrative Code, Title 19, Part 1, Chapter 13, Subchapter F, Rule §13.105

Gap between Students' and Policymakers' Expectations

Students do not generally know about the completion agenda or the role community colleges might play in their quest for a baccalaureate. The local community college seems to be an inviting place to explore careers and higher education, although this may result in extra credit hours and a more lengthy time-to-degree. Students are not aware of policies, policymakers' expectations, and the consequences for not taking a more linear path within an expected timeline. The literature confirms students are influenced by their family and by their early educational experiences. The college expectations of students strongly influence their degree attainment (Goldrick-Rab & Pfeffer, 2009; Pike, Hansen & Childress, 2014). Research on community college students also reveals that baccalaureate expectations are influenced by student backgrounds, motivational beliefs and community college experiences (Wang, 2013). The completion agenda is focused on students progressing through the pipeline to the baccalaureate, with the default assumption that students should all progress at similar rates. However, students' baccalaureate degree attainment is dependent on a number of factors, all of which influence time to degree and the number of credit hours that do not apply directly to their degree. Ignoring student differences jeopardizes the efficacy of policies, and produces unremarkable completion outcomes.

The number of certificates and associate's degrees available to students are abundant, and providing student choice is generally desirable. However, the number of degree pathways sometimes also means that students who change their major might complete courses that do not transfer. "The missions and functions of community college[s] have historically been comprehensive. In addition to serving students who intend to transfer, vocational and technical education, continuing education, remediation, and community services" are also offered to meet students' needs (Wang, 2013, para. 10). Some students are not sophisticated about the differences between workforce education/technical credit and academic credit; or that there may be a penalty for accruing too many hours at the community college. This may be exacerbated by having a need for developmental coursework, or by engaging in the process of exploring careers. Students may encounter "significant negative consequences due to their lack of knowledge of the transfer process and not being well advised that included having to repeat courses, taking additional courses, delaying time to transfer and/or degree completion, and costing more money" (Fann & Marling, 2012, p. 36).

The community college may provide a convenient, safe, friendly environment where students grow in confidence and build social capital through academic integration and interacting with faculty and advisors (Wang, 2013). Participants shared that students are not completely cognizant of the expectation that they should leave the community college with no more than 60 hours of transferrable credit that directly apply to their degree plan. Students do not realize that they are expected to know the program and the university they intend to attend from the first moment they enter the community college if they intend to graduate on time. Participants stress that time to degree and excess hour problems may be caused by students' indecision and by the changing of their majors. Students are not sophisticated enough to understand the complexities of the transfer pathway and the consequences for lacking that knowledge. The problem may be compounded when they receive conflicting information about transfer from institutions (Fann & Marling, 2012).

Student knowledge and experiences with state policies. Throughout the interviews, participants perceived transfer students as uninformed and naïve of policies, becoming enlightened only when negative impacts ensue, and when it is too late to avoid the consequences. These perceptions align with the findings of Fann and Marling (2012) during interviews with Texas transfer students who stated they were unaware of policies until after they transferred or received penalties. The negative impact usually includes financial penalties for the student. From the policymakers' standpoint, the policies are intended to prevent particular student behaviors. However, these expectations are lost on students, as they are unaware of them until too late.

For example, students classified as Texas residents pay in-state tuition rates. However, there is a state policy that allows institutions to charge out-of-state tuition rates when a student attempts at least 30 hours over the credit hours required for a degree.

> The student facing [penalties for excess hours or repeating courses] doesn't know their path forward, or doesn't have the time and resources to study and research it as carefully. Students are negatively impacted, and blindsided sometimes by those financial restrictions.
>
> —*Legislative Staff Member*

> I do think it is unfair to a student if they are not aware of those policies, and so they encounter them once they have already bumped up against those thresholds. I think that making students aware of the limitation on dropping how many courses you can drop is just information they should have at the beginning so that they know that this is a busy time for their family, they should only take two classes that semester. They can make more informed choices.
>
> —*Legislative Staff Member*

The perceptions that students receive inadequate information and advising concerning policies also reoccurred throughout the interviews.

> Students and institutions can be financially penalized with some of the things like three-repeat rules, excess credit hours. They're a barrier to the students. They're not enforceable in terms of the policy responsibilities that institutions have. But in the application of those stated policies, the students are the ones who suffer the most because colleges don't necessarily worry about that. Colleges are worried about that now, and are taking actions to remedy the situation, but before they had no direction from legislature, for example, nor from the coordinating board. Basically, the movement to take care of some of this is starting at the local community college level and it's becoming more and more of something that they're looking at.
>
> *—Professional Association Member*

Native Versus Transfer Students

Transfer students do not fare well when compared to native students earning their baccalaureate. "Transfer students [require] more than two additional years to complete their degrees, when compared with their university native peers. Time-to-degree data for individual Texas public universities show that no university has been able to graduate transfer students in the same time period as it graduates native students" (THECB, 2014c, pp. 11-12). Participants of this study attribute this to inefficiencies and inequities in the transfer pathway. Transfer students arrive on the community college campus with varying degrees of academic readiness, resources, and frequently change their aspirations along the way. These challenges combined with university support systems (financial aid, scholarship, orientation, and advising) designed for incoming first-year students rather than transfer students, compound the problem. One of the greatest challenges for students was identified as the excess credit earned at community colleges prior to transfer, indicative of the quality of advising.

> It's crazy. Students are transferring into universities with eighty or ninety credits. They are at an associate's degree-and-one-half at the time of transfer.
>
> *—Legislative Staff Member*

I think advising is the key component, either investing in more advising, helping students understand which courses are credit-bearing to advance their degree, and which are in the elective category, so that you don't have students transferring with 80 or 90 credits. They should be out of community colleges at 60 or 70 credits. You don't need that many credits to get an associate's degree.

—Legislative Staff Member

The problem I saw is that the legislature put a limit to their associate degrees, and that was one of the big impediments for the bachelor degrees. An average numbers of hours of somebody who came out of community college was 90 hours. There's no way you can get only 30 hours more for a bachelor degree. So people transferred with a lot of hours, and I'm not sure how many people understand what that's about. It's about how many hours the state paid for. It doesn't matter that they didn't complete, it doesn't matter that they cannot be applied to your degree. The state paid for them.

—Coordinating Board Staff Member

Inequitable university environment. Transfer students face an environment where institutions, faculty and the curriculum are more inwardly focused on traditional students; an environment that fails to consider the best interest of the transfer student who has yet to arrive or who may never arrive on their campus. All participants stated that institutions and advisors do not adequately inform students of state policies or aid. Participants hold students less responsible than institutions for complying with the current system. Participants assume students are not aware of the consequences for enrolling in excess hours or changing their major, and blame institutions for not being more forthcoming with students. Policymakers believe that advising and transition services are not the same from institution to institution, and are concerned that additional advising inequities may exist among academic departments within the same institution. Transfer students land in an environment not focused on them, but rather on new first-year students. Institutions expect transfer students to be more college-savvy, and the environment may not provide transfers the support to propel them forward as those who enter a university as a first-year student.

I don't think the advising is very good. I don't think students really know what to do when they are ready to transfer. Many of the schools send students to computers to show them what will transfer and what classes to take. If I were in a university, I would spend a week with an orientation to show them how a university works, where things are, deadlines, etc., because they come from a smaller campus, with smaller classes. Universities place them in huge classes where nobody will know their names and it isn't easy to speak to professors, that is the big difference between universities and community colleges. Universities do this [orientation] for their freshmen, but not their transfers. The fact that they've been to a community college doesn't mean they know how to navigate the university.

—Coordinating Board Staff Member

There is not continuity for that swirling student. Whatever campus they land on may not be equally focused on the transfer student.

—Legislative Staff Member

Decentralized systems may disadvantage transfer students. The completion agenda emphasizes reducing the time to degree, and increasing graduation rates. Both of these measures seem elusive to transfer students, who face the unexpected challenges of the independent, decentralized nature of higher education in Texas. Transfer students move between institutions that are autonomous and independent of each other. Native students do not face this experience. The faculty are responsible for the curriculum development on their own campus, but yet stakeholders expect students to transfer seamlessly from one institution and degree program to another. A decentralized matrix of independent, autonomous institutions contribute to low completion rates, excessive credit hours, and more time to degree for the transfer student.

Policymakers understand the decentralized nature of higher education in the state contributes to the problem, but they are hesitant to use policy to fortify the transfer pathway. Practices in reverse transfer, common course numbering systems, and articulation agreements are preferred over prescriptive practices. This more passive approach prevails, assuring less urgency than the completion agenda implores.

We impose so much as a legislative body on institutions already. If we were in control of what universities could do, we would have equalized mediocrity.

—*Legislative Staff Member*

You have to be careful. It is always a balancing act. You could say everybody [institutions] has to increase their graduation rates and then the next day, everybody is going to increase their admission standards. So, you want to balance that out . . . and also in making sure students can get through in a timely fashion. Not all students can get through. Not everyone is going to be able to enroll full-time and that's something that has to be acknowledged. Life does get in the way.

—*Legislative Staff Member*

Disparities in resources and curriculum at community colleges. The completion agenda places high expectations on community colleges and their efficacy in supporting students through to graduation. The funding formula for institutions is marked with metrics that shift more resources to research institutions and universities than to community colleges, although community colleges educate more than half of the students participating in higher education in the Texas. The institutions that serve the growing population of students with fewer financial resources and lower levels of college preparation are expected to do more with less, while simultaneously serving academic and workforce education demands. There is a consensus that the state needs to match its expectations and commitment to education, and move towards equitable funding for higher education and especially for community colleges.

If you look at what the distribution of funds is between community colleges and four-year institutions, or the general education institutions, they get three point something billion dollars, and community colleges only received under a billion dollars.

—*Professional Association Member*

If you look at funding from [the] macro perspective [of] community colleges, they are not going to be able to sustain this kind of funding model for very long. And if so, institutions are going to have to either shoot up taxation rates so that they can get the income or they will have to get it from the backs of students' tuition.

—Professional Association Member

Community colleges are the only ones in the higher ed system that are flexible enough to meet the needs of any population that comes into our communities. They are open enrollment, unlike restrictive universities. Serving the demographic shift is going to fall on the back of the community colleges. They are not being supported appropriately by the state to do this work.

—Professional Association Member

FINDINGS RELATED TO THE LITERATURE

The study aligned with the literature review in most areas. The decentralized system of higher education contributes to many of the problems transfer students face. The autonomy and independence of institutions is helpful for serving local communities, developing strategic planning, and funding; but the transfer student is disadvantaged by this system (Richardson et al., 1999; Habley, 2012). The state does identify that there is a problem, but there are barriers to seamless transfer as enumerated in the literature review and confirmed in the interviews.

I think it's improving slowly. I definitely would say it's improving, but there's a long way to go. I think that there's been a lot more attention around articulation policies, and just transfer, like common course numbering or all of those policy aspects from the state or the local level. I don't really think those things make transfer easier for students.

—Legislative Staff Member

Participants confirmed that the completion agenda and accountability initiatives are at the forefront of policymaking focused on saving the state financial resources (CPUPC, 2010; Hamilton, 2013a; Handel, 2013; Mangan, 2013).

Policymakers are aware of the baccalaureate gap for transfer students as the literature suggests (Hamilton, 2013b). State legislators have attempted through various policies both to address the baccalaureate gap, and to decrease the amount of time students remain in college (Kisker et al, 2011). These policies attempt to reduce the cost of higher education for the state and the student (Martinez, 2004). As confirmed by the participants, the transfer pathway remains important to community college students and to the economy in producing a better qualified, skilled workforce (Handel, 2013; THECB, 2014a).

> Texas is one of the most vibrant states economically and it is because of our higher education system. We have to act. Every moment we do not act means that somebody's stopping out, dropping out, or having a negative experience. We cannot afford that luxury if we are going to maintain a strong middle class.
>
> —*Professional Association Member*

> That's what makes me so passionate about being involved in community colleges. We are changing lives; we even get success. But one of the quotes I heard at a national conference is deep in my psyche. Vice President [Joe Biden] said "*Community college is the pathway to the middle class.*" And that resonates with me because the talk we had thinking about the middle class that it is starting to evaporate. Only if community colleges are supported will the middle class be sustained.
>
> —*Professional Association Member*

IMPLICATIONS FOR POLICY

Transfer advisors, admissions officers, financial aid officers, orientation staff, faculty and administrators can all help policymakers create better policies using the knowledge gleaned directly from their work with transfer students. A task force representing an equitable cross-section of institutions and representative of these stakeholders may hold promise for practical solutions. These stakeholders have a unique perspective regarding the actual problems within the transfer pathway. Ideas and innovation must be organically developed for legislative committees engaged in future policy discussions. However, this approach could have limited results. According to some participants, policymakers tend to legislate based on anecdotal experiences of key stakeholders or ideologically lean towards the least restrictive approach, despite the best data and consultation. Unless the legislators are serious about data-informed solutions, the task force's efforts would likely be in vain.

Recommendations for Policymakers

Institutions are accountable for the inefficiencies students face on their campus, and formula funding should encourage institutions to be more efficient and thereby enhance students' success. Participants stated if funding is not tied to transfer success, institutions will not prioritize their approach to serving transfer students and their success. Additionally, an important change should occur in the calculation of graduation rates at the federal and state levels. Transfer students are not currently included in the calculation of IPEDS graduation rates, and do not reflect reality. Metrics should acknowledge community colleges' efforts in successfully sending their students to the university for further studies. Likewise, metrics should also calculate the university's success in supporting the transfer student through to the baccalaureate. If decreasing the baccalaureate gap for transfer students is a priority, then meaningful metrics would measure transfer success at the community college and university level. Institutions will prioritize their resources to align with formula funding and rankings success. Extrinsic motivations in the form of incentivized funding would impact institutional priorities to assure transfer success on each campus. The calculations for graduation should better reflect the realities of completion on both ends of the pathway.

Carrots and sticks prevail. Policymakers are focused on saving money and graduating students quickly; and the current transfer policy structure uses a "carrots and sticks" to accomplish the goals. Policymakers use extrinsic motivations to prevent excess credit. The current policies imply that students and institutions will not comply without a punishment or a reward. However, the punishments are more financially punitive for students, and appear to protect the institution from financial loss by allowing higher tuition fees for excess hours.

Policymakers may prefer to implement change utilizing less restrictive policies, but the impact on community colleges should be reevaluated. If improving transfer success and outcomes is a priority, then a more prescriptive policy needs to include additional resources, with a more prescriptive transfer infrastructure at the state-level focused on reducing inefficiencies, despite the tendency of the state to prefer institutional-level controls. Transfer occurs between institutions, so no single institution can be solely responsible or accountable for a student's success. Presently, students do not have access to a neutral party for transfer advice. Advisors tend to be inherently biased towards their institutional employer, and thus are not able to provide students with an objective perspective. A positive framework for change should focus on building interconnections, and incentivizing institutions to cooperate to support student success.

A mismatch with consumer market demands. Stark differences exist between the market's demands for innovation and creativity and how policymakers treat curricula as homogenous. Policies tend to assume students and programs are similar. The transfer initiatives in Texas, such as the Fields of Study Curriculum and Core Curriculum, assume curricular alignment and course transferability, while the market and consumers value institutional creativity. Thus, institutional autonomy competes with the Fields of Study Curriculum and its more prescriptive solutions. To preserve institutional creativity and autonomy, technology might provide a potential solution. If the state developed a statewide transfer system, students would be able to compare institutions and degree plans against their earned credit to make informed decisions. Technology could illustrate degree pathways between institutions, guide the timing of the transfer, and offer neutral information to students without institutional bias. Investing in a technological solution could preserve institutional curricular creativity and provide students information on how many hours are still required to earn their baccalaureate at the point of transfer. Such a system could save students time and money, and save state resources by reducing excess credit hours.

Policymakers and policy influencers need to consider the gap in expectations and research ways to help students develop more realistic expectations. College students in a democratic society are adults with free will and the freedom to explore career options in their *pursuit of happiness*, while policymakers are stewards of millions in taxpayer money, charged to allocate money in the best interests of the state. Policymakers in Texas created thresholds of taking 30 hours of excessive credit hours, limits on repeating a course no more than two times without penalty, and limits of dropping a maximum of six courses while earning an undergraduate degree program. They have attempted to quantify and limit the amount of time students may spend exploring degree options. These policies imply that students have similar experiences, expectations, and goals as they work towards their degree. The policies are meant to modify behavior, but the reality is that students are not aware of them early enough in their college career to respond as intended. Policymakers believe students are not aware of the policies, and yet seem oblivious to the irony that the efficacy of these transfer policies is dependent on students' awareness of the policies.

Policies should differentiate between native students and transfer students. Native students do not experience the same barriers as transfer students, and have significantly better outcomes. Furthermore, not all students enter college with the same skills or knowledge, and they will not progress at the same rate. Policymakers should consider mandatory advising throughout a student's career, helping to assure students stay on track. Advising and providing information about what is expected in order to graduate on time could modify student behavior. Currently, students are frequently lacking information at critical decision times during course selection periods.

With the known disparities between native student progress and transfer student progress (THECB, 2014c), should policies for excess credit hours be equally applied to both populations? Transfer students face excess credit hour penalties more frequently than native students due to the loss of credit at transfer and the inefficiencies in the transfer pathway. Consideration should be given to providing more equitable consequences to transfer students until inefficiencies in the transfer process are removed.

IMPLICATIONS FOR PRACTICE

Transfer students experience inefficiencies that cause either the loss of credit or earning excessive credit, and these inefficiencies should be identified and addressed. Issues generally originate from the curriculum differences between and among four- and two-year institutions; workforce education courses; course numbers used and unique courses. Solutions should occur both at the local level and the state level, and must include faculty involvement. Solutions should be student-focused, and require participants to see the *big picture* of what their work will accomplish for thousands of students statewide by reducing the time to degree; and the resulting positive effects on the state economy. Solutions will require compromise from community colleges and universities as well as their respective faculty.

At the local level on community college and university campuses, institutions should talk to advisors and students to evaluate if their campus is transfer-friendly, and any inefficiency should be addressed.

Student-Friendly Publications

Institutions can do simple things to improve the student experience, and many of them do not require significant financial investments. A coordinating board member suggested that institutions review publications and college catalogs to confirm they are student-friendly and accurate. The use of student focus groups to identify problems should also be done on campus websites, including information requests, financial aid websites, and navigation and search functions. Institutions should review their information from the perspective of the transfer student, assuring a centralized location for transfer articulation agreements. Several legislative participants noted that colleges and universities do not adequately warn transfer students about tuition limits and course repeat policies. Improving communication to students would help increase awareness of these policies.

Targeted Student Services

Universities should equitably allocate resources and financial aid for incoming first-year and transfer students. Likewise, orientation and engagement activities should be as intensive for transfer students as first-year students. Institutions should not assume that transfer students are prepared to navigate the process without support and should devote more resources to engaging new transfer students and providing frequent, individualized advising. Students should be advised of their "expected" linear path and of the penalties for taking credits off the path. Students should be informed of these policies and penalties repeatedly during advising and through websites and publications.

Engagement of Community College Faculty

Community colleges must do a better job educating students about the transferability of workforce education and technical courses, and community college faculty should examine the academic and technical degrees on campus to see if there are ways to reduce the number of credits available that do not transfer. Even if a student does not originally intend to transfer when enrolled in workforce courses, what happens if they later pursue a baccalaureate? Are there better ways to align the curricula at the community college level to ameliorate the problems caused when a student decides to pursue a degree beyond the technical associate degree in applied sciences?

Know Your Students

Institutions can improve if they analyze student data. The performance of transfer students should be regularly monitored by community colleges and universities to identify inefficiencies in services or curricula, and to find solutions to reduce the number of students falling off their transfer pathway to the baccalaureate. Institutions do not bear all of the responsibility for transfer student outcomes; students are responsible for changing majors. Sometimes "life gets in the way," but institutions should support students through detours caused by personal issues with more intrusive, frequent advising. Support with career planning may lessen the occurrence of major changes and reduce the enrollment in nontransferable courses that do not apply to a bachelor's degree.

RECOMMENDATIONS FOR FUTURE RESEARCH

Future research should explore what policymakers understand about the challenges students face with financial aid, transportation needs, childcare and self-care. Most policymakers had a traditional college experience, and this may hinder their understanding of realities faced by today's community college and transfer students. How do policymakers' past personal experiences in higher education shape their perceptions of students? The same question may be asked of other stakeholders including those advocating for the completion agenda. Do their experiences mirror the experiences students face today? Did they attend community college or public universities? Future research should examine the expectations of institutions, policymakers, and students, and how these expectations drive policy decisions and priorities for allocating resources.

Research should identify disparities in resources or focus between incoming first-year and transfer students at the university level. The general disparity of resources is not limited to institutional decisions, but also includes state formula funding models, national graduation rate metrics, federal and state financial aid allocations, and scholarship availability. All of these resources tend to emphasize a traditional incoming first-year student over a transfer student. Research on these disparities should also analyze their effects on special populations of students.

Workforce Education versus Academic Credit

Future research on the curriculum inefficiencies at Texas community colleges could explore the following questions: Do employers know the difference between an Associate of Science/Arts degree and the Associate of Applied Arts and Science degree earned at Texas community colleges? Do community colleges design curriculum based on local needs? How does the formula funding model foster differences between technical, workforce education courses and transferrable, academic courses? Are the differences in formula funding driving the agenda to enroll students in programs/courses that may not transfer? With the technological advances today, are some technical degrees more similar to academic, transferrable associate degrees?

Future research should identify inefficiencies that lead to earning excessive credit hours and an unacceptable time to degree. How could degree completion be enhanced by improved efficiencies of curriculum and services by institutions or a statewide systemic change? Since students face barriers and confusion with workforce education credit, it may be time for Texas to realign the curriculum. Research exploring the number of transfer students impacted by these barriers could quantify the money lost by the state and enumerate the negative impact on time to degree for students.

Policymakers write policies that they hope will influence behavior and decrease time to degree. However, punitive financial aid penalties force some students out of college. Future research should consider the effects of financial aid penalties on vulnerable, at-risk populations of students. Studies should also examine whether transfer students more heavily carry the consequences of these punitive financial aid policies in the decentralized higher education system in Texas, and also examine whether the policies are counterproductive. If transfer students are affected more negatively than native students, then findings could be used to modify policy to be more equitable. Future research should continue to enumerate the economic benefits of improving the efficacy of the transfer pathway for the state, institutions, and students.

CONCLUDING REMARKS

This study reinforces the literature, supporting the thesis that the completion agenda drives policy decisions, thus creating an expectations gap. Participants stressed that reducing the time to degree for students is a top priority for policymakers, but students may have other priorities.

However, the completion agenda is heavily focused on measuring native students who start at the university their first year, and do not transfer; or those that complete an associate degree at a community college. Transfer students have been ignored in completion and performance funding metrics, and this influences institutional priorities. For community colleges, the focus has been on graduation rates, because there is no credit for helping students transfer into universities.

The completion agenda negatively impacts transfer students. The completion agenda has little tolerance for vertical alignment curricular problems, technical versus academic course selections and other inequities in the system. The inefficiencies of the transfer pathway encourage students to earn excessive credit hours and delay a timely graduation. Time to degree metrics indicate students are at a disadvantage if they start at a community college before attending the university. However, the metrics do not fully explain the complex realities community college students face, including employment and family responsibilities. A slower pace to graduation may sometimes have less to do with institutional factors, but the completion agenda is undiscerning.

The inefficiencies in the Texas transfer pathway are not a glamorous topic vying for news headlines. The challenges inherent in the transfer pathway are complicated, with tedious, complicated answers. The topic doesn't attract the interest of the general public and the press as much as other topics like "guns on campus." The problems of the transfer pathway are difficult to explain, and do not offer much "low hanging fruit" for legislative committees. The problems exist, and students bear the brunt of the problems as time carries on with no systemic change in Texas.

There is a disconnect in what higher education people are excited about and what the public is really excited about. I think transfer stuff can get lost in the weeds there a little bit, because it is wonky and complicated. It is not as easy to solve like "guns on campus." **You can't fix transfer with a few words.**

—Higher Education Journalist

There is hope of gradual improvement with each legislative session, as aspects of the problems are tackled piecemeal. The transfer pathway is drastically better than it was twenty to thirty years ago according to participants of this study, but much work remains to be completed. For those involved in decreasing transfer inefficiencies, society will be served best by institutions and faculty thinking in the interests of all students, and not only those currently on their own campus. Until institutions and faculty resist the urge to remain inwardly focused, we will lack a cross-institutional curricular alignment that serves transfer students and the state.

All stakeholders should keep the students' best interests at the center of their work. As more students attend college at multiple institutions throughout their career, higher education must adjust to a fluid, mobile student population and must develop curriculum that is more mobile as well. Improving curriculum cross-institutional alignment is the shared stakeholder expectation, as it can benefit the state's economy while it simultaneously serves the best interest of students.

REFERENCES

Altbach, P. G., Reisberg, L., and Rumbley, L. E. (2010). *Trends in global higher education: Tracking an academic revolution.* A report prepared for the UNESCO 2009 World Conference on Higher Education. Paris, France: UNESCO and Rotterdam.

American Association of Community Colleges. (2014). *2014 fact sheet.* Retrieved from http://www.aacc.nche.edu/AboutCC/Pages/fastfactsfactsheet.aspx

Argyris, C., & Schön, D. A. (1996). *Organizational learning II: Theory, method, and practice.* Reading, MA: Addison-Wesley.

Bardach, E. (2009). *A practical guide for policy analysis: The eightfold path to more effective problem solving* (3rd ed.). Washington, D.C.: CQ Press.

Bers, T. H. (2013). Deciphering articulation and state/system policies and agreements. In J. Marling (Ed.), *New directions for higher education, 2013*(162), 17–26. doi:10.1002/he.20052

Brint, S. (2011). Focus on the classroom: Movements to reform college teaching and learning, 1980–2008. In J. Hermanowicz (Ed.), *The American academic profession: Transformation in contemporary higher education* (44–91). Baltimore, MA: John Hopkins University Press.

Cohen, A. M. & Kisker, C. B. (2010). *The shaping of American higher education: Emergence and growth of the contemporary system.* San Francisco, CA: Jossey-Bass.

CollegeBoard. (2006). *Community colleges—Places so close can take you so far* [Brochure]. New York, NY: Author.

CollegeBoard. (2011, July). *Improving student transfer from community colleges to four-year institutions—The perspective of leaders from baccalaureate-granting institutions.* New York, NY: Author.

CollegeBoard, Center for Innovative Thought. (2008, January). *Winning the skills race and strengthening America's middle class: An action agenda for community colleges.* Report to the National Commission on Community Colleges. New York, NY: Author.

Complete College America. (2011, September). *Time is the enemy: The surprising truth about why today's college students aren't graduating . . . and what needs to change.* Washington, D.C.: Author.

Council of Public University Presidents and Chancellors. (2010, November). *Improving student transfer rates from Texas' public community colleges to public general academic institutions: Recommendations addressing participation and success.* Retrieved from http://www.cpupc.org/images/Transfer_Report_Nov_2010.pdf

CPUPC Community College Student Transfer Committee. (2008, September 22). *Improving Texas community college student transfer rates to general academic institutions: A report featuring recommendations for the coordinating board, higher education institutions, and the state.* Retrieved from http://www.cpupc.org/images/CPUPC_Student_Transfer_Report_9-08.pdfDougherty, K.J. (2003). Community colleges and baccalaureate attainment. In F.K. Stage, D.F. Carter, D. Hossler, E.P. St. John (Eds.), *Theoretical perspectives on college students* (223–242). Boston, MA: Pearson Custom Publishing.

Dougherty, K. J., Jones, S. M., Lahr, H., Natow, R. S., Pheatt, L., & Reddy, V. (2013, August). *Envisioning performance funding impacts: The espoused theories of action for state higher education performance funding in three states* (Working Paper No. 63). New York, NY: Community College Research Center.

Dowd, A. C., Cheslock, J. J. & Melguizo, T. (2008). Transfer access from community colleges and the distribution of elite higher education. *The Journal of Higher Education, (79)*4, 442–472.

Fann, A. (2013). Campus administrator and student perspectives for improving transfer policy and practice. In J. Marling (Ed.), *New directions for higher education, 2013*(162), 27–38. doi:10.1002/he.20052

Fann, A., & Marling, J. (2012). *The efficacy of state transfer policies.* Austin, TX: TG Philanthropy.

Flaga, C. T. (2006). The process of transition for community college transfer students. *Community College Journal of Research and Practice, 30*(1), 3–19.

Goldrick-Rab, S., Pfeffer, F.T. (2009). Beyond access: Explaining socioeconomic differences in college transfer. *Sociology of Education, 82*(2), 101–125.

Habley, W. R., Bloom, J. L., & Robbins, S. (2012). *Increasing persistence: Research-based strategies for college student success.* San Francisco, CA: Jossey-Bass.

Hamilton, R. (2013a, February 12). Gordon Gee: The TT interview. *The Texas Tribune.* Retrieved from http://www.texastribune.org

Hamilton, R. (2013b, October 29). Community college group launches Texas Success Center. *The Texas Tribune*. Retrieved from http://www.texastribune.org

Handel, S. J. (2007). Second chance, not second class: A blueprint for community-college transfer. *Change: The Magazine of Higher Learning, 39*(5), 38–45.

Handel, S. J. (2013). The transfer moment: The pivotal partnership between community colleges and four-year institutions in securing the nation's college completion agenda. In J. Marling (Ed.), *New directions for higher education, 2013*(162), 5–15. doi:10.1002/he.20052

Howell, M. A. (1999). *Effects of legislative mandates for site-based management implementation on espoused theory and professional practice, as perceived by selected elementary school principals and teachers in Bexar County, Texas* (Order No. 9943499). Available from ProQuest Dissertations & Theses Global. (304562301). Retrieved from http://search.proquest.com/docview/304562301?accountid=7113

Keierleber, M. (2014, April 7). 4-year colleges' views of transfer credits may hinder graduation. *The Chronicle of Higher Education*. Retrieved from http://www.chronicle.com

Kiley, K. (2012, December 11). Texas university supporters release data on outcomes to counter Perry's reforms. *Inside Higher Ed*. Retrieved from http://www.insidehighered.com

Kisker, C. B., Wagoner, R. L. & Cohen, A. M. (2011, April). *Implementing statewide transfer & articulation reform: An analysis of transfer associate degrees in four states*. Report #11-1 by the Center for the Study of Community Colleges. Oak Park, CA: Center for the Study of Community Colleges.

Leslie, B. (2015, July 2). Improving transfer from community college to university: Critical for driving up completion rate. *The Evolllution*. Retrieved by: http://evolllution.com/opinions/improving-transfer-community-college-university-critical-driving-completion-rate/

Mangan, K. (2013, January 23). Report calls for renewed focus on raising college-completion rates. *The Chronicle of Higher Education*. Retrieved from http://chronicle.com

Mangan, K. (2014a, March 3). Two-year colleges are urged to capitalize on their time in the spotlight. *The Chronicle of Higher Education*. Retrieved from: http://www.chronicle.com

Mangan, K. (2014b, August 20). When students transfer, credits may not follow. *The Chronicle of Higher Education*. Retrieved from: http://www.chronicle.com

Martinez, M. C. (2004) *Postsecondary participation and state policy: Meeting the future demand.* Sterling, VA: Stylus Publishing.

McGuinness, A. C. (2005). The states and higher education. In P. G. Altbach, R. O. Berdahl, & P. J. Gumport (Eds.), *American higher education in the twenty-first century: Social, political, and economic challenges* (115–160). Baltimore, MD: John Hopkins University Press.

Mullin, C.M. (2012, October). *Transfer: An indispensable part of the community college mission* (Policy Brief 2012-03PBL). Washington, D.C.: American Association of Community Colleges.

Pascarella, E. T. & Terenzini, P. T. (2005) *How college affects students: A third decade of research.* San Francisco, CA: Jossey-Bass.

Patton, M. Q. (2002). *Qualitative research & evaluation methods.* Thousand Oaks, CA: SAGE Publications, Inc.

Pike, G. R., Hansen, M. J., & Childress, J. E. (2014). The influence of students' pre-college characteristics, high school experiences, college expectations, and initial enrollment characteristics on degree attainment. *Journal of College Student Retention: Research, 16*(1), 1–23.

Richardson, R. C., Bracco, K. R., Callan, P. M. and Finney, J. E. (1999). *Designing state higher education systems for a new century.* Phoenix, AZ: The American Council on Education and Oryx Press.

Richardson, Jr., R. and Martinez, M. (2009). *Policy and performance in American higher education: An examination of cases across state systems.* Baltimore, MA: Johns Hopkins University Press.

Schmidtlein, F. A. & Berdahl, R. O. (2005). Autonomy and accountability: Who controls academe? In P. G. Altbach, R. O. Berdahl, & P. J. Gumport (Eds.), *American higher education in the twenty-first century: Social, political and economic challenges* (71–90). Baltimore, MD: John Hopkins University Press.

Simone, S. A. (2014). *Transferability of postsecondary credit following student transfer or coenrollment* (NCES 2014-163). Washington, D.C.: National Center for Education Statistics and U.S. Department of Education. Retrieved from http://nces.ed.gov/pubsearch

Texas Higher Education Coordinating Board. (2014a). *Agency info— Mission, vision, philosophy and core values.* Retrieved from www.thecb.state.tx.us

Texas Higher Education Coordinating Board. (2014b). *2014 Texas public higher education almanac: A profile of state and institutional performance and characteristics.* Retrieved from http://www.thecb.state.tx.us

Texas Higher Education Coordinating Board, Workforce, Academic Affairs and Research. (2014c). *Texas general academic institutions: Increasing successful community college transfer.* A report to the Texas legislature Senate Bill 1, 83rd Texas legislature. Retrieved from http://www.thecb.state.tx.us

Texas Higher Education Coordinating Board. (2015). *Summary of higher education legislation—84th Texas Legislature.* Retrieved from http://www.thecb.state.tx.us

The Texas Tribune. (2013, April 16). Higher ed outcomes: Tracking eighth-graders' post-secondary success. *The Texas Tribune.* Retrieved from www.texastribune.org

Trow, M. (2010). *Twentieth-century higher education: Elite to mass to universal.* M. Burrage, (Ed.) Baltimore, MD: John Hopkins University Press.

Tuition for Repeated or Excessive Undergraduate Hours, Texas Education Code, Chapter 54, Subchapter A § 54.014 (2005).

Wang, X. (2012). Factors contributing to the upward transfer of baccalaureate aspirants beginning at community colleges. *The Journal of Higher Education, (83)*6, 851–875.

Wang, X. (2013). Baccalaureate expectations of community colleges students: Socio-demographic, motivational, and contextual influences. *Teachers College Record, 115*(4), 1–39.

Wellman, J. V. (2002, August). *State policy and community college-baccalaureate transfer.* National Center Report #02-6. Washington, D.C.: The National Center for Public Policy and Higher Education and The Institute for Higher Education Policy.

Zusman, A. (2005). Challenges facing higher education in the twenty-first century. In P. G. Altbach, R. O. Berdahl, & P. J. Gumport (Eds.), *American higher education in the twenty-first century: Social, political and economic challenges* (115–160). Baltimore, MD: John Hopkins University Press.

8

FACTORS, PRACTICES, AND POLICIES INFLUENCING STUDENTS' UPWARD TRANSFER TO BACCALAUREATE-DEGREE PROGRAMS AND INSTITUTIONS: AN OVERVIEW OF A MIXED-METHODS RESEARCH PROJECT[1]

Robin R. LaSota, Ph.D.

ABSTRACT

This article summarizes findings from an explanatory, sequential mixed-methods research project to assess factors that influence the likelihood that community college students will transfer to baccalaureate-granting institutions. It also presents promising practices in colleges and states aimed at improving upward transfer, particularly for low-income and first-generation college students. The quantitative analysis of this study features a multi-level random-effects model designed to better understand how factors such as students' academic and social integration, community college characteristics and expenditures, and state transfer policies influence community college students' 2/4 transfer probability over a six-year period, utilizing the Beginning Postsecondary Study 2003–2009. Comparative case studies of six community colleges in three states (Florida, Georgia, and Washington) also provide insights regarding the ways in which community colleges and state policy leaders are engaged in experimentation and innovation to improve students' 2/4 transfer, and how they use data to inform decision-making on this issue.[2] Case study analyses also examine

1   With thanks to my dissertation advisor, William Zumeta, and my dissertation committee members, Robert Abbott, Michael Knapp, Margaret Plecki, and Jennifer Romich. This research was supported by grant funding from the Institute of Education Sciences and the Association for Institutional Research. The complete dissertation is available from ProQuest Dissertation and Theses database.

2   Georgia does not have community colleges. Rather, the University System of Georgia has 15 "access institutions" that are primarily associate's degree granting institutions, and most offer limited baccalaureate degrees. My case study institutions include two of these access institutions. However, findings for this presentation draw primarily from Florida and Washington colleges. As part of Complete College Georgia, the University System of Georgia partners with the Technical College System of Georgia (TCSG) to improve postsecondary success outcomes. TCSG consists of 25 technical colleges with two university system technical divisions in USG and 31 satellite campuses. Among nearly 49,000 awards conferred in 2011 in the TCSG, 12% were associate's degrees, 63% were technical certificates, and 25% were high school

practices occurring in community colleges and state policy circles designed to augment the historical, longitudinal, multi-level analysis of factors influencing community college students' transfer to baccalaureate-granting institutions, using nationally representative (BPS) data. The case study design compared positive-performing institutional and state-level exemplars to average (and rising) exemplars to illustrate how the implementation of policies and practices in the field influenced student transfer outcomes.

WHY FOCUS ON COMMUNITY COLLEGE STUDENTS' UPWARD TRANSFER?

According to the National Center for Education Statistics (2011), six out of ten students who initially entered public two-year colleges in the U.S. never transferred over the six-year period from 2003–2009 (Table 6.0-B). However, two-thirds of the students who never transferred expected a bachelor's degree at the time of initial enrollment. Forty percent of community college entrants transferred, but only 61% of these were upward transfers to four-year institutions, 36% were lateral transfers, and 3% were downward transfers from a four-year to a two-year institution. The total percentage of upward transfers is only 26.6%; 17% of entering public two-year college students transferred to public four-year institutions, another 5% transferred to private nonprofit four-year institutions, and another 4.6% transferred to for-profit institutions (some four-year institutions are in this group), based on a nationally representative sample of entering college students in the Beginning Postsecondary Study (BPS) (NCES, 2011, Table 6.0-B).

At the height of the 2007–2011 enrollment boom, about 7.8 million students enrolled in community colleges in the U.S. in 2011 (Mullin, 2012). Substantial economic and social benefits accrue to individuals with higher levels of educational attainment, particularly bachelor's degrees (Goldin & Katz, 2008; Bureau of Labor Statistics, 2011). Labor market returns correlate strongly and positively with each additional degree earned, and occupational forecasts show that the majority of jobs (63%) will require some postsecondary education (about one-fourth of them requiring BA degrees or higher) (Carnevale, Smith, & Strohl, 2010). As minority and

---

equivalency diplomas. Note that most of Florida's community colleges have their own baccalaureate degree programs in specialized occupational fields, including one of the case study colleges selected in that state. For simplicity, I refer to colleges as community colleges throughout the paper, though different institutions may offer some range of baccalaureate programs or be in the process of obtaining approval for a bachelor's degree program(s).

low-income individuals represent the fastest-growing demographic groups in the United States and disproportionately enroll in community colleges, research studies that inform policy and practice to improve transfer rates of community college students to four-year institutions (often called "2/4 transfer") will be valuable.[3] Low rates of transfer, coupled with labor market demand for individuals with a bachelor's degree or higher and heightened economic returns for at least a bachelor's level of education, indicate the tremendous importance of strengthening systems of support for upward transfer for community college students.

FACTORS INFLUENCING COMMUNITY COLLEGE STUDENTS' UPWARD TRANSFER

The quantitative strand of the research project contains findings from a multi-level random effects model that estimates how individual student factors, public two-year college characteristics,[4] and variations in statewide articulation and transfer agreements may contribute to the probability that community college students will successfully transfer to a four-year institution (2/4 transfer). Two types of quantitative analyses were performed to predict community college students' likelihood of transferring to a four-year institution: 1) research on student characteristics and their choices relevant to transfer, and 2) research on state and community college characteristics relevant to transfer. Student-level factors appear to be more important in predicting student outcomes than institutional or structural factors, according to Bailey, Jenkins, & Leinbach (2005). However, these researchers note that "the possibility remains that these relationships are constrained by the data available to include in statistical models and how these models are constructed," (Goldrick-Rab, 2010, p. 457). Roksa (2009) noted substantial confusion and incoherence in the transfer literature, as a result of data and methodological limitations: "Surveying the transfer literature reveals the diversity of definitions, measurements, data, and analytical methods used that makes it virtually impossible to arrive at any coherent conclusions" (p. 2470). Nonetheless, various hypotheses have been examined to identify influential predictors of students' upward transfer probability.

---

3   See recent population projections from Johnson and Lichter (2010) and college enrollment projections by WICHE, (2013). Provasnik and Planty (2008) report on differences in community college enrollment by race, ethnicity, income status, etc.

4   These institutions may also be called community colleges, primarily associate's granting institutions, or access institutions. For simplicity, I will refer to them as community colleges.

Analyses for this study are drawn from the Beginning Postsecondary Study (BPS) 2003–2009, a nationally representative sample dataset of first-time beginning college students. The number of individuals in the sub-sample of community college students (rounded to the nearest 10) equals 5,010. Additional institution-level variables come from the Integrated Postsecondary Education Data System (IPEDS) and the remaining college and state variables come from other national data sources. Within this nationally representative sample, students' upward transfer probability varies across colleges and across states. Upward 2/4 transfer probability across the national BPS sample is about 26% over the six-year period. See Figure 8.1 for an overview of the predicted probabilities of student, college, and state factors affecting students' upward transfer from community college to baccalaureate programs and institutions. LaSota and Zumeta (2015) provide additional information about the findings of the analytical models, including model equations, data tables, and variable descriptions.

Influential Student Factors

Six factors over which students can exert control are positively associated to increase the probability that a student will transfer (based upon the subject-specific model, with slopes allowed to vary for sub-populations,[5] no predictors of randomly varying slope added):[6]

1. Students who attend college full-time rather than part-time;

2. Students who work less than 20 hours per week;

3. Students who declare a major in STEM, arts and social/behavioral sciences, or education in the first year, compared to students who are undeclared or a business major;

4. Students who earn relatively higher GPAs;

---

5 Sub-populations of students that vary in 2/4 transfer probability by college and state are: (1) low-income, first generation to earn a BA in his/her family; (2) first-generation, not low-income students (compared with not low-income, not first generation students); and (3) students who declare a health/vocational/technical-oriented major (vs. business or undeclared). Sub-populations that vary in 2/4 transfer probability by state but not college are: students who planned to transfer compared to students who did not plan to transfer in 2003–2004. Results were derived from multi-level regression with random intercepts and random slopes with all student characteristics (selected to vary one at a time with state policy characteristics and community college characteristics in the intercepts).

6 Population-average results define regression coefficients to be interpreted as the expected change in the outcome associated with a one-unit increase in the relevant predictor holding constant other predictors, but without controlling any random effects. The unit-specific or subject-specific model holds constant the other predictors and controls random effects (Raudenbush & Bryk, 2002, p. 334), and estimated effects are adjusted for individual differences (Hu et al., 1998). Subject-specific results are selected in order to present findings in terms of the change due to the covariates for a specific group of individuals (e.g. students who planned to transfer).

5. Students who meet with an academic advisor "often" or "sometimes" compared to students with little or no such contact (weakly significant, p<.10); and

6. Students who participate in sports (weakly significant, p<.10).

Factors that are negatively associated with transfer include the need to complete remedial courses in the first year of college. Finally, factors that did not explain variance in 2/4 transfer probability for this population include students who participate in study groups, students who meet informally with faculty outside of class (e.g. office hours), and students who participate in arts and clubs.

Influential College Characteristics

Although few community college characteristics and state policy variables demonstrate a statistically significant difference in students' six-year 2/4 transfer probability, two institutional characteristics of the primary two-year college attended have been identified that helps to account for the variance in students' 2/4 transfer probability (in both population-average and subject-specific models):

1. The college's average proportion of associate's degree completions in health and vocational fields was negatively related to the college's 2/4 transfer rate (weakly significant in the subject-specific model, no slope predictors added, p<.10).

2. The college's average transfer-out rate was a positive predictor of 2/4 transfer probability.

College characteristics that did not explain variance in transfer probability for the overall population were: percent of full-time faculty, percent of full-time students, faculty-to-student ratio, community college enrollment size, per-student expenditures on instruction, per-student expenditures on student services, status as a minority-serving institution, distance to nearest public four-year institution or nearest non- or less-selective public four-year institution, and average transfer-in rate of the nearest public four-year institution. Gross and Goldhaber (2009) found certain institutional factors impactful, including expenditures on instruction and student services, percent of tenured faculty, and student-to-faculty ratio, but used an older dataset (the National Educational

Longitudinal Study, NELS 1988–2000). Stange (2012) did not find evidence that per-student instructional expenditures improved transfer probability. Among four-year institutions, Webber and Ehrenberg (2010) found that per-student expenditures on student services positively influence BA degree attainment, particularly for institutions with lower entrance test scores and higher Pell grant expenditures per student, although these findings are not directly relevant since community colleges were not examined in this study. Student services programs at four-year institutions, particularly those with more academically under-prepared and low-income students, tend to have better systems of support than those established thus far at community colleges.

Influential State Factors and Articulation Policies

Similar to other researchers' findings, this analysis found that most state transfer policies demonstrate little or no effect on the probability of transfer, even after controlling for state wealth (gross state product per capita, see next paragraph). State articulation and transfer policies generally include several components, as catalogued by the Education Commission of the States (ECS) in 2001 and 2010. ECS transfer policy components are: presence of articulation and transfer legislation; cooperative agreements among institutions and/or departments at 2- and 4-year institutions; transfer data reporting to state higher education commissions, departments, and authorities; transfer incentives and rewards (such as priority admission and scholarships); presence of a statewide course articulation guide; common core curriculum; and common course numbering. State articulation and transfer policy components have binary coding in the ECS catalogue and some degree of correlation (all less than 0.3) with each other across states, which poses a challenge for discerning effects of individual policy components.[7] The policies' existence and strength of implementation are not measured annually.

Gross state product per capita is strongly correlated (0.6, p<.001) with the proportion of bachelor's degree holders in state's population, and uniquely explains significant variance in transfer probability across states (before and after controlling for state articulation/transfer policies). Relative to the average, a student in a state with one standard deviation higher gross

---

[7] The only significant correlation was between presence of a state transfer guide and transfer-related incentives (correlation=0.3, p<.05).

state product per capita showed increased transfer probability by +35% greater odds. The reason to control for gross state product per capita is suggested by Anderson et al. (2006) who documented an association in the increase of gross state product with a decline in state expenditures in higher education and the expansion of comprehensive articulation agreements. As stated by Anderson et al. (2006),

> In an effort to help manage a somewhat inevitable fiscal crisis in public higher education—which is attributable in part to the state underfunding—statewide articulation agreements were adopted or modified during this period [1978–2000] to generate new cost-effective pathways for states to educate baccalaureate-bound students. (p. 434)

Contrary to the hypothesis that higher local unemployment would increase students' likelihood of pursuit of a bachelor's degree to boost their long-term earning potential, Kienzl, Wesaw, and Kumar (2011) also found that a higher unemployment rate produced a negative effect on transfer. They theorized that students may be unwilling to continue on to a four-year institution due to other economic impacts (which may be associated with higher unemployment, state/county economy, etc.) such as reduced financial aid or cutbacks in services at community colleges. Neither the proportion of two-year to public four-year college tuition averaged over 2003–08, nor the proportion of community college enrollment relative to the adult population in the state, were significant predictors of transfer probability. Kienzl et al. (2011) similarly found that the tuition differential between two-year and public four-year institutions no longer mattered in the BPS:2009, even though this factor (i.e. a larger differential) negatively impacted students' transfer probability in the earlier BPS:2001 cohort. This may be due to students having a higher awareness of financial aid opportunities nearly a decade later, and increases in Pell grant awards during the period (ACE, 2012).

In the random-intercepts and slopes, subject-specific model with no slope predictors added, none of the state articulation policy components explained variance in six-year 2/4 transfer probability. However, when all the state articulation/transfer policy components were added to explain variance in slopes for sub-populations, the only component that was significant was common course numbering (for first generation students, regardless of income level).[8] Since only eight states reported common course numbering during this period across two and four-year systems, it may be a proxy for broader statewide policy discussions and innovations not picked up by the state policy measures themselves. For the four states in the dataset with 30 or more students represented in the data with common course numbering (Florida, Mississippi, Texas, and Wyoming), common course numbering (as one aspect to a broader set of state articulation/transfer policies) proved to be positively associated with increased transfer probability. The other four states (Alaska, North and South Dakota, and Idaho) are not represented in BPS or have only a few students in the data.

For first-generation students who are not from low-income backgrounds (relative to students who were neither first-generation nor low-income), the presence of common course numbering in a state may indicate a substantial increase in the odds of upward transfer, after controlling for gross state product (wealth), which is also a factor associated with increased 2/4 transfer probability. This study found a positive association between the presence of a statewide transfer guide and the average student's transfer probability in the model with fixed effects, randomly varying slopes. According to ECS (2010), 26 states have developed state transfer guides that describe transfer and articulation requirements and provide students with answers to questions about the transfer process. Although this measure does not account for students' access to or degree of use of the state transfer guide, it serves nonetheless as an indicator of a statewide effort to consolidate and purposefully assist students in the transfer process.

State transfer guides are a tangible representation of a state's commitment to the transfer process. Such guides would not exist if it were not for relationships developed to support better articulation and transfer between two- and four-year institutions. Similarly, common course numbering would not exist without intention at the state-level to bolster upward transfer access and success. For example, the development of a common course numbering system requires systematic review of courses by faculty at both two- and four-year institutions, and a high level of sustained coordination by articulation professionals to align course curricula relative to agreed-upon outcomes. These findings suggest that it is

---

8 As described by the Education Commission of the States (2001, 2010), identical course numbering for similar courses between two-year and four-year institutions facilitates ease of transfer, and reduces numbers of students taking non-transferable credits.

the relationships built among faculty, administrators, and staff at two- and four-year institutions around these articulation/transfer policy initiatives that positively impact upward transfer, not the state transfer guide or the common course numbering scheme.

Figure 8.1

Predicted Probabilities of Upward Transfer, i.e. 2/4 Transfer of Factors Significant In the Multi-Level Regression

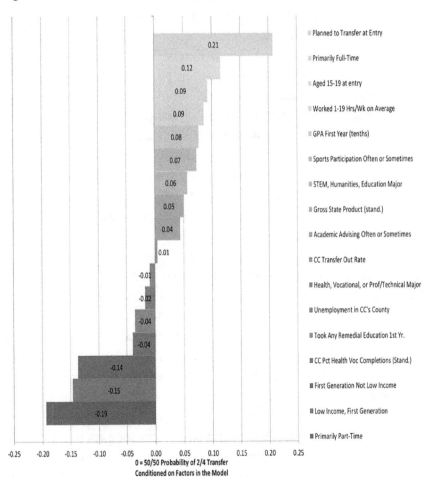

CASE STUDY ANALYSES

This research project utilized case studies of community colleges with success in increasing transfer rates among students from low-income and other underrepresented students. Several questions frame this case study approach: (1) To what extent is theoretical and empirical research used in community colleges' program design and modification? (2) In what ways are innovative practices included as part of a systemic organizational effort that influences student experiences? (3) What organizational factors may support innovative practices for transfer success? (4) In what ways do state policies and college practices increase students' upward transfer?

Washington, Georgia, and Florida were selected as priority case study states. These states have notable policies in promoting student success in transfer (Moore, Shulock, & Jensen, 2009; Finney, Perna & Callan, 2012). Above-average colleges were identified from outliers of regression analyses of colleges' cohort-based transfer rates in each state, controlling for student population characteristics, such as percent of Pell recipients, percent of African-American and Latino students, and percent of students placed in developmental courses (where available). In addition, Aspen Prize data and input from state higher education policymakers were used to supplement regression analyses.

Washington is one of the few states in which half or more of its postsecondary students are enrolled in community colleges. (50% per The National Center for Higher Education and Public Policy, 2011). It has cooperative agreements with all four-year institutions (public and private) in the state, which provide transfer students (who earned AA and AS degrees) top priority in the admissions process (ECS, 2010). Florida and Georgia also enroll a large proportion of students in community colleges (28% and 35%, respectively, of students in higher education enrolled at two-year colleges in 2007-08). Florida has a progressive articulation agreement that allows AA degree graduates from state-approved Florida community colleges to be admitted as juniors to any state university as long as the university has space, money, and curriculum to meet students' needs (ECS, 2010). In Georgia, students who complete the core curriculum at an institution in the University System of Georgia are guaranteed full credit in transfer at all public two-year and four-year colleges and universities, provided students do not change majors or programs of study (ECS, 2010).

The case study analysis began with a series of semi-structured interviews with institutional administrators, program developers, faculty leaders, institutional researchers, and student services leaders from each case study institution. These interviews were used to gain insight about transfer practices, their use of data to guide decision-making, and their strategic planning efforts aimed at increasing 2/4 transfer among low-income students. Additional interviews were conducted with state policy officials working on improving state articulation and transfer pathways, policies, and incentives. These state-level interviews aid in deepening our understanding of new strategies being implemented to increase 2/4 transfer, and provide additional context of historical factors that may improve or constrain the state's effectiveness in improving community college students' transfer outcomes. Understanding state policies is important in terms of understanding the constraints affecting the selected community colleges' institutional capacity and effectiveness in improving 2/4 transfer rates.

In total, I spoke with 179 individuals across the three states and six colleges. I interviewed twenty state policy analysts and leaders in one-hour interviews (n=9 in FL; n=5 in GA; n=6 in WA). In my visits to colleges, I spoke with 110 administrators, faculty, and staff. Administrator interviews included presidents, vice presidents of academic affairs and student affairs, directors of institutional effectiveness and research, directors of pre-college education, academic deans, and leaders of student support programs, such as TRIO. Faculty who participated in my study were generally involved in student advising or instructional reforms designed to improve students' progression towards transfer. College interviews also included student affairs advisors, TRIO staff, and academic support staff. Across the six colleges, I talked with 49 students (nine individual one-hour interviews, forty students in focus groups). I spoke with no fewer than six students at each college, who were TRIO eligible or in a similar support program such as Brother to Brother (Georgia), MESA (a STEM support program for low-income, minority and female students in Washington), and specialized support programs in Florida. Generally, I worked with the vice president of academic affairs to secure participation from all the key informants from the study, and in Florida, I worked with the chiefs of staff.

Next, I used analytic memos on initial findings from each of the states and their institutions (Emerson, Fretz, and Shaw, 1995) as the basis for making theoretical generalizations from specific experiences, perspectives, and interpretations shared by participants. I also developed summary tables, charts, and figures related to each of the areas of case study analysis: (1) academic advising, (2) data use, (3) support for learning and innovation, and (4) the role of state articulation and transfer policy. This summary highlights case study findings about the interdependence between state articulation and transfer policies, and college-level innovation.

Case Study Findings

Problem-identification, solution-finding, and innovation in the design and implementation of the college's system(s) of support for students' upward transfer generally began with dialogue among administrators, staff, faculty, and students in the colleges I studied. Although I use the term "system of support for students' upward transfer," each college in my study is in a different stage of creating a comprehensive, coordinated system of support for transfer. None of the colleges I studied had a robust, comprehensive, and coordinated "system of support for students' upward transfer." However, all colleges had some individual components and practices that assisted students in making an effective transition to upper-division coursework and bachelor's degree programs/institutions. Moreover, each of the colleges in the study have as part of their mission the goal to support students in achieving success in their chosen field and job, which may or may not include pursuit of a bachelor's degree.

Role of State Articulation and Transfer Policy

The degree of commitment on the part of a state to improve upward transfer is driven by several factors: (1) the proportion of students' enrolled with transfer intentions relative to the college's transfer mission, (2) the commitment of college leaders on improving the 2/4 transfer rate, and (3) the interdependence of supply/demand forces in the local higher education economy influencing the degree of institutional effort towards recruiting and retaining transfer students to nearby four-year institutions from both institution types. Interdependent and reciprocal relationships inform the nature of systems of support for upward transfer among the state's articulation and transfer policy networks. These relationships connect leaders within local associate's granting and baccalaureate-granting institutions, the leaders of major-related programs, and employers in those fields. Macro-level policy efforts, such as state actions related to Complete College America and state legislation designed to improve bachelor's degree completion and postsecondary-workforce alignment, shape the degree to which college-level frameworks are successful and new institution-wide practices are adopted. (See Figure 8.2)

Figure 8.2

Overview of Inter-Dependent Relationships between State Articulation and Policy Context, Local Economies, and Leadership of Two- and Four-Year Institutions

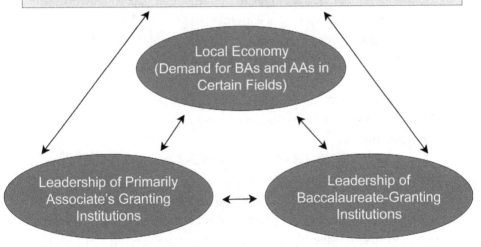

While state articulation and transfer policies may not increase the probability that students will successfully transfer to a four-year institution, it seems reasonable to assume that the efforts of influential policy actors positively affect the college-level implementation of programs and practices that may ultimately improve overall student upward transfer rates. This is noticeable with respect to college-level reforms of developmental education and the policy supports offered for such reforms at the state level (in all three states). For example, efforts of Florida college student services leaders led to the formulation of Florida H.R. 7135, which requires mandatory transfer advising before students reach thirty hours of credits in their associate's degree program.[9] To the extent that state articulation/transfer policies reflect a significant positive relationship with students' upward transfer rates, these efforts appear to be correlated with the depth, focus, and adaptability of collaborative relationships supporting transfer between primarily associate's degree granting and four-year universities that are also reinforced by state-level networks and policy-making circles.

New solutions are also being generated to support progression from pre-college education to college-level coursework, course grades of C or better in those college-level courses, term-to-term retention, and associate's degree completion. In states such as Florida, Georgia, and Washington—which all have relatively strong and progressive state-level policy systems for articulation and transfer—the college-level brainstorming and solution-finding seems to be highly interactive with principles affirmed or created at the state-level. For example, Florida's college-level experimentation with new advising practices coincides with that state's recent legislative mandate that ensures all students receive transfer advising before earning thirty credit hours. Creation and development of institution-to-institution articulation agreements and university-based partnerships at community colleges in Washington is reinforced by state-level policymaking, specifically with respect to a mandate for the creation of specific major-related pathways for articulation/transfer.

The quantitative analysis of predictors of students' upward transfer in BPS noted that the presence of common course numbering policy is associated with much greater odds of transfer for first-generation students. For the whole population of community college entrants, the presence of common course numbering does not demonstrate a positive association

---

9   One of the provisions of Florida legislation passed in 2012 (H.R. 7135) requires that every college in the Florida College System (FCS) have a plan in place for mandatory transfer advising by the time students earn thirty college credits towards their AA degree. Specifically, the law "requires the Articulation Coordinating Council (ACC) to have each FCS student identify a desired baccalaureate degree, by institution of interest, by the time the student earns 30 credits. The FCS institution must then notify the student of degree program prerequisites," (Lehr, McColsky, & Woodruff, 2012, p. 21). This legislation was touted by Florida's Higher Education Coordinating Council as "the most comprehensive postsecondary legislation since 1995," (2012, p. 4).

with upward transfer probability. After all, common course numbering is present in only four states represented in the dataset (Florida, Mississippi, Texas, and Wyoming). From the case study analysis, which included Florida, my hypothesis was that the robust communications and problem-solving involved in the creation of step-by-step pathways towards baccalaureate degree attainment (including the creation of common course numbering) positively impacted students' upward transfer rather than the mere existence of common course numbering.

Common course numbering would not exist without the state-level intent to bolster upward transfer access and success. The development of a common course numbering system requires systematic review of courses by faculty at both two- and four-year institutions, and a high level of ongoing orchestration to align dynamic course curricula relative to agreed-upon outcomes that constitute the basis for particular transferable courses (and their corresponding numbers). Other states have sought the advice of Florida's policymakers on designing common course numbering systems in their state, as Florida's common course numbering system model is highly regarded as a national exemplar.

The framework for the state-level performance funding in operational or planning stages also has an influence on the way in which upward transfer is prioritized. Among the three states in this case study research, only Washington has a performance-based funding system in place, and the allocation of dollars tied to those performance metrics is relatively small (1–2%). The Washington Student Achievement Initiative (SAI), however, does not include 2/4 transfer as one of the funding-based measures, which may largely be due to the ambiguity about data validity and reliability relative to the P-20W longitudinal data system that is being developed by the state. Now that the Mutual Records Transcript Exchange (MRTE) has obtained full participation in spring 2013 from the public four-year institutions, and the data management issues are better clarified, inclusion of the 2/4 transfer outcome in the SAI may be re-visited. When faculty discussed the SAI's influence on their work advising students about transfer and generally improving the system of support for transfer, faculty expressed the opinion that SAI is largely symbolic, and not an important driver for changes in their teaching, advising, or leadership.

Academic leaders in Florida and Georgia were highly attuned to proposals for performance-based budgeting and subsequently shaped their practices to align with emerging priorities and proposals at the state level. For example, at one Florida college, the chief student affairs officer shared,

> As a college, we have decided we're going to work as if our funding is going to be based on retention . . . students who pass their courses with As, Bs, and Cs, and who show up for the next semester, graduate, or go to the next level . . . transfer has taken on a whole new meaning. We used to say, "Well, we've done our part, you got your AA," . . . but now that we confer baccalaureate degrees, transfer is even more important . . . the majority of our transfer students to our baccalaureate programs are all native students who got their AA degree here.

As another example, Georgia higher education system leaders worked on "developing an outcomes-based funding model for higher education in Georgia," building from the Tennessee model which earmarks the majority of higher education funding to performance metrics (Higher Education Funding Commission, 2012). Academic leaders in the Georgia colleges that participated in this study expressed how the current policy context has dramatically shaped the creation of their "college completion plans," a requirement of all institutions in the University System of Georgia as central to the Complete College Georgia initiative. In 2013, Georgia's proposed framework included "formula dollars awarded for successful transfer and completion is prioritized over progression." The proposed definition of successful transfer by the Higher Education Funding Commission (2012) at the time was:

> The number of students who transferred out to any public, private, or out-of-state institution who had accumulated at least 15 earned credit hours. Metric calculated based on student enrollment at College A during year 1 (summer, fall, spring year 1) and transfer enrollment found later in year 1 or year 2 (fall, spring, year 2). This does not include a student who accumulated hours through dual enrollment programs and then enrolled at another institution. The number of credit hours accepted by the institution the student transfers to, does not factor into this outcome. The National Student Clearinghouse and/or GA AWARDS (Georgia's Academic and Workforce Analysis and Research Data System) should be used to track transfers. (p. 9)

This measure does not specify upward transfer (from lower-division to upper-division coursework, or the equivalent of 2/4 transfer), yet it signals to colleges a monetary value for supporting students' access and success through their transfer and eventually to their desired degree. The outcome-funding proposal also specifies a state mechanism for tracking students' transfer, which anticipates how essential measuring this function is in order to accurately award "credit" for the transfer in the outcome-funding formula.

QUALITATIVE ANALYSES

In 2011, University of Southern California researcher Alicia Dowd concluded that, "Although community colleges and the transfer function are often construed as the embodiment of democratic opportunities for access to higher education, transfer is primarily something affluent students do," (p. 219). Nevertheless, case study findings from this research show that at least three states (Florida, Georgia, and Washington), are actively involved in developing innovative transfer policies and practices to improve transfer for all students. Still, colleges also face numerous challenges in attempting to close the upward transfer gap between students from underserved groups (e.g., first-generation, low-income, ethnic/racial minority students) and students from more affluent backgrounds. One of the most influential challenges to improving students' upward transfer is that states and colleges each prioritize the transfer outcome differently with respect to performance or outcomes funding, and with respect to their own transfer-intending populations.

Colleges with higher transfer rates have implemented a range of practices such as mandatory advising, early bird advising, and early warning advising systems generally targeted at first-time, full-time students and/or students placed into developmental education courses. Despite these innovations, many students do not have the access and support they feel they need for focused and strategic transfer planning. For example, data show that students who are enrolled part-time experience barriers with financing higher education, succeeding in pre-college or college-level courses, and managing multiple demands of work and family responsibilities. In addition, many students find the supports offered in their community college insufficient.

With support from organizations such as Achieving the Dream and Complete College America, states and colleges have developed better ways to access and utilize data on students' upward transfer. Challenges persist, however, in gathering reliable data on first-generation status (since self-reported data may not be reliable and there is a lack of consistency in defining first-generation status). In addition, there are challenges disaggregating student outcome data (such as students' upward transfer) by low-income status or need for developmental education coursework in math, reading, or both. Once gaps are identified based on disaggregating cohort-based transfer rates by population sub-groups, the next challenge faced by colleges is to develop meaningful interventions. Colleges face budgetary constraints when adding incentives and resources to student services programming and faculty responsibilities. Colleges also face additional pressures from state policies, such as in Georgia, which mandated consolidation of eight institutions to better streamline administrative operations, improve cost-efficiency, and leverage resources across the University System of Georgia to increase postsecondary-workforce alignment in major fields. In Florida, colleges must respond to new legislation requiring transfer advising by the time a student reaches thirty credit hours and colleges must revise general education curriculum offerings in response to a state mandate to reduce the general education core curriculum from 36 to 30 hours. Washington's continuing revisions to articulation requirements by major require that colleges regularly update their advising practices in each of the major fields as policy changes occur. No matter what the policy mandates, a persistent challenge remains for colleges to coordinate consistent, reliable implementation of articulation and transfer policies at scale among their student population, particularly those who are vulnerable and/or under-performing.

The college case studies also suggest that other states should incentivize colleges to design research-based innovations and measure effectiveness with meaningful comparison groups. Together, states and colleges may achieve higher transfer rates—particularly among vulnerable student populations—when student success data are used to support decision-making around existing and new programs, and services targeted at increasing students' degree completion and transfer outcomes. Research suggests that students less likely to transfer (such as first-generation students) may benefit from initiatives that facilitate consistent dialogue among faculty and administrators responsible for the articulation of lower- and upper-division courses and programs, including the planning required to develop common course numbering plans. For example, Florida's success in helping students transfer can be traced to some degree on its commitment to craft a common course numbering scheme nearly fifty years ago. However, every state has the opportunity to build upon its own history with respect to articulation and transfer systems to strengthen transfer, including the coordination of associate's degree and bachelor's degree programs.

MIXED-METHODS ANALYSIS

While the quantitative analysis in many ways affirms prior research about the ambiguous or unknown effects of state transfer and articulation policies, the case studies offer some insight regarding state policies that may improve transfer student outcomes, especially for students from vulnerable populations such as first-generation college students. Students are largely disconnected from state policymaking with respect to articulation and transfer, and experience only the effects of these efforts as reflected in the ease with which they are able to transfer and/or enroll in a particular field of study. What matters most to the majority of students is having a positive, supportive experience with the college faculty and staff with whom they interact to address whatever barrier they are experiencing, relative to their own motivation for succeeding in college and transferring to a bachelor's degree program. State articulation and transfer policies do not tend to address this key factor, but college leaders concern themselves with this issue to a high degree. Some of the largest barriers to creating engaging and personalized learning environments have to do with the difficulties of managing multi-campus colleges, extremely large enrollments (such as more than 10,000 students), an increasing number of adjunct and part-time faculty, and extremely large (such as 1,000 to 1) student-to-advisor ratios.

From the quantitative analysis in this research project, policy intervention would likely be most strategic if directed at helping high school students create specific plans for obtaining a bachelor's degree in a specific field and outlining a specific transfer pathway. Research from the Community College Research Center (Jaggars & Fletcher, 2013) indicate that community college students may have a more difficult time solving transfer-related advising scenarios than with completing tasks related to choosing a program of study based on prior achievement and desired salary objective. This suggests it would be worthwhile for high schools to offer student success courses generally offered for first-year college students as a way of building transfer intentions and plans earlier. Transfer intention and full-time attendance were the two student-level characteristics most positively associated with upward transfer probability from the quantitative strand, which implies that further intervention to increase full-time, continuous enrollment would also be extremely beneficial. Reform of financial aid policies and packaging—particularly for community college entrants—would be needed in this effort, particularly because many community college students are loan averse and/or working 20 or more hours a week (a factor negatively associated with upward transfer).

The case study analysis offers insights for improving the use of transfer data for decision-making when allocating resources and planning interventions to increase students' upward transfer. However, the larger issue around improving upward transfer is generating increased individual and collective responsibility among both two- and four-year institutions. As states develop performance or outcome-based funding models and build longitudinal student data warehouses to track student degree completions, transfer, and labor market outcomes, colleges will need to respond to this increased accountability with strategic and innovative change. This article offers some promising strategies, interventions, and practices among colleges with above-average transfer rates designed to promote student transfer, especially among students from underrepresented groups who are more likely to begin their pursuit of a baccalaureate degree by first attending a community college.

REFERENCES

American Council on Education (2012, July 31). *Pell grant funding history (1976 to 2010)*. Retrieved from http://www.acenet.edu/news-room/Documents/FactSheet-Pell-Grant-Funding-History-1976-2010.pdf

Anderson, G. M., Alfonso, M., & Sun, J. C. (2006, March). Rethinking cooling out at public community colleges: An examination of fiscal and demographic trends in higher education and the rise of statewide articulation agreements, *Teachers College Record, 108*(3), 422–451.

Bailey, T., Jenkins, D., & Leinbach, T. (2005). *What we know about community college low-income and minority student outcomes: Descriptive statistics from national surveys.* New York, NY: Community College Research Center.

Bureau of Labor Statistics. (2011, May). *Education pays...* Washington, D.C.: U.S. Department of Labor. Retrieved from http://www.bls.gov/emp/ep_chart_001.htm

Carnevale, A. P., Smith, N., & Strohl, J. (2010). *Help wanted: Projections of jobs and education requirements through 2018.* Washington, D.C.: Center for Education and the Workforce, Georgetown University. Retrieved from http://www9.georgetown.edu/grad/gppi/hpi/cew/pdfs/fullreport.pdf

Dowd, A. (2011). Improving transfer access for low-income community college students. In A. Kezar (Ed.), *Recognizing and serving low-income students in higher education: An examination of institutional policies, practices, and culture* (217–231). New York, NY: Routledge.

Education Commission of the States. (2001). *StateNotes: Articulation and transfer policies.* Denver, CO: Author. Retrieved from http://www.ecs.org/clearinghouse/23/75/2375.htm

Education Commission of the States. (2010). *StateNotes: Transfer and articulation policies.* Denver, CO: Author. Retrieved from http://www.ecs.org/html/Document.asp?chouseid=9070

Emerson, R. M., Fretz, R. I., & Shaw, L.L. (1995). Processing fieldnotes: Coding and memoing. In *Writing ethnographic fieldnotes* (142–168). Chicago, IL: University of Chicago Press.

Finney, J. E., Perna, L., & Callan, P. (2012, January). *The state review project II: State policy leadership vacuum: Performance and policy in washington higher education.* Philadelphia, PA: National Center for Higher Education and Public Policy and the Institute for Research in Higher Education. Retrieved from http://www.gse.upenn.edu/irhe/srp

Florida Department of Education. (2011, October). State articulation manual.

Goldin, C. & Katz, L. F. (2008). *The race between education and technology.* Cambridge, MA: Belknap Press for Harvard University Press.

Goldrick-Rab, S. (2010). Challenges and opportunities for improving community college student success. *Review of Educational Research, 80*(3), 437–469.

Gross, B. & Goldhaber, D. (2009). *Community college transfers and articulation policies: Looking beneath the surface.* CRPE working paper #2009_1. Seattle, WA: Center on Reinventing Public Information.

Higher Education Funding Commission. (2012). *Developing an Outcomes Based Funding Model for Higher Education in Georgia* [PDF document]. Retrieved from https://www.gainesvilletimes.com/news/incentive-based-funding-possible-for-ga-colleges/

Hu, F. B., Goldberg, J., Hedeker, D., Flay, B. R. & Pentz, M. A. (1998). Comparison of population-averaged and subject-specific approaches for analyzing repeated binary outcomes. *American Journal of Epidemiology, 147*(7), 694–703.

Jaggars, S. & Fletcher, J. (2013, April 30). *Navigating a sea of choices: The community college student perspective.* Presentation delivered at the American Educational Research Association conference, San Francisco, CA. New York, NY: Community College Research Center, Teachers College, Columbia University.

Johnson, K. M. and Lichter, D. T. (2010, Spring). *The changing faces of America's children and youth. Issue brief no. 15.* Durham, NH: Carsey Institute, University of New Hampshire. Retrieved from http://www. carseyinstitute.unh.edu/publications/IB_Johnson_ChangingFaces.pdf

Kienzl, G., Wesaw, A. J., & Kumar, A. (2012, December). *Understanding the transfer process: A report by the institute for higher education policy for the initiative on transfer policy and practice.* Washington, D.C.: CollegeBoard and Institute for Higher Education Policy.

LaSota, R. (2013). *Factors, practices, and policies influencing students' upward transfer to baccalaureate-degree programs and institutions: A mixed methods analysis.* Retrieved from ProQuest Dissertations and Theses. (UMI Number 3608859).

LaSota, R., & Zumeta, W. (2016). What matters in increasing community college students' upward transfer to the baccalaureate degree: Findings from the beginning postsecondary study 2003–2009. *Research in Higher Education, 57*(2), 152–189.

Lehr, S. M., McColsky, E., & Woodruff, E. (2012, May 7). *2012 Legislative session, Final session report.* Jacksonville, FL: Florida State College. Retrieved http://www.fscj.edu/district/government-relations/assets/documents/final-leg-rpt.pdf

Moore, C., Jensen, C., & Shulock, N. (2009). *Crafting a student-centered transfer process in California: Lessons from other states.* Sacramento, CA: Institute for Higher Education Leadership & Policy.

Mullin, C. M. (2012, February). *Why access matters: The community college student body.* AACC Policy Brief. Washington, D.C.: American Association of Community Colleges.

National Center for Education Statistics (NCES). (2011). *Six-year attainment, persistence, transfer, retention, and withdrawal rates of students who began postsecondary education in 2003–04.* (NCES 2011-152). Washington, D.C.: U.S. Department of Education, Institute of Education Sciences.

National Center for Higher Education and Public Policy (2011, June). Affordability and transfer: Critical to increasing baccalaureate degree completion. *Policy Alert.* San Jose, CA: Author. Retrieved from www.highereducation.org

Provasnik, S. & Planty, M. (2008). *Community colleges: Special supplement to the condition of education 2008* (NCES 2008-033). Washington, D.C.: National Center for Education Statistics, Institute of Education Sciences, U.S. Department of Education.

Raudenbush, S. & Bryk, A. S. (2002). *Hierarchical linear models: Applications and data analysis methods* (2nd edition). Thousand Oaks, CA: SAGE Publications, Inc.

Roksa, J. (2009). Building bridges for student success: Are higher education articulation policies effective? *Teachers College Record, 111*(10), 2444–2478.

Stange, K. (2012, Winter). Ability sorting and the importance of college quality to student achievement: Evidence from community colleges. *Education Finance and Policy, 7*(1), 74–105.

Webber, D. A. & Ehrenberg, R. G. (2010). Do expenditures other than instructional expenditures affect graduation and persistence rates in American higher education? *Economics of Education Review, 29,* 947–958.

Western Interstate Commission for Higher Education (2013, April). Demography as destiny: Policy considerations in enrollment management. *Policy Insights.* Retrieved from http://www.wiche.edu/info/publications/PI-knocking2013.pdf

Wine, J., Janson, N., & Wheeless, S. (2012). 2004/09 *Beginning postsecondary students longitudinal study (BPS: 04/09): Full-scale methodology report* (NCES 2012-246). Washington, D.C.: National Center for Education Statistics. Retrieved from http://nces.ed.gov/pubs2012/2012246_1.pdf

Robin R. LaSota, Ph.D. *is currently a Senior Research Scientist at the Development Services Group, Inc.*

AFTERWORD

Stephen J. Handel, Ph.D.

As the chief admission officer for the University of California (UC) System, I am sometimes asked why UC enrolls so many students from California community colleges, especially given the sky-high number of applications places like UCLA and Berkeley receive for admission into their first-year class. The questioner's subtext—always unacknowledged and often quite innocent—is that traditional first-year students are more worthy of admission to an elite four-year institution than students who attend a community college. Is it not self-evident that a high school student who has met UC's exacting selection requirements is more entitled to admission than an individual who attends a college with no admission requirements at all?

There's a lot to unpack in a question like that one. I usually respond that first-years and transfers do not compete for space at UC; both constituencies are critical to our educational commitment to California. I also say that UC's enrollment of community college students is the result of the progressive insights of education leaders who saw over a century ago that higher education had value for *all individuals*, not simply those who could afford it. I also offer my personal bias that colleges and universities ought to be accessible to anyone who is willing to commit herself to the challenges inherent in earning a baccalaureate degree.

With that as my professional moniker, it should come as little surprise, then, that *Transition and Transformation* (and its earlier companion volume) is something more than an opportunity to publish the work of thoughtful researchers who have devoted themselves to illuminating an important avenue of higher education access for community college students. Of course, that alone would be reason enough. However, for my co-editor,

Eileen Strempel, and myself, this devotion to transfer is something of a professional calling, regardless of how modest our ultimate outcomes or influence. This calling compels us to see the transfer process as a definable, distinct, and necessary topic for scholarship and critique.

The higher education literature is, of course, replete with the work of distinguished scholars throughout the U.S. who have advanced our understanding of community colleges, four-year institutions and the transfer process that links them. Moreover, I wish to avoid any impression there are not others equally committed to transfer, who have influenced our thinking and stirred our commitment to research and scholarship on this topic. Since the beginning of the community college movement over a century ago, writers and researchers have been engaged in an ever-expanding dialogue around questions of higher education access, productivity, and accountability. That work—like all good scholarship— informs the questions we ask today and the methodologies we employ. It is upon the shoulders of those visionary individuals that *Transition and Transformation* was conceived and developed.

Our aim with *Transition and Transformation* has been to drill deeper and communicate more widely the importance of the transfer process for community college students seeking the baccalaureate degree. Of course, the transfer student is now a ubiquitous phenomenon within U.S. higher education. The trajectory of today's college students is often characterized as the prototypical "swirling" student who does not necessarily follow the traditional transfer pathway (community college to four-year institution), but moves among several different types of postsecondary institutions before ultimately earning a degree. We acknowledge the validity of that experience, but believe it can be honored best by highlighting the traditional two- to four-year institutional pathway. It is *that* unique and bold lived experience of educational access that continues to stir the heart of this writer who, three decades ago, benefitted from the profound, life-changing impact of a college education by transferring from a community college to a four-year institution to earn his degree.

In recent years, I have been approached by education leaders in countries as diverse as the Netherlands, Canada, and China about the transfer pathway. I am asked, "How can you allow students who begin at an institution with no selection requirements to gain admission at a four-year institution whose standards are higher for first-year students? And how can these transfer students compete against their peers who usually have had stronger high school preparation for college and benefitted from a more competitive undergraduate curriculum?" That such open access institutions exist and that transfer students succeed is not just surprising to my international colleagues, but often unbelievable.

One could make a persuasive argument that the community college itself is the most important variable in the transfer equation. Of course, community colleges are transformative institutions in themselves, not simply because they offer the transfer option, but also because they offer a variety of terminal degrees and certificates that prepare students directly for employment in the workplace. Yet the unique aspect of the community college is the transfer element and its linkage to four-year colleges and universities. Vocational schools, technical institutes, for-profit entities, and apprenticeships parallel what goes on in the modern community college and are essential members of a diverse educational system. The authentically radical notion, however, is the access community colleges provide for students into the nation's most sought-after four-year institutions via the transfer pathway.

I am not aware of other highly selective postsecondary education systems that trade in this kind of opportunity—and optimism.

Despite its innovative genesis, the transfer pathway underperforms. The lack of a direct object in the previous sentence highlights the dilemma. An effective transfer pathway has many masters, but none who will own up to an obligation to do better by students who wish to transfer and earn a four-year degree. Even to the non-expert, two- and four-year institutions are jointly responsible for transfer students. Community colleges must effectively prepare students for the upper-division, and four-year institutions must commit to admitting and acclimating qualified students. Within America's diverse higher education ecosystem, however, there is little oversight of the process, even if there are extraordinary examples of two- and four-year institutions working in harmony and efficiency to serve transfer students. For every partnership between Santa Monica College and UCLA, there are dozens more transfer partnerships that languish. State legislatures and even the federal government often intercede, but their solutions, however well intended, rely on policy instruments (common course numbering systems, for instance) that miss the mark precisely because they have nothing to do with education and everything to do with regulation. Still, we must be mindful of policymakers' frustration with our treatment of transfer students and, more importantly, be responsive and creative in our solutions to better serve them.

The U.S. higher education system today, whatever its faults, is seen collectively as the most impressive in the world. Part of the reason for this has been the steady focus on scholarship that raised important questions about our educational system and devised ways to improve it, whether that be in pedagogy, curriculum, academic preparation, financial aid, or equity and access more broadly. We should build a similar initiative around transfer, not simply as an *extension* of the community college mission or merely an *obligation* of four-year institutions that seek a boost in enrollment. Rather, we should examine transfer as a distinct process that links American higher education in a web—not of regulation and obligation—but of collective mutuality; a like-minded constituency that advances educational opportunity, especially for students from underrepresented groups, promotes economic vitality for all Americans to earn a family-sustaining wage, and supports a society that values democracy, security, and sustainability.

That is why books like this one—and the newly minted researchers whose work is highlighted—are so important. Not only for the findings they offer, but also for the critical lens that they focus on the transfer pathway. My authentic disappointment with an underperforming transfer pathway is almost always counterbalanced by the knowledge that talented practitioners and researchers are diving into this area more than ever before, providing a broader and more incisive conversation about the transfer pathway.

In a career that is at best stalwart and steady, whatever success I have had is due in large measure to the recognition of the transformative power of this invention called "transfer." Although *Transition and Transformation* is a modest contribution to the broader transfer effort, it involves the sustained commitment of progressive education advocates, whose expertise lights the way for future improvement. I thank the authors who participated in this project for sharing their research and insights, including my inspiring co-editor, Eileen Strempel, who invited me to join this project despite my pitiful excuse that I "did not have time." "Who does?" she replied. Her gentle and gracious insistence was the impetus I needed and the result has been one of the most satisfying of my career. Both Eileen and I thank our colleagues at the National Institute for the Study of Transfer Students, especially Judith

Brauer and Janet Marling, whose leadership made these monographs possible, along with the talented editors and publishers at the University of North Georgia Press who made manifest the research presented in this volume. All of us hope this book inspires and excites you and, in doing so, advances the progress of the transfer pathway.

CPSIA information can be obtained
at www.ICGtesting.com
Printed in the USA
BVHW040417180519
548585BV00002B/61/P

9 781940 771472